D1715368

Purloined
Letters

Purloined Letters

Cultural Borrowing
and
Japanese Crime Literature,
1868–1937

Mark Silver

University of Hawai'i Press • Honolulu

Library of Congress Cataloging-in-Publication Data
Silver, Mark.
 Purloined letters : cultural borrowing and Japanse crime literature,
1868–1937 / Mark Silver.
    p. cm.
 Includes bibliographical references and index.
 ISBN 978-0-8248-3188-2 (hardcover : alk. paper)
  1. Detective and mystery stories, Japanese—History and criticism.
2. Japanese fiction—19th century—History and criticism. 3. Japanese
fiction—20th century—History and criticism. 4. Japanese fiction—
Western influences. I. Title.
 PL726.55.S63 2008
 895.6'3087209—dc22
                    2007048339

Designed by Lucille C. Aono

Printed by Edwards Brothers, Inc.

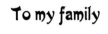
To my family

Contents

Acknowledgments

It is a pleasure to express my gratitude to the many people who played a role in the making of this book. Edwin McClellan taught me how to read Japanese literature and what it means to work to a high standard. As I was writing the dissertation on which the book is based, he was patient, wise, and encouraging, and he saved me from many errors. He also arranged for me to spend ten months under the tutelage of Etō Jun (then of the faculty of Keiō University), who found time in a famously busy schedule for weekly meetings during which he listened to my ideas and answered my questions about the texts I was working with. The impromptu lectures he gave me in his office (on everything from the history of autopsy and Edo period cures for leprosy to silent film and Japanese tabloid journalism) were always an embarrassment of riches, and I could not help wishing that his audience were far larger. The memory of his generosity spurred me on throughout the remainder of the project.

I could not have enjoyed the benefit of Etō Jun's counsel without the financial assistance of the Japan Foundation, which provided a generous dissertation-research fellowship. Etō Jun's students, particularly Shigeta Mariko and Yamada Junji, were a source of intellectual stimulation during my stay in Japan, and they were no less generous than their mentor. Shigeta Mariko showed me the ropes at the National Diet Library. Yamada Junji and his family saw to it that my New Year was properly full of mah-jongg and visits to crowded shrines.

While I was in Tokyo, Suzuki Sadami and Gonda Manji both kindly agreed to meet with me to listen to my ideas and offer suggestions. After I had returned to the States, the latter also mailed me a number of useful books. Shimazaki Yukiko and Masui Yukimi generously took me into their circle and did much to make my visit the pleasure it was. They also endured my peppering of them, sometimes at odd hours, with phone calls about the meaning of difficult passages in Japanese.

ix

Back at Yale, I was again the grateful beneficiary of a fellowship, this time from the Yale Graduate School. Chie Chao and Yamaguchi Eitetsu, both of the Japanese language staff at Yale, graciously helped with still more questions about difficult passages.

Edward Kamens' scholarship has long been a model to me. I could not have made head nor tail out of Kanagaki Robun's writings without his instruction in literary-style Japanese and the time I spent in his seminar reading premodern texts. I am also grateful to him for the comments he offered on my dissertation and for his advice since. I might never have written on crime literature at all if Alan Tansman had not said he thought it was a good idea. Both he and Jeffrey Kinkley made helpful comments on early drafts of my work and gave me encouragement when I needed it most. Richard Torrance made perceptive comments on a version of some of the material in Chapter 5.

Dan O'Neill read and commented on an early draft of Chapter 3 and also got me thinking about *Takahashi Oden*'s basis in actual events. Miryam Sas was there at the beginning. She mailed a book from Japan on one occasion and posed sharp questions on a number of others. Wei Zhuang seemed to be constantly on the lookout for materials relevant to my project. I am grateful to her for bringing the work of Wada Shigejirō to my attention. Grace Chang took an interest from the first. She provided stimulating conversation, friendship, and moral support, as well as hatching many welcome diversions.

My colleagues at Colgate University and Connecticut College, including Gloria Bien, Yōichi Aizawa, Yukari Hirata, Jing Wang, John Crespi, Amy Dooling, Yibing Huang, Alexis Dudden, Dale Wilson, Jim Austin, Tek-wah King, and Hisae Kobayashi have all been sources of inspiration in varied ways, and I am grateful to each of them. I have also benefited from my contacts with Amanda Seaman, Sari Kawana, and Kyōko Ōmori, whose own work on Japanese detective fiction has provided helpful perspective.

Pamela Kelley, my editor at the University of Hawai'i Press, guided me through the review of my manuscript with professional calm, and she has made the entire process of publication smoother than I imagined it could be. The press' anonymous readers provided informed and incisive comments that helped me reshape and improve nearly every chapter of the book. Susan Stone did a superb job of copyediting, correcting numerous inconsistencies and infelicities without being heavy-handed in the least; she also prepared the index.

Earlier versions of sections of the book have appeared in previous publications. Part of Chapter 2 first appeared in "The Lies and Connivances of an Evil Woman: Early Meiji Realism and *The Tale of Takahashi Oden the She-Devil,*" *Harvard Journal of Asiatic Studies,* vol. 63, no. 1 (June 2003):

5–67. Parts of Chapters 2 and 3 have previously appeared in "Putting the Court on Trial: Cultural Borrowing and the Translated Crime Novel in Nineteenth-Century Japan," *Journal of Popular Culture,* vol. 36, no. 4 (Spring 2003): 853–885. An additional part of Chapter 3 was first published in "The Detective Novel's Novelty: Native and Foreign Narrative Forms in Kuroiwa Ruikō's *Kettō no hate,*" *Japan Forum,* vol. 16, no. 2 (July 2004): 191–205.

The R. F. Johnson Fund and the Department of East Asian Languages and Cultures at Connecticut College both helped defray some of the costs of publication.

On a more personal note, I wish to thank my family, to whom I dedicate this book. My brother, Peter Silver, followed the project closely even as he was absorbed with finishing a book of his own. His willingness to listen and react as I talked things through was more valuable than I can say. He continually amazed me with his ability to throw off ideas in the way a Roman candle throws off stars of fire. My parents, George and Jane Silver, have been everything a son could hope for. I am thankful for their understanding, their belief in me, and their cheerful willingness to read through the manuscript at the various stages of its development. Each made countless helpful suggestions. My father also deserves special mention for playing the role of deus ex machina (god from the telephone) on half a dozen desperate occasions when I ran into trouble with my computer. My sister-in-law, Mona Fixdal, was both encouraging and inspiring as she, too, finished a book with what seemed to me the efficiency of a well-oiled machine. My niece, Celia, exerted her own sprightly influence as she grew along with the manuscript. My ultimate debt of gratitude, however, is to my wife, Lucy Kaminska-Silver, who has not only become the pillar of my life, but who also tolerated a great deal of nonsense as I finished writing and revising.

Note on Names
and Romanization

Japanese names, when they are given in full, generally appear surname first (the customary Japanese order). Exceptions have been made in bibliographic citations listing works in English by an author with a Japanese name. In these cases the author's name appears as it does on the title page of the work cited.

When referring to Japanese authors who use pen names, I have followed the Japanese practice of calling them by their first name rather than by surname in cases where the full name is not given. For example, Ihara Saikaku is referred to after his first mention as "Saikaku" rather than "Ihara." Authors who did not use pen names, in contrast, are referred to after first mention by surname (Kume Masao, for example, is "Kume" rather than "Masao").

All Japanese names and words have been romanized using the system of *Kenkyūsha's New Japanese-English Dictionary,* fourth edition, with slight modification. Rather than using a hyphen to separate the palatal "n" from a succeeding vowel, I have used an apostrophe ("Tanizaki Jun'ichirō" rather than "Tanizaki Jun-ichirō"). And I have omitted the macron from familiar place names ("Tokyo" and "Osaka" rather than "Tōkyō" and "Ōsaka").

Introduction

Cultural Borrowing and
Japanese Crime Literature

This book is about what happens when writers work in the shadow of a culture they see as more advanced and powerful than their own. When Japan ended its policy of self-imposed isolation in the late nineteenth century, a newly emerging political leadership, alarmed and embarrassed at Japan's apparent backwardness, set to work catching up with the West. To Ōkubo Toshimichi, a member of the famous Iwakura legation dispatched in 1871–1873 to study life in Europe and America, Japan's need to throw off the legacy of its insular past and turn outward was clear. "All the countries of the world are...propagating...'civilization and enlightenment,'" he observed, "and they lack for nothing. Hence," he bluntly declared, "we must imitate them."[1] As a deliberate policy for bridging the gap between Japan and the West, imitation would prove to have complex ramifications—indeed understanding the modes and meanings of cultural imitation is a central concern of this book. But the policy's immediate effect was clear and dramatic. Japan began a process of Westernization that encompassed everything from the nation's systems of law, government, and education, to industry and commerce, to architecture, literature, and the arts, as well as the more mundane aspects of everyday life, such as diet, bathing, clothing, and hairstyles.

In the realm of literature, writers and critics such as Tsubouchi Shōyō (1859–1935) and Futabatei Shimei (1864–1909), newly inspired by the example of Western novels, pioneered the modernization of the Japanese written language and Japanese narrative. But the very premise of this project—that Japanese literature needed to be modernized to accord with Western models—virtually guaranteed that their writings would be measured

1

against the models that had inspired them and that they would be found wanting. Shōyō's novel *Tōsei shosei katagi* (The Characters of Modern Students, 1886), for example, was judged by a contemporary Japanese reviewer to be "respectable, but only if one considers that it was written by a member of a second-tier civilization." The reviewer added: "It does not compare to the works being produced by authors from first-tier civilizations in the West."[2] This early judgment upon Shōyō's novel has been long-lived. Donald Keene, writing in the 1980s, observed that "the realism of *Tōsei shosei katagi* is exceedingly limited.... Tsubouchi's conception of 'characters' remained closer to the character books of [Tokugawa period writer] Ejima Kiseki than the character of Gertrude in *Hamlet;* he presented a collection of types rather than complex individuals."[3] The late-nineteenth-century episode of contact between the Japanese and Western literary worlds set up a continuing pattern, on both sides of the Pacific, of conceiving literary relations in starkly binary terms and of casting Japan as the inferior, imitative member of the East-West pair. The historical inequality in geopolitical, technological, and military power between Japan and the West has, in other words, been mirrored in the prevailing assessments of literary value and in the dominant explanations of the flows of literary influence. This tendency has perhaps been most conspicuously visible in the modern novel, and it has received considerable scholarly attention in that arena.[4]

But if highbrow writers such as Futabatei Shimei, Tsubouchi Shōyō, or (later) Akutagawa Ryūnosuke found themselves trapped in the shadow of their Western models, and if they often found themselves judged by a decidedly Eurocentric standard, the problems faced by writers working in the genre of detective fiction (in Japanese, *tantei shōsetsu*) were still more acute and persistent. A writer such as Futabatei, who saw himself as remaking Japanese prose fiction in general, could draw with relative freedom upon native traditions of narrative in his work. He whimsically began his novel *Ukigumo* (Floating Clouds, 1887–1889), for example, with an extensive listing of contemporary mustache styles, a rhetorical flourish firmly in the tradition of Japanese *gesaku* narrative (literally, "playful writing"). Writers of detective fiction, in contrast, were working in a genre that employed an imported and novel narrative structure, one whose relative fixity meant it could not so easily withstand hybridization with native Japanese forms and still remain true to itself. This imported narrative structure, now familiar to any reader of the whodunit, was built of two interlocked stories: the story of an investigation and the story of the crime that comes to light through that investigation.[5] This narrative structure had no native precedents in Japan when the first translations of detective stories appeared in the 1880s. Early

Japanese detective writers were thus keenly aware of their status as borrowers from Western sources and of the inevitability of comparison with those sources.

These circumstances of the detective story's production would give it special cultural weight for Japanese authors and critics, despite the tendency to view it as an essentially popular and frivolous entertainment. For many Japanese observers, it became a test case for measuring Japan's fitness to call itself a modern nation, a cultural touchstone for Japan's national identity, its national competence, and its place in the world. The critic Hirabayashi Hatsunosuke (1892–1931) is best known for his association with the proletarian literature movement in Japan, but in the final decade of his life he wrote a number of detective stories and critical essays on Japanese detective fiction. His observations in one such essay from 1925 indicate the range of concerns the genre could sweep before it: "There are certain social conditions that stand as prerequisites for the development of detective fiction," Hirabayashi wrote, in an effort to explain what he saw as the stunting of its growth in Japan. "Development of a scientific civilization, the development of reason, the development of an analytical spirit, the development of a methodical spirit [are all necessary]. There must also be scientific methods used in investigations, court procedures based on the use of incontrovertible physical evidence, and a nation whose order is maintained by the rule of law."[6]

Each of the preconditions for detective fiction that Hirabayashi stipulated would have had special resonance for his audience, given Japan's particular historical legacy. By the 1920s, no one would have suggested that Japan did not live under "the rule of law," but that was a comparatively recent development. It was only in 1911 that the last vestiges of "extraterritoriality" had been expunged from the treaties between Japan and the Western powers. Under the provisions of these unequal treaties, foreigners on Japanese soil had been subject to the laws of their home country—not to Japanese law—precisely because the consistency, logic, and fairness of the Japanese judicial system were suspect in the eyes of the treaty makers. Hirabayashi's stipulation that court procedures in a detective novel be based on "incontrovertible physical evidence" was a grim reminder that the Japanese judicial system had, before the reforms of the Meiji period (1868–1912), relied far more heavily on torture and forced confession than on physical evidence or forensic medicine. For Hirabayashi, the investigations carried out by detectives had to be scientific, rational, analytical, and methodical if they were to measure up to Western models. By implication, Japanese authors and their audience had to have these qualities as well; the shortcomings of the Japanese detective novel were, for Hirabayashi, short-comings of Japan. "The reason the detective novel hasn't developed in Japan," he went on to say in the same essay, "is . . . that Japanese civilization is scientifically infantile and primitive. That is the root cause of all the reasons people give for the lack of the detective novel's development in Japan."[7] Hirabayashi's views—which are not only the views of a critic, but also the self-criticism of an author—suggest how persistently the question of inter-national comparison could dog writers working in this borrowed genre.

Detective fiction's development in Japan is thus an instructive case of literary borrowing between "unequal" cultures. Not only does the absence of a native equivalent allow us to fix the moment of the genre's arrival in Japan. The genre's distinctive narrative structure also allows us to trace its subsequent absorption in the way that a radiologist might trace the move-ments of a marker dye in the body of a patient. This makes for a consider-ably clearer picture than is possible in studies of more nebulous literary phenomena, such as the spread of realism or naturalism. The picture that results from such a tracing prompts one central conclusion: Japanese liter-ary borrowing in the arena of detective fiction has been remarkably and richly varied in spite of the circumstances of its production—circumstances that all but forced Japanese writers into the role of imitator by their choice of genre.

In some cases, as Hirabayashi Hatsunosuke's essay shows, one does see evidence of a subtle cultural imperialism—not only what seem to be Japa-nese attempts at wholesale imitation of Western models but an accompany-ing self-criticism that suggests the Japanese have completely internalized a set of Western, Eurocentric cultural norms. In other cases, one sees evidence of a resistance to Western cultural influences that threatens to alter or sub-vert the borrowed narrative form without apology. In still other instances, one sees the borrowed form put to creative uses in the local, Japanese, context—uses that could not have been anticipated in their original Western one—and that defy categorization as either imitation or resistance.

These complications suggest that the conventional models of cul-tural borrowing and cross-cultural influence, in their persistent focus on the poles of cultural imperialism and colonial resistance, have succumbed too easily to the siren call of monolithic consistency. This is partly because monolithic consistency has an inherent attractiveness. But it is also because the study of highbrow literary influence has occupied center stage in the academy for so long. Broadening our perspective to include peripheral genres such as the detective story can have the salutary effect of upsetting conventional assumptions about the movements and meanings of interna-tional and intercultural literary cross-currents.

One noteworthy trend in the scholarship of "unequal" literary relations has been a focus on questioning the fundamentally binary model of influence that underlies such condescending judgments as the one leveled against Tsubouchi Shōyō ("respectable for a second-tier nation"). Miryam Sas, in her study of Japanese surrealism, points out that traditional studies of cultural borrowing "tend to emphasize a single direction of influence and thus lose sight of the process of cultural exchange as a complex and intricate series of relations."[8] Lydia Liu, too, has championed the notion of what she calls "translingual practice," or a rethinking of translation in order to emphasize the "productive distortion" of "host languages," rather than employing the notions of "source" and "target" languages, with their implication of a one-way flow.[9]

Such insights are indispensable for understanding certain episodes in the history of Japanese detective fiction. For instance, Kuroiwa Ruikō (1862–1920), an early translator of Western detective novels (treated in Chapter 3), produced translations in which we see not only the Japanese host language, but also Ruikō's local political context yielding a quirkily creative product that can by no means be written off as mere mimicry of a Western original. And yet, in other instances, such as that of Edogawa Ranpo (1894–1965) and his contemporaries (treated in Chapter 5), there is little evidence of the sort of exchange or mutual influence that Sas and Liu find in the development of the more self-consciously literary genres they work with (surrealist poetry for Sas and modernist prose for Liu).

Certainly there is no parallel in detective fiction to *japonisme,* the late-nineteenth-century European fascination with the Japanese arts that exerted such influence on Claude Monet and Vincent van Gogh. The Oriental influence on the Western detective story during this period, such as it was, had nothing to do with technique and everything to do with content. The Orient generally figured within stories only as the mysterious "Other" that required investigation and explanation. In Arthur Conan Doyle's Sherlock Holmes stories, for example, China is evoked as an exotic hinterland. Readers are meant to feel astonishment at the breadth of Holmes' knowledge when it is shown to encompass even this outer limit, as it does in "The Red-Headed League" (1891). In the story Holmes performs his customary astonishing recitation of facts about a prospective client, deducing, among other things, that the man has been in China: "the fish you have tattooed immediately above your right wrist could only have been done [there]," he announces. "That trick of staining the fishes' scales of a delicate pink is quite peculiar to China."[10] Alternatively, the Orient could serve as a source of malicious impulses or as an enabler of their enactment. In Conan Doyle's story "The Speckled Band" (1892), it is both. The morose Doctor Roylott is a returnee from Calcutta, and Holmes recognizes the snake that the doctor unleashes on his step-daughter as "a swamp adder!...the deadliest snake in India."[11] Later, in the mid-1930s, John P. Marquand would put the Japanese detective Mr. Moto at the center of a long-running series of detective novels, but again this is no more than a device to lend the works an exotic atmosphere; anyone looking for signs that Marquand's plots or prose were influenced by Japanese detective writers will be disappointed.

Japanese detective writers in the 1920s and 1930s therefore stood in a very different relationship to their Western models than did Kuroiwa Ruikō, the early translator. Much of what the writers of the 1920s and 1930s produced was haunted by anxiety about standing up to a judgmental Western gaze—a gaze that, in a further twist, must have been almost wholly imaginary, given the linguistic and cultural barriers. In this case, a model of cultural influence suggested by Shu-Mei Shih—what she calls "asymmetrical cosmopolitanism"—seems more apt than those proposed by Sas and Liu. Shih sees Chinese modernist writers as having entered into "the global arena in a leap of imagination." She explains that she "emphasize[s] the imaginary nature of this dialogue, because...it was very much a one-sided affair, with the Chinese gesticulating energetically without really getting seen or heard."[12] The one-sidedness Shih describes reaches an extreme in Japanese detective fiction of the 1920s and 1930s. In this literature one often sees a self-conscious imitativeness that is much less at ease with itself than the adaptive creativity in Kuroiwa Ruikō's mid-Meiji translations. Writers in this later generation were extremely well-versed in European and American detective fiction (Edogawa Ranpo, for example, is known to have maintained exhaustive and systematic catalogs of the ruses employed by murderers in foreign detective stories). But this familiarity was not especially liberating. Indeed, it often resulted in works that seem haunted by doubts about their qualifications for membership in a genre that Japanese writers and critics still tended to view as fundamentally Western.

In the case of Ranpo's generation, then, one does at times see a remarkable consonance between literary relations and international power relations. In the 1930s, especially—just as Japan is staging its most aggressive bid to join the club of modern, imperial nations once and for all—Japanese detective writers were carrying out their replication of Western techniques and conventions with a self-consciousness that reached new heights. These works suggest that relations of political power strongly shaped Japanese detective writers' sense of what was most worth doing in their chosen genre.[13] But at the same time they also reflect the ambivalence that accompanied Japanese admiration of Western cultural achievement.

Anxious Imitation and Cultural Identity

Edogawa Ranpo's novella *The Pomegranate* (*Zakuro*, 1934) demonstrates how large ambivalent imitation and anxiety about cultural identity could loom in Japanese detective stories of the 1930s.[14] The story's playful but keenly self-conscious imitativeness represents only one possible mode of response to the problem of writing in a borrowed genre. Nonetheless, Ranpo's story illustrates its particular mode of response with great clarity, and it therefore usefully establishes the broader parameters of this study. Ranpo's story is deeply affected from the start by the problem of positioning itself in relation to Western precedents in the genre of detective fiction. *The Pomegranate* does not only recycle plot elements taken from a Western example of the genre. By focusing on a case of murder involving suspected impersonation, the story makes imitation, originality, and eventually national identity into explicit themes. Its meditations on these themes give it a distinctly self-referential quality so that the story's ending, in which the main character confesses to two fraudulent impersonations, takes on an unmistakable resonance when read in light of Ranpo's own incorporation of borrowed material into the story.

Signs of self-referentiality crop up in the story almost immediately, in the framing narrative with which it begins: this framing narrative sets *The Pomegranate* up as a story about telling a story. The first-person narrator, a former detective, explains how he recently had occasion to recall one of his most interesting cases. While on vacation at a hot spring, he tells us, he struck up a conversation with a man he had noticed reading a detective novel. This man, named Inomata, introduced himself as a connoisseur of crime and detection. Asked by Inomata to recount one of his past triumphs, the detective settled on the ten-year-old Case of the Sulfuric Acid Murder, which he tells for us as he told it to Inomata.

At the center of the case is the corpse of a man killed by forced ingestion of sulfuric acid. When the body is discovered, the victim's identity cannot be determined because his face has been so burned by the acid as to be unrecognizable. The victim's fingerprints are taken but match none on file.

A day later, the detective hears from a woman named Tanimura Kinuyo. Her husband, Tanimura Man'emon, is the owner of a generations-old beancake (*manjū*) business. Kinuyo is alarmed because her husband is missing. She is convinced that he is responsible for the murder and that the victim is a man named Kotono Sōichi. Kotono and Man'emon have been archrivals since childhood. Kotono's family also runs an equally old beancake business, and the two enterprises are in direct competition.

She tells the detective that she last saw her husband early on the morning after the body was discovered, as he was leaving their bedroom to go on a business trip. The previous afternoon and night he had shut himself in his study to work until very late, but she has realized he could have left the house without her knowledge. Kotono it turns out, is also unaccounted for, never having returned home on the night the murder occurred. Since the kimono worn by the corpse proves to be one of Kotono's, everything points to Tanimura Man'emon's guilt. A manhunt for him, however, proves fruitless. The police are at their wit's end when the detective has a breakthrough.

On a visit to Kinuyo, he discovers a fingerprint on a page of her husband's diary. The print is distinctive, and he recognizes it as a match for a print from the faceless corpse. In light of this discovery, the detective arrives at a new theory about what happened: it was not that Tanimura Man'emon killed Kotono but rather the reverse—the faceless corpse is that of Tanimura, and it is Kotono who was his murderer. No one had considered this possibility before, since Tanimura had been at home with Kinuyo—or so she thought—the morning after the corpse was discovered. Kotono, the detective now realizes, must have killed his rival Tanimura, disfigured his face with acid, exchanged clothes with him, and then gone to Tanimura's house, where he then impersonated his own victim. By sleeping with his rival's wife Kinuyo and making an early morning departure, Kotono made it appear that he himself had been killed. When the detective questions her, Kinuyo has to admit that she never had a good look at the man in her dark bedroom that night and that, moreover, he seemed more tight-lipped than her husband usually was. Now it is Kotono who is put on the wanted list.

There is, however, another reversal in store. Inomata, after hearing the detective's solution to the case and learning that the ten-year-old search for Kotono has turned up nothing, suggests still another way of looking at the facts. Perhaps, he suggests, the fingerprint in the notebook was planted by Tanimura in order to lead the detective to his theory about Kotono's impersonation. Since Kotono had sometimes visited Tanimura's house, it would have been easy for Tanimura to cause Kotono to handle various objects and leave his fingerprints on them. Tanimura could then have carefully removed any remaining fingerprints of his own. After killing Kotono and returning home to his own bedroom, Inomata explains, "Tanimura would behave as if he were Kotono impersonating [Tanimura]; without saying a word and while taking the most careful precautions not to show his face…he would have consummated the strangest possible of illicit bonds with his very own wife."[15]

After presenting this alternative solution to the mystery, Inomata offers the most convincing of proofs that it is correct, and he does so by revealing yet another impersonation. He suddenly reaches into his mouth and removes a full set of false teeth, altering the shape of his face dramatically. ("His face became so pathetic as to induce disbelief at the extreme changes possible in human appearances.") Inomata asks the detective to study his face carefully: "First, imagine that my eyelids are not creased. Imagine the eyelashes much thicker. Think of the nose as being a bit flatter. Now get rid of the beard, and in its place grow thick, short-cropped hair on my head.... Well? You don't see? Is there no such face anywhere in your memory?"[16] Inomata turns out not to have been a casual visitor to the hot spring who has met the detective by chance; he is Tanimura Man'emon himself. After killing Kotono, he reveals, he left his wife Kinuyo to run off with another woman, who has recently died. With nothing left to live for, he announces, he has searched out the detective to make a gloating confession before taking his own life. He then immediately makes good on his intentions, hurtling himself from the high rocky precipice where the two have been seated and plunging into the river far below.[17] The story takes its title from its most gruesome image—that of Inomata's bloody remains spreading over the surface of the river, which the narrator likens to the sight of a cross-sectioned pomegranate.

The impersonation at the center of this case—the one by the killer of his own victim—is inspired by one of the seminal works in the tradition of the English golden-age detective novel *Trent's Last Case* (1913), by Eric C. Bentley.[18] In Bentley's book, John Marlowe, secretary to the wealthy financier Sigsbee Manderson, is desperate to clear himself of suspicion in Manderson's death. By wearing Manderson's clothes and mimicking his voice during two carefully planned encounters with Manderson's butler and his wife, Marlowe makes it appear that Manderson was still alive hours after he had in fact died. By changing the supposed time of Manderson's death, he is able to divert attention from his own role in the affair.

Ranpo has, of course, worked variations on this material. In Bentley's book there is no corpse defaced by acid, and there is no sexual encounter between Marlowe and Mrs. Manderson. (Manderson and his wife are estranged; Marlowe pulls off his impersonation by briefly exchanging words with her while she lies half asleep in the next room.) And Ranpo's story goes Bentley's one better—or is at least more convoluted—in its solution. Ranpo's killer, rather than impersonating his victim, only pretends to be impersonating his victim. Ranpo has borrowed other things from *Trent's Last Case*, too. The idea of making a man leave fingerprints without his knowledge, a lecture on particularly distinctive types of fingerprints, the idea of dentures dramatically changing a man's appearance, and the confession by the true killer that bowls the detective over at the story's end are all important elements of Bentley's original.

But Ranpo forges the truly unmistakable link to Bentley near the beginning of his story, when Inomata first attracts the narrator's attention at the hot spring. Inomata is reading a novel at that moment, and it is none other than *Trent's Last Case*. When the detective's eye falls upon the spine of Inomata's book, the title of Bentley's book and Bentley's own name are reproduced, in capital roman letters, within the Japanese text of Ranpo's story.[19] Later, after Inomata has revealed his past, Ranpo has his character rather laboriously explain that he was holding Bentley's book in order to influence the detective, through "a memory present beneath consciousness," to respond with the story of Tanimura and Kotono when invited to recount a case.

Ranpo's incorporation into the story of these references to Bentley points to the potential ambiguity of many acts of cultural borrowing. One might read the references as knowing and ironic gestures toward the fundamentally imitative and repetitive nature of the detective story itself, based as the genre is on a relatively limited set of conventions. Or one might read them as an homage to a story that has been so influential as to act as a persistent memory beneath consciousness for a host of subsequent practitioners. Then again, one might read the references to Bentley as a playful nose thumbing at Bentley's dominant status, an act of appropriation carried off with the intent of ostentatiously going Bentley one better. The story certainly revels in its own virtuosic spinning out of dizzying hypothetical possibility and in its conspicuous reworking of Bentley's materials.

Interpreting the meaning of such gestures becomes largely a matter of discerning the spirit in which they are made, and it can be difficult to do so while avoiding entrapment in the well-known "intentional fallacy" of impugning psychological motives to authors based on their works. Nonetheless, Ranpo's literary diary provides some telling clues about the circumstances of this story's composition, clues that suggest Ranpo was acutely aware of his status as a marginalized heir to Bentley. In addition—and more important—the story itself is so conspicuously preoccupied with the theme of guilty impersonation that even if one cannot be certain of the spirit in which the references to Bentley have been made, their ultimate effect is to suffuse the text with an uneasy self-consciousness about the literary impersonation the story perpetrates. Emphasizing this uneasy self-consciousness in Ranpo's work has about it a semblance of ethnocentrism that may make some readers uncomfortable. But there is in fact considerable evidence to suggest that Ranpo was powerfully fixated on Western models and that his

difficulty in fighting through the anxiety of their influence left him peren-
nially dissatisfied with his own work. To gloss over this aspect of Ranpo in
the name of avoiding all semblance of ethnocentrism seems no less grave
an offense than ethnocentrism itself.

Ranpo's famously detailed literary diary, which he published in increasingly longer versions as he lived out the latter half of his life, devotes several
pages to his composition of *The Pomegranate* and its reception. In the diary
Ranpo explicitly mentions his debt to Bentley, saying that, "at that time,
though I should have done so sooner, I read Bentley's *Trent's Last Case* and
was extremely impressed." He continues: "I sketched out a plot [for *The
Pomegranate*] with the idea that I was showing how I would have handled
the trick in [*Trent's Last Case*] if it had been my own, demonstrating how the
work would turn out if it were rewritten in the Japanese style. It was not so
much a matter of imitation as it was a matter of saying, 'Have a look at how
I would treat this same trick.'"[20] One might conceivably read this as a statement of positive and triumphant cultural appropriation. Yet Ranpo appears
here to be fending off the accusation of copying ("It was not so much a matter of imitation..."), which suggests a perception on his part that his story
appeared derivative, as does the hypothetical premise on which he says his
composition of it was based ("I was showing how I would have handled the
trick in that work *if it had been my own*").[21]

Indeed it is the latter reading that takes on the greater weight when
one attends to other signs of dissatisfaction with the story's derivativeness
in Ranpo's diary account. Ranpo's account makes mention more than once
of his having committed to a deadline for delivery of the piece without
any fresh ideas in mind. "Although I was excited at the request [from the
journal *Chūō kōron*]," he writes, "nothing that could be called a new con-
cept came to me."[22] Reflecting on his completed novella a few lines later,
he remains unenthusiastic: "[*The Pomegranate*] didn't have any ingredient
in it that would enable me to display it with a flourish and announce, 'This
is my new work.'"[23] Ranpo also reproduces at considerable length, in the
style of a scrapbook, contemporary reviews of *The Pomegranate* from several
leading Japanese newspapers and journals, including the *Yomiuri*, the *Tokyo
Asahi*, and *Bungei shunjū*. These reviews are overwhelmingly negative. They
refer to the story's cheapness, its tired recycling of tricks, its consequent
mustiness, and Ranpo's evident decline as a writer.[24] "This work uses the
device of fingerprints," one of these reviews observes, "which has gotten
quite old by now, and looking beyond this it has little in the way of new
flavor.... The detective story is prone, no matter what one does, to smell-
ing like an adaptation of Western material" (*dōshite mo seiyō dane no hon'an
kusaku naru*).[25] Ranpo's response to these reviews is notably resigned: "That

The Pomegranate is done in my same old style and that it has nothing new in it," he says, "the author himself has acknowledged."[26] And at the end of this section of his diary, Ranpo records that the publication of *The Pomegranate* prompted him to "think that I could no longer write anything that detective story readers would read and that I no longer had the desire to write detective stories."[27] In fact, this realization seems to have been temporary, since Ranpo continued to turn out commercially viable serialized works in the genre for some years to come. Nonetheless, the evidence in his diary provides ample support for a reading of the *The Pomegranate* that emphasizes its self-conscious preoccupation with originals and copies and, by implication, with its own literary debts to Western predecessors.

And indeed, for all of the story's verve and brio, these preoccupations are everywhere apparent in the text of *The Pomegranate*. The story can be read as an elaborate, troubled meditation on the differences between imitations and originals, and on the threats to personal and cultural identity implicit in the denial of those differences.

Imitation and originality first come into the story as the crux of the rivalry between the beancake businesses owned by Tanimura and Kotono. Both families claim to have the original recipe for "Mujina" (literally, "badger") beancakes. The families' storefronts are side by side, and they both display large signs with identical (and therefore mutually contradictory) slogans proclaiming "Original Mujina Beancakes." Neither family wants to be stigmatized as an imitator, and the generations-old feud over the issue has resulted in incidents of violence and sabotage. With this thematic material, Ranpo installs in the story a starkly binary notion of originality and imitation. The dispute over which family is the originator and which is the imitator is never resolved, but it is clear that in the world of the story each family must be one or the other, that the status of originator is superior to that of imitator, and that the distinction matters enough to become a motive for murder.

The figures of Tanimura and Kotono themselves, set up as nearly interchangeable versions of each other, further underline the problematic of originals and copies. It is this basic interchangeability that creates the initial confusion over the identity of the faceless corpse and of the killer. The story's fascination with originals, copies, and personal identities becomes truly baroque when it presents the competing, mirror-image-like theories of the charade played out in the Tanimuras' bed. We are invited in these passages to contemplate first the possibility that Kotono, as a copy of Bentley's character Marlowe, made himself into a copy of Tanimura, and then the possibility that Tanimura made himself into a copy of Kotono copying him as a copy of Marlowe would.

This episode carries the story across the boundary between realism and farce. It stretches credulity to the breaking point to imagine that Tanimura's wife, Kinuyo, could be fooled by either man. That the story crosses this boundary anyway suggests its deep concern with the question of whether a copy could somehow pass as a viable original. It is particularly telling in this regard that the story should end up presenting as its solution the scenario in which Tanimura engages in an act of double impersonation, thereby rendering the bedroom charade an essentially harmless deception between husband and wife rather than an act of half-recognized rape or adultery. In this scenario the distinction between impersonator and original proves false; the supposed copy turns out not to have been a copy at all.

Read as an allegory of Ranpo's own borrowing from Bentley, this scenario—the very one in which Ranpo has introduced the additional reversal beyond Bentley—becomes a sort of self-absolution, a vindication of Ranpo as an original in his own right and a wish-fulfilling enactment of precisely the sort of reconciliation between originator and imitator that had seemingly been ruled out as an impossibility in the perpetual feud between the families of Kotono and Tanimura.

But subsequent developments in the text threaten to undermine this admittedly dubious self-absolution. By the story's end, the paradigm of absolute distinction between impersonator and original reasserts itself, and Tanimura, as we have seen, confesses to his crime and plunges to his death. Tanimura not only confesses to the murder of Kotono (by which he hoped to obviate the latter's threat to his own claim of originality in beancake making); he also confesses to another impersonation—an impersonation that is not reducible, as his earlier one is, to impersonation of himself.

In the course of this confession, Tanimura explains that immediately after the murder he escaped to Shanghai and in the ten years since has lived under a false identity, "eras[ing]," as he puts it, "the man Tanimura from the world and creat[ing] an entirely new and separate person." He continues:

There are some very good hospitals in Shanghai. They are mostly run by foreigners, and I picked out, from among the ones that were, the most convenient dentist, eye doctor, and plastic surgeon, and paid visits to them faithfully. First I...drastically thinned my hair....Next I had my eyelashes made much thicker. Then the nose. As you know, my nose was, besides being flat, not much to look at. I had them, by means of rhinoplasty, create for me this Grecian nose. Then I thought about changing the lines of my face....I had all my teeth taken out...and put in a full set of dentures with gums made thick where they had been thin before....After growing the beard, all that was left was the eyes. Eyes are a real bother to disguise. First I had surgery done to

> change the creaseless lids to creased ones....I sacrificed one of my
> eyeballs...[and] had a glass one [put in]....In other words my face is,
> in every respect, an artificial creation.[28]

Ranpo loads Tanimura's transformation into Inomata with conspicuous sig-
nifiers of ethnicity and cultural identity. At the story's opening, when the
detective tells us how he first met Inomata at the hot spring, he describes
the connoisseur of crime as "somehow not quite Japanese" (*doko to naku
nihonjin-banare*).[29] Tanimura's story confirms that the narrator has every
reason to form this impression. Tanimura presumably effects his transformation into Inomata to disguise his old identity; but in doing so, he takes
on—almost, under the logic of this story, as a matter of course—a new,
artificially assumed identity as a quasi-Westerner, or as an Asian-Western
hybrid. (And it does seem clear that the cultural categories in play here are
not much more specific than the "Asian" and the "Western.") The plastic
surgery Tanimura has performed on his nose renders it more prominent,
"Grecian" rather than Japanese. The surgery performed on Tanimura's
eyes rids him of his Asian creaseless lids. These surgeries are carried out
in hospitals run by presumably Western "foreigners," and Tanimura is then
able to hide in the cityscape of Shanghai. This last detail, given Shanghai's
reputation in the 1930s as a site of quintessential cosmopolitanism, suggests a fantasy of acceptance in a zone of cultural ambiguity, a zone where
one's claims to hybridity, being relatively commonplace, would not come
under especially close scrutiny, and where a Japanese might successfully
impersonate a part-Westerner.

   Having first effected a self-absolution in which copy and original collapse into one, the story now undoes that self-absolution by exposing the
copy as an obvious imitation. In Tanimura's second impersonation—the
one made possible by his plastic surgery—there is a starkly obvious difference between his own Japanese identity and the Western, or quasi-Western,
identity he attempts to assume. No longer harmlessly impersonating himself, Tanimura is now guiltily impersonating another and must resort to
conspicuously artificial methods in order to do so.

   If we read this segment of the story for its implications concerning
Ranpo's own borrowing from Bentley (a maneuver that the story's own self-
referentiality invites), Ranpo here seems to represent himself as a full-
blown impersonator, one that—given the glass eye, the dentures, and the
rhinoplasty—has become a vaguely monstrous hybrid. (This hybridity is consistent with that of Ranpo's punning pen name, which also hints at an act
of only partially successful impersonation. Ranpo's actual name was "Hirai
Tarō." "Edogawa Ranpo" is a slightly distorted rendition, in the Japanese

phonetic system, of "Edgar Allan Poe.") In this case Ranpo's bid to position himself as a Japanese participant in the genre of Western detective fiction, to offer something in the style of the work that defines that genre, almost seems determined to doom itself to failure. Ranpo's story all but insists that, once its claims to belong to the genre of detective fiction are closely examined (just as the narrator closely examines "Inomata's" face), the result will be the revelation of a well-disguised fraud; not only will the story collapse into an imitation of *Trent's Last Case*, we will realize that it has actually advertised this eventuality almost from the beginning, where Bentley's title first appears in the text. Carrying this reading to its logical conclusion, the burst of bloody remains on the surface of the river at the story's end serves not only as a sign of Inomata's suicide but of the anxiously self-destructive tendencies of *The Pomegranate* itself. It is a strangely apt image to set above the whole as its title.

This story's continual mulling through of its own position vis-à-vis Bentley and its nearly obsessive, self-conscious fixation on the problem of imitation and originality are typical of much of Ranpo's writing. As Chapter 5 demonstrates, Ranpo's stories present an impressive array of variations on the basic theme of impersonation, regularly expanding it to include the themes of cultural hybridity and monstrosity.

The self-consciousness and the undercurrents of anxiety in Ranpo reflect more generalized Japanese anxieties of the 1920s and 1930s: anxiety over Japan's place in the modern world, over the meaning of Japan's Westernization and the threats it posed to Japanese cultural identity, and over the mixed success of Japan's attempts at colonial expansion in a manner that both followed Western example and asserted Japanese interests. (Cosmopolitanism was not all that Shanghai signified for readers of *The Pomegranate*. The city was also a site of such Japanese imperialist aggression as the first Shanghai Incident of 1932, an attack designed to support the larger colonial project in Manchuria.)

The Pomegranate together with Ranpo's larger oeuvre thus aptly sets up the central questions of this study: How persistently do "borrowed" literary genres maintain their exotic identity after they have begun to filter across intercultural boundaries? If Japanese detective writers tended to view their genre as an essentially Western one, how did they place their own work within the membership of that genre? And to what extent do national identity and relations of international power become significant subtexts for authors writing in a genre that is not only borrowed, but borrowed from a culture that they perceive as more powerful than their own?[30]

Ranpo's oeuvre does not, however, by any means provide the only answers to these questions. Although many of Ranpo's works offer striking examples of the self-consciousness that the task of writing in a borrowed genre could provoke in Japanese writers, it would be wrong to let the patterns of response represented in Ranpo overshadow other possible patterns. In fact the close match discernible in the 1930s between the Japanese emulation occurring at the national level and the sorts of emulation one finds in writers such as Ranpo poses a potential danger to students of "unequal" literary relations. The fit here between international power relations, on the one hand, and textual production and consumption, on the other, may prompt us to assign too much weight to those power relations in our analysis of cross-cultural influence and to overlook the possibility of other, quite different, configurations of cultural interchange and borrowing. Such an exclusive focus on any one mode of response (whether uneasily imitative or radically subversive) risks falsifying the variety of Japanese borrowing in the arena of crime literature and impoverishing our understanding of Japanese cultural borrowing in general.

Overview

The primary focus of this book is the description and assessment of Japanese writers' responses to the problem of writing in the borrowed genre of detective fiction. But since sources of information in English on Japanese detective fiction are so limited, it also has the secondary aim of tracing the development of Japanese detective fiction in Japan from its early native antecedents (in the seventeenth and eighteenth centuries) to the outbreak of the second Sino-Japanese War in 1937.[31]

I begin, in Chapter 2, by describing the state of Japanese crime literature before the detective story's arrival. Tokugawa era (1600–1868) crime literature was dominated by the tradition of courtroom narratives such as Ihara Saikaku's *Honchō-oin hiji* (Trials in the Shade of a Cherry Tree, 1689) and the anonymous *Ōoka seidan* (Ōoka's Rulings). These stories were written in a climate of authoritarian legal thought, and they generally glorified the state's authority as it was embodied in the wise judges at these stories' center. In contrast to the classic detective story's mystification, traditional courtroom narratives tended to use omniscient narrators who identified the guilty parties early in the narration, thus shifting the suspense away from the question of the culprit's identity to the question of how the judge would discover it—which he inevitably did. The portrayal of these judges as such unfailingly clear-sighted men tended to shore up a prevailing belief in the infallibility of a justice system that was in fact full of possibilities for abuse. When the justice system was overhauled in the early Meiji era (1868–1912) as part of Japan's attempt to attain the status of an "enlightened" nation, the gathering and interpretation of physical evidence for trials superseded the previous emphasis on forced confession. The detective story's popular acceptance in Japan shortly thereafter was in part explainable by a new fascination with this process of evidence gathering.

The other noteworthy native precedent to the detective story is the criminal biography. During the early Meiji era, in particular, there was a boom in such works, especially the biographies of so-called *dokufu*, or "poison women"—alluring, silver-tongued, female flimflammers and murderers. This boom was set off in part by the rise of the tabloid press and in part by the new, Westernizing Meiji government's abolition of legal status distinctions. The anxiety of a society newly confronted with true social mobility found a natural focal point in women such as the notoriously protean Takahashi Oden, who was beheaded in 1879 for allegedly stabbing and robbing a used-kimono dealer after posing as the agent for a client. But these criminal biographies, groundbreaking though they were in such areas as their incorporation and publication of court documents (which would have remained secret under the Tokugawa regime), made no mystery of the identities of the criminals they chronicled.

Mysteries using the characteristic interlocking narrative structure did not appear in Japanese until 1887, when such American works as *XYZ: A Detective Story* (by Anna Katharine Green) and Edgar Allan Poe's "Murders in the Rue Morgue" were partially translated. Chapter 3 focuses on such early translations, particularly those published by Kuroiwa Ruikō, by far the most prolific Meiji period translator of detective stories. Pirating most of his material (thanks to the lack of international copyright agreements), Ruikō turned out dozens of serialized translations and adaptations of American, French, and English detective novels in his newspaper *Yorozu chōhō* (Morning Report for the Masses). Many of these translations were notably free, falling into a category of literature that came to be known as *hon'an-mono*, or adaptations, rather than adhering to the standards of faithfulness we now associate with translation. These adaptations stand out for Ruikō's wholesale grafting into them of original material and for the uses to which Ruikō put the works in his own, quite local context. Ruikō's adaptation of Émile Gaboriau's *L'affaire Lerouge* as *Hito ka oni ka* (Man or Devil? 1888), for example, has an entirely new ending calculated to turn the novel's story of confusion over the true culprit in a murder case into a political tract attacking the death penalty, which Ruikō viewed as feudal, unenlightened, and prone to error.

In Ruikō's hands, the translation *Hito no un* (People's Luck, 1894, based on an unidentified English detective novel) also became a critique of the Japanese Meiji period justice system. He published his translation in serial form on the same pages of the paper in which he was running coverage of the Sōma scandal, a sensational real-life murder trial involving a huge inheritance and an allegedly insane family patriarch. Ruikō's trial coverage relentlessly accused the wealthy Sōma family of having greased the wheels of the justice system with bribery. By introducing a crucial interpolation into his translation, Ruikō underlined the striking parallels between the fictional story (in which an inheritance dispute also looms large) and the real one. He thus used his translation to add weight to the critique of corruption in the Japanese justice system that he was carrying out in the adjacent editorial and news columns of the paper.

In both cases Ruikō's changes in the course of adaptation illustrate the complexity of his acts of cultural borrowing, which were never mere mimicry of the dominant Western culture. Ruikō's ideals as a muckraker and his indignation at the faults of the Japanese legal system were inspired by a modern, Western view of the relations between citizens and the state. But the uses to which he put the cultural artifacts he appropriated were quirkily creative in their own right and wholly unpredictable on the basis of the artifacts themselves. This element of unpredictability and flexibility in Ruikō's appropriations becomes especially clear through examination of a third translation of Ruikō's, *Kettō no hate* (The Consequences of a Duel, 1889, based on Fortuné du Boisgobey's *Les suites d'un duel*). Here Ruikō again uses European culture as an intermediary for Japanese self-scrutiny, but he does so in a way that makes France into an object of ethnographic curiosity rather than a model to be emulated, and a stand-in for the pre-Enlightenment self that Japan has left behind.

Chapter 4 treats Okamoto Kidō (1872–1939), a Kabuki playwright who saw the detective story as essentially Western and modern but put it to ends that were thoroughly nativistic and protradition. Directly inspired by Arthur Conan Doyle, Kidō wrote, beginning in the 1910s, a hugely popular series of sixty-eight detective stories set in the old city of Edo (as Tokyo was known before the Meiji period). Kidō's stories are narrated as the nostalgic reminiscences of Hanshichi, a private investigator retired from service in the old city of Edo. He continually punctuates his storytelling with wistful observations about the irreversible changes that have occurred since the downfall of the shogun. The stories are thus suffused with longing for a Japan that has been all but erased by the incursions of modernity. The solutions to the mysteries in these stories also turn, as a rule, on some forgotten detail about Edo culture so that the stories become self-contained lessons in (and records of) Japan's premodern history. These solutions, moreover, are arrived at by decidedly unscientific means, and Hanshichi takes a pride in his hunches that sets him in direct opposition to Sherlock Holmes' embodiment of Western, post-Enlightenment rationality.

The nativistic longing in these stories is further heightened by their latent unease with early Western incursions onto Japanese soil. One story, for example, re-creates a scene in which a Japanese mob stones a group of foreign visitors to Edo; another centers on hooligans posing as "barbarian expellers" who extort money from the citizens of Edo in order to support their systematic assassination of Westerners. By restaging such episodes of violence but also stopping short of unambiguously endorsing them (the second story, for example, eventually reveals the barbarian expellers to be frauds), Kidō's works reveal a striking ambivalence toward Westernization.

In addition Kidō's use of the series form—in which each story ritualistically repeats elements of all the others in the series—also gives his stories an especially backward-looking feel. Since each story is full of stock gestures made familiar by repetition in earlier stories, and some stories even involve sophisticated play on the expectations of readers who know the earlier stories in the series, they point just as insistently to their own, invented past as they do to Japan's historical one. Indeed, the stories can be understood ultimately as an attempt to insulate Japan from Western modernity by creating an imaginary, remembered world that is as easily comprehended (Hanshichi's hunches are never wrong) as it is culturally pure. Kidō's stories thus show that what begins as an imitation need not end up as one. Like Ruikō before him, Kidō put a borrowed form to unexpected uses. But where Ruikō was mostly motivated by Western-style liberalism, Kidō was motivated by a nativistic conservatism that seems to have reflected a more generalized Japanese discomfort with the cultural sacrifices required by Westernization and modernization, a discomfort that was not yet so prevalent during Ruikō's career.

Chapter 5 takes up the detective fiction and critical essays produced in the 1920s and 1930s by Edogawa Ranpo and his contemporaries. These works suggest that, as Japan's modernization progressed, Japanese detective writers were increasingly troubled both by cultural changes affecting the Japanese national identity and by their position as practitioners of a borrowed genre, a position that, as we have seen, could lead them to self-indictment for what they saw as a fatal lack of originality. Ranpo's stories, in particular, show with special acuteness the effects of a dual anxiety about Japan's cultural hybridity and about their own hybridity as narratives. His stories repeatedly revisit the themes of impersonation, double identity, and monstrous hybridity, and these themes regularly become associated in some nightmarishly twisted way with Japan's Westernization and with his stories' own place in the shadow of Western literary models.

Ranpo published many of his stories and serialized novels in the magazine *Shinseinen* (New Youth), one of a number of post–World War I mass-produced magazines for young urbanites. The magazine devoted much of its space to detective fiction and also to critical essays on the genre. Many of these essays were suffused by the same ambivalence evident in Ranpo's stories. In particular, the question of why Japan had failed to produce a "good" detective novel becomes in these essays a constant refrain. For this generation, the detective novel clearly comes to represent modernity and rationality, and the failure to produce a novel equal to those of the West becomes an embarrassing sign of Japan's rootedness in the premodern world. These essays, not only by Ranpo and the critic Hirabayashi Hatsunosuke, but also by Kozakai Fuboku, Katō Takeo, and even the well-known novelist Satō Haruo, offer explanations for this "failure" ranging from the dearth of locking rooms in traditional Japanese architecture (a handicap when it comes to writing locked-room mysteries) to the supposed inability of Japanese to engage in close logical reasoning. This sense of inadequacy evidently still haunted Ranpo as late as 1951, when he wrote that even on the eve of the second Sino-Japanese War (1937–1945), Japanese detective writers were "subject to an unspoken criticism that there were no real detective novels in Japan."[32] Ironically, the cosmopolitanism of the writers in this generation seems to have left them perpetually frustrated with their own seeming inability to be anything more than a second-rate version of the Western writers they admired.

The concluding chapter of the book reviews the responses laid out in the previous chapters to the problem of writing in a borrowed genre and summarizes the case in favor of a more nuanced understanding of the processes of intercultural literary borrowing. This case rests on my contention that the conventional notions of imitation and cultural imperialism are incomplete at best and cannot be applied equally to all the instances of borrowing that this book explores. The asymmetry in power between Asia and the West was perhaps a necessary condition for the importation and subsequent adaptation of the classic detective novel in Japan. And Japanese writers' views of their place in the genre were no doubt shaped by Japan's frustrated ambition to gain equal footing with Western powers by replicating their legal system and their pattern of imperial conquest, a frustration that culminated most acutely in the writings of Ranpo and his generation.

But an impulse toward emulation at a national level did not translate straightforwardly or consistently into emulation at the level of particular texts, and it would be a mistake to confer upon Ranpo and his generation the status of a teleological (rather than a merely chronological) endpoint for the development of the detective novel between the Meiji Restoration (1868) and the outbreak of the second Sino-Japanese War (1937). Ranpo's continuing reputation as the father of the Japanese detective novel should not allow him to overshadow a more balanced and inclusive understanding of borrowing by Japanese detective writers during this period as a whole. Although they arrived at starkly different results—one essentially modern and the other essentially antimodern—Ruikō and Kidō stand together as significant counterweights to the tendencies one sees in Ranpo and his contemporaries.

The single gravest mistake we can make in trying to understand the cross-cultural flow of literary influence is to become fixated on a single model of how such influences occur. To let Ranpo's crises of identity and self-perception—or, for that matter, Kuroiwa Ruikō's devil-may-care élan or Okamoto Kidō's unapologetic subversion of the detective genre's post-Enlightenment rationality—dominate our view of these influences is to give short shrift to the multiplicity of the processes of borrowing, to the vagaries of intercultural transfer, to the historical moment at which the borrowing occurs, and to the temperaments and purposes of individual writers. The variety of responses that the writers treated here exemplify, and the variety of uses to which they put their borrowings, show that no one model—whether of Japanese imitativeness or of Japanese cultural triumph, whether of cultural imperialism or of quasi-colonial resistance—adequately encompasses the richness of the possible goings-on at intercultural boundaries, even in a case (such as that of the Japanese borrowing of the detective novel) in which the Western origin of the genre and the perception of international inequality that accompanied its borrowing might seem likely to exert a determinative power.

Affirmations
of Authority

Premodern and
Early Meiji Crime Literature

Although the basic narrative structure of the detective story was new to Japan when Kuroiwa Ruikō (1862–1920) and other translators began reproducing it in the mid-1880s, there were certain elements of continuity between the preexisting native tradition of crime narrative and the newly imported genre. There were also significant things—in addition to narrative structure—that distinguished the two. This chapter examines the native tradition, presenting an analysis of these continuities and differences in order to provide historical context for the developments of the 1880s and the following decades.

The two major forms of crime narrative in circulation before the detective story arrived in Japan were the courtroom narrative, based on a Chinese tradition of stories about wise judges, and the criminal biography, which enjoyed a surge of popularity in the early Meiji period (1868–1912) thanks to the contemporaneous rise of tabloid journalism. Both these genres set precedents for the representation of the Japanese justice system that would later be rudely broken by Kuroiwa Ruikō. But of these two antecedents to the Japanese detective novel, criminal biography is the more significant reference point. It was, for one thing, in the market formed by readers of criminal biography that early translators of detective fiction saw the best chance of commercial success. "I saw that readers were tiring a bit of the [Kanagaki] Robunesque stuff, and I wanted to show them what was available in the West," Kuroiwa Ruikō is known to have remarked, referring to the leading writer of criminal biography.[1] But, more important, such biographies represented the state of the art of Japanese crime writing when translations of detective fiction were first introduced to Japan in the 1880s. This chapter therefore devotes considerably more attention to criminal biography (focusing particularly on Kanagaki Robun's *Tale of Takahashi Oden the She-Devil*, 1879) than to courtroom narratives.

In the earliest major examples of Japanese courtroom narrative, those of Ihara Saikaku (1642–1693), the justice system is essentially infallible. In later examples, such as those afforded by the anonymous *Ōoka seidan* (Ōoka's Rulings), some cracks in this façade become visible, but they are hastily papered over. And in early Meiji period criminal biography, there is a hybridizing of new and old. On the one hand, such biographies could incorporate documents, such as official court verdicts and records of criminal testimony, that would not have been made public before the Meiji government began its Westernizing reform of the court system.[2] If these documents implied a plausible alternative story, one at odds with the story told by their framing narrative, such biographies could hint at shortcomings in the justice system. But on the other hand, these biographies drew such stark lines between good and evil, and their official portrayal of the justice system tended to be so celebratory, that it seems unlikely these hints were actually intended to register with contemporary readers. Although there were significant differences among these premodern and early Meiji examples of crime literature, they ultimately projected similar ideologies in that they all affirmed the authority and the wisdom of the justice system's agents. In contrast (as Chapter 3 explains) Kuroiwa Ruikō positioned himself in his translations and adaptations of Western detective fiction as an antiestablishment muckraker, and his portrayals of the justice system were accordingly critical.

One of the most significant precedents set by early Meiji period criminal biography was its premise of referentiality. With the burgeoning of an industry in Japanese tabloid journalism, criminal biographies increasingly played up the appeal of their basis in real events, even though liberal embellishment of those events was the rule rather than the exception. This tendency to straddle the divide between the real world and a fictional one would become a hallmark of Kuroiwa Ruikō's translations and adaptations of detective fiction, which he often deployed to political ends.

A final noteworthy feature of early Meiji period criminal biography is its exploration of the social consequences of Japanese Westernization as they played out in an arena beyond the justice system, that of the status system. The dismantling of the old feudal status system was a central part of the Meiji government's program of civilization and enlightenment. One result of this change was that anxieties about the resulting social mobility manifested themselves in an increasing fear of the imagined criminality such mobility might enable, a fear writ large in the criminal biographies of the day. This exploration of social and cultural anxieties would continue in much subsequent detective fiction, particularly that of Okamoto Kidō (treated in Chapter 4) and that of Edogawa Ranpo (treated in Chapter 5). In the hands of these authors, crime narrated in the imported form of the detective story became an arena not only for the playing out of writers' own preoccupations with literary theft, but also for the exploration of more generalized social and cultural anxieties arising from Westernization, including anxiety about the hybridization or outright loss of Japanese tradition and identity.

Tokugawa Period Courtroom Narratives
(the Seventeenth Century)

Ihara Saikaku is probably best known for his early novella-length tales of desire and transgression, most notably *Five Women Who Loved Love (Kōshoku gonin onna)* and *The Life of an Amorous Man (Kōshoku ichidai otoko)*. But later in his life he published a collection of forty-four courtroom narratives under the name *Honchō ōin hiji*, or *Trials in the Shade of a Cherry Tree*, which is the most famous example of traditional Japanese courtroom narrative. This title, as Thomas Kondo and Alfred Marks have pointed out, is a variation on the title of the thirteenth-century Chinese classic *T'ang ying pi shih*, or *Trials in the Shade of a Pear Tree*, by Kuei Wang-jung.[3] The term *hiji* in Saikaku's title, a direct transfer into the Japanese phonetic system of the Chinese words *pi shih*, means "comparing things." Kuei Wang-jung's work grouped related cases together in pairs in order to reflect the actual contemporary Chinese practice of rendering judgments based on comparisons of the particulars of a case with those of other, precedent-setting cases. With one exception, Saikaku's stories themselves, however, seem to have been based on some combination of his own imaginings and actual Japanese trial records, rather than on his Chinese source text.[4] Some of Saikaku's stories can be traced to the *Itakura seiyō* (Essentials of the Administration of Itakura), a collection of trial records and stories concerning Itakura Katsushige and his son Shigemune, both of whom served as Kyoto Shoshidai (a regional deputy, in Kyoto, of the Tokugawa Shogunate) between 1601 and 1654.[5]

In Saikaku's hands, the Japanese justice system, as it is embodied in the character of the magistrate that he puts at center stage, is essentially infallible—even when keeping this idea alive requires a certain amount of contrivance. The ideology of infallible justice projected by Saikaku's stories was in perfect accord with the image projected as a matter of policy by the administrators of the actual Tokugawa era (1600–1868) justice system.

In the city of Edo, for example, shogunal policy called for criminal suspects to go through a preliminary interrogation at the hands of low-level functionaries before they could be brought to the *shirasu,* the "courtyard of white sand," in the residence or offices of the local administrator who would pass final judgment upon them.[6] As Daniel Botsman has reported, these low-level functionaries often acted on orders to extract a confession through torture before a session on the *shirasu,* because too-frequent findings of innocence at the *shirasu* would "imply that officials did not *already* know whether a person was guilty or not, and…fallibility of any kind was something the warrior state was loath to admit." Once the local administrator rendered a verdict of guilty, he would propose a punishment to his superiors; these proposals were often modified, but guilty verdicts themselves seem to have been overturned seldom or never. Botsman quotes records of an 1804 case of petty theft that suggest a self-serving logic lurked behind this consistency: if after a guilty verdict has been rendered, the ruling in this case reasons, "it is announced that the matter, which has been recommended for punishment, does not in fact constitute a punishable offense, the fear and respect felt by the contemptible common people will naturally be diminished."[7]

Given the emphasis placed by the Tokugawa regime on maintaining its aura of infallible authority in judicial matters, it is not surprising that formal confession should have been the gold standard for settling the guilt of a suspect. A confession (assuming, of course, that it is true) removes the necessity of constructing a narrative of guilt based on potentially ambiguous evidence and lends an air of certainty to the judgment rendered. So central was this notion to the Tokugawa era justice system that, if a confession could not be extracted before a suspect's appearance on the white sand, there were formalized procedures for resorting to judicial torture during that latter stage of the proceedings. Torture was explicitly limited to four varieties: whipping *(muchiuchi),* crushing the legs of the kneeling prisoner with heavy stone slabs *(ishidaki),* tying the prisoner into painfully contorted positions with rope *(ebizeme),* and suspension of the prisoner's entire body weight by a rope attached to the wrists after they had been bound behind the back *(tsurushizeme).*[8]

Whatever the actual record of this system was in avoiding judicial errors, it was surely haunted by their specter at every turn. Not only did reliance on torture pose the obvious danger of innocent prisoners confessing to crimes they did not commit simply to escape pain. The resort to capital punishment as the penalty for such crimes as arson or, in the case of a servant, causing injury to one's master considerably upped the stakes of an error even in cases concerning relatively light offenses.[9] The desire to instill fear in the lower classes by projecting an aura of infallibility compounded the dangers still more by creating an incentive to prize unwavering judgments over correct ones. Read in this light, Ihara Saikaku's courtroom narratives begin to look suspiciously like official propaganda or the results of censorship. Or perhaps they are simply a set of wishful fantasies about the fairness of a judicial system that must have been ripe for abuse. In any case, the result is that their representation of the justice system projects an ideology that is completely of a piece with that projected by contemporary official policy.

In Saikaku's *Honchō ōin hiji,* virtually every story moves toward a denouement that underlines the clearsightedness of the magistrate (referred to simply as *gozen,* or His Lordship) and the infallibility of the justice system. It is a consistent feature of the stories in this collection that the magistrate will test litigants or defendants in some clever and unexpected way. When a large sum of money is stolen during a New Year's celebration, for example, he commands the ten men who were present at the party to appear in court with their wives or, in the case of the unmarried, a female relative. The couples are told that they are all being held responsible for the theft, and each couple is made to carry a large drum along a circuitous route through the streets, which are lined with jeering onlookers. Unbeknownst to the couples, the magistrate has concealed inside the drum an eavesdropping midget priest. When the guilty couple take their turn carrying the drum, they fall to grousing at each other and eventually incriminate themselves within the priest's hearing. The priest reports back to His Lordship, and the couple have no choice but to confess.[10]

In another case, a corpse impaled by an arrow is found in the street. His Lordship interrogates two known enemies of the victim, but both give satisfactory accounts of themselves. He then tells the victim's widow to bury the arrow together with the man's body and make her peace with his death. But he has not in fact given up on the case. A year later, he instructs the woman to go to the neighborhood where her husband was found and to raise a false alarm over a supposed burglar. Most of the neighbors rush into the street carrying clubs, but one is holding a bow and arrow. The waiting police seize this man and his weapons. His Lordship then orders that the body of the widow's husband be exhumed. The arrow buried with him is compared to those in the possession of the man in custody. When the arrows prove identical, the suspect confesses to the murder and is executed shortly thereafter.[11]

The magistrate in Saikaku's stories thus has enormous discretion, and his methods are often devious. Yet these methods nearly always result in unambiguous confessions of the guilty—confessions, moreover, that are won not through torture but through mental acuity and an unfailing understanding of human nature. In spite of their having been composed against the background of an actual justice system that offered ample opportunity for error and abuse, the stories in this collection are all variations on the theme of the magistrate's benevolent, infallible wisdom. One never has the slightest sense that any of the power vested in the magistrate might be excessive or ill-placed. It is the bedrock principle of these stories' imaginary world that this power is always properly wielded in the name of promoting the common welfare.

Courtroom Narrative in Eighteenth-Century Japan

Ōoka's Rulings (Ōoka seidan), a later, eighteenth-century, collection of courtroom stories, allows much more anxiety about potential miscarriages of justice into its imaginary world than does Saikaku. But if anything these stories are even more emphatic than Saikaku's in their affirmations of official infallibility. Whenever things threaten to go awry in the administration of justice—a surprisingly regular occurrence in these stories—the clear-sightedness of the judge saves the day.

Ōoka's Rulings contains sixteen anonymous stories recording cases from the jurisdiction of Ōoka Tadasuke (renamed Ōoka Echizen in the stories), an actual city commissioner *(machi-bugyō)* who judged cases in Edo from 1717 to 1736. The collection may have taken its present form as late as the 1850s, but it is known to have circulated underground as *utsushi-bon*, or hand-copied manuscripts, beginning in about 1769.[12] This underground circulation suggests that the threat of censorship hung over the collection. It is possible that it did so simply because it was illegal to commit to paper any representation of a shogunal official, not because it trafficked in especially subversive representations. That said, this collection does acknowledge far more explicitly than Saikaku's the danger of potential judicial error. But then again, these errors are always either corrected by the story's end or shown not to have been errors at all. It is for this reason that the stories seem to affirm the authority of the justice system even more emphatically than Saikaku's. Where Saikaku's stories never admit the possibility of error at all, the stories in *Ōoka seidan* admit it but then vehemently—perhaps a little too vehemently—deny that it is a cause for concern.

"The Story of Hikobei the Haberdasher" ("Komamonoya Hikobei no den"), set in the year Kyōho 9 (1724), is typical in its adherence to this pattern. In the story the title character is, on the basis of circumstantial evidence, accused of the murder and robbery of a rich but old and frail townswoman. Hikobei's arrest takes his neighbors by surprise. They rally round him, saying, "It's probably a mistake of some kind—you'll be cleared before long" *(ōkata mono no machigai naran ni yori, yagate kiyoki karada ni naru beshi)*.[13] And even as he is locked up in prison to await his interrogation, the narrator affirms his innocence, describing the arrest as one carried out *tsumi naku,* or "without crime" (p. 488). Naturally, Hikobei refuses to confess to the crime even when the commissioner confronts him with the evidence against him. He is then tortured. "Rather than endure the pain," the narrator now tells us, "he confessed to a crime he didn't commit" *(mujitsu no tsumi o hikiuke),* set his seal on the deposition, was decapitated, and had his head put on public display (p. 490). When his faithful son Hikosaburō goes to retrieve his father's remains from the execution ground, he overhears two passing palanquin bearers talking about the case. "Hey, Sukejū," one says to the other, "that haberdasher Hikobei who was beheaded here...that was a big mistake. The one who killed that woman had to have been Kantarō" (p. 496).

At the son's request, the palanquin bearers agree to present their evidence before the commissioner, and this Kantarō is eventually induced to confess his crime in court, at which point the story must revisit the issue of the innocent father's death. Criticism is now allowed to heap upon the commissioner. One character who previously testified against the innocent man approaches the bench: "It's only natural that he [Hikosaburō] should think of me as his enemy and bear me a grudge for having killed his innocent father. If that is so, couldn't the same be said of the commissioner who ordered an innocent man to his death? But since you are a noble gentleman that will probably be the end of the matter" (pp. 514–515). The two palanquin bearers also come forward with what is at first a gentle rebuke: "Even he who is known as the most skillful commissioner under the heavens will make a mistake (just as the master Kōbō Daishi could with his calligraphy), so do not take this as an insult. But what are you going to do about the dead Hikobei?" *(ikaga asobasaruru ya)* (p. 515). Shushed by Ōoka Echizen, they then become defiant: "'We will not be quiet. Hikosaburō has grounds for complaint *(mōshibun).*' [Others too] now came forward, and they raised a ruckus all the more pointedly" (p. 515).

Faced with this protest at the injustice of his court, Ōoka Echizen is now allowed to extricate himself from what looks like a bad situation in the most convincing way possible: he produces Hikosaburō's father, still alive after all. Despite the man's confession, the commissioner explains, there was something amiss in the man's way of speaking and in his looks, so he secretly kept the man alive and placed another criminal's head on display instead. The head, we are here reminded, had been unrecognizable, and it had been given out at the time that Hikobei had been disfigured by a disease contracted in prison.

This story, then, only flirts with the idea of a gap in the administration of justice; after this flirtation the legal system is made whole again and the suspected breach shown not to have occurred at all. Anxiety about possible injustice under a system of torture and capital punishment is allayed at the story's end by the clear-sightedness of the commissioner himself. There is no soul-searching here about the difficulty of coming to the truth or even about how heavily justice hinged upon the chance encounter of the faithful son and the two palanquin bearers at the execution ground. Even when the protest is raised, the justice system itself is not put into question. Indeed, the utter lack of irony in the narration can be astonishing, as when the torture of Hikobei, who has refused to confess, is described as being begun "for lack of any alternative" *(zehi naku)* (p. 490).

In *Ōoka's Rulings,* the sense of seamlessness in the administration of justice is often further heightened by the stories' narrative structure. Most of the stories assume the form not of the "whodunit," but of a "how's the judge going to find out whodunit." They show, in other words, the commissioner Ōoka Echizen moving toward a conclusion that the reader already knows is correct. When his verdict subsequently matches what the reader has already been shown, the commissioner's authority is buttressed by the reader's foreknowledge. The case in the story "Echigo Denkichi no den" (The Story of Denkichi of Echigo), for example, concerns two headless corpses and the attempt by an enemy of the title character to pin the hapless victims' murder on him. But the scene of the killing and this enemy's depositing of a pair of blood-soaked sandals at Denkichi's house are narrated in all their particulars before the trial scene ever begins. So when Ōoka Echizen sets about his interrogation, it is not to arrive at a surprise identification of the culprit, but rather to arrive at what the story has set up as a foregone conclusion.

Early Meiji Period Criminal Biography

The confidence these seventeenth- and eighteenth-century courtroom narratives projected in the justice system was carried forward into early Meiji period criminal biography as well, even though it was somewhat less central a theme. Indeed, one notable side-effect of these biographies' new concern with journalistic accuracy was that their attempts to project this traditional confidence could be inadvertently undermined by their own inclusion of documents (such as the actual testimony of criminals themselves) that

offered alternatives to the official story of guilt justly punished. But as a
rule these tensions were not openly acknowledged in the narrative. In their
visibly strained attempt to hold together competing narratives of the life
of the criminal and the legitimacy of the court, these biographies became
a sign of the extraordinary transition that Meiji society had undertaken, a
transition that was itself fraught with tensions between the traditional and
the modern.

The earliest Meiji crime writing was dominated by a form known as *dokufu-mono*,
or "stories of poisonous women." The *dokufu-mono* were criminal biographies that narrated the colorful exploits of female outlaws such as the notorious flimflammer and seductress Takahashi Oden, who was beheaded in
1879 after being convicted of using her feminine wiles to con and murder
a used-kimono dealer. *The Tale of Takahashi Oden the She-Devil* (*Takahashi
Oden yasha monogatari*, 1879) by Kanagaki Robun (1829–1894) is the most
famous version of Takahashi Oden's life and the most famous example
of the *dokufu-mono* genre. The genre's popularity ensured that the *dokufu*
quickly became a well-known and predictable type: silver-tongued, alluring,
cunning, defiant, usually oversexed, and quick to steal or kill or both.

The earliest example of the genre is generally thought to be a three-day
serial that appeared in 1876 in a newspaper started by Kanagaki Robun,
the *Kana-yomi shinbun* (Phonetic Reading Newspaper). The story appeared
under the title "Onna tōzoku Otsune no den" (The Story of Otsune the
Female Thief). Soon after, in the same paper, there appeared the serial
"Torioi Omatsu no den" (The Story of Omatsu the Strolling Musician).
Omatsu was a woman of the outcast *(hinin)* class whose crimes, when compared to those of other heroines of the *dokufu* genre, are tame—mostly
theft and chicanery helped along by her good looks. All the same, her story
too proved popular and sensational enough to warrant the issue, in February and March 1878, of a revised stand-alone version, titled *Torioi Omatsu
kaijō shinwa*, or *A New Tale of Omatsu the Strolling Musician at Sea*. (The book
took its name from an episode in which Omatsu, having fallen into the sea
in a scuffle with a man making unwanted advances, is then picked up by a
steamer bound for Kōbe.) That same year Okamoto Kisen (1853–1882)
published a story in the *Tōkyō sakigake* (Tokyo Herald) called "Yoarashi
Okinu hana no adayume" (The Beautiful Vain Dreams of "Night Storm"
Okinu). The story's heroine fatally poisoned her husband and attempted
the same on a second man. She was tried and executed for her crimes at
the age of thirty. Okinu's story too enjoyed great success, and in keeping
with what was fast becoming the usual pattern, it was revised for publication in book form, in the spring of the following year. The titles of books

being brought out as late as the mid-1880s suggest that the boom in *dokufu-mono* was still alive and well a decade after "The Story of Otsune the Female Thief": a writer named Suzuki Kanejirō, for instance, came out with *Meiji dokufu den* (Stories of Meiji Poison Women) in 1886.[14]

The emergence of a thriving tabloid newspaper industry during this same period played an obvious role in heightening the popularity of such stories and creating a demand for them. The forerunner to the modern tabloid was the broadsheet *(kawaraban),* a special edition usually printed up in response to a particular event (including such things as fires and earthquakes, but also criminal executions). With the country's opening to foreign trade and its exposure to Western journalism, however, such broadsheets were quickly superseded by newspapers with regular weekly or daily publishing schedules. Some of the impetus behind such newspapers was political: as popular agitation for representative government increased with the rise of the Freedom and People's Rights Movement, the printed editorial became a supplement to traditional public speechmaking. Technological innovation was also a catalyst. Japanese movable type became commercially viable in the 1860s, and in 1870 the *Yokohama mainichi shinbun* (Yokohama Daily Newspaper) appeared as the first paper to use the new technology.[15] The mass-circulation tabloid was not far behind. In 1874 Kanagaki Robun, realizing that traditional *gesaku* prose (which had been his stock in trade) was becoming outmoded, announced he was becoming a journalist.[16] He first joined the *Yokohama mainichi shinbun* as a part-time reporter and then started the *Kana-yomi shinbun* the following year. Increases in literacy rates and in the disposable incomes of city dwellers also supported the market in tabloids. And it was a corollary of this market's growth that the hunger for sensational news should also grow. Reports of violent crimes, trials, and executions all filled the bill handsomely. This increase in the representation and contemplation of public events in print media created a new register of public opinions and anxieties, and it was only natural that serialized criminal biography in the pages of the tabloids should reflect this trend.[17]

Viewed in light of the subsequent developments in the genre of detective fiction, the most important aspects of the stories of poison women (and of tabloid criminal biography in general) were their blurring of the lines between truth and fiction, their use of criminality in particular as a focal point for social anxieties of the early Meiji period, and their sometimes inadvertently compromised portrayal of the justice system. All of these elements of Meiji period criminal biography are clearly evident in Kanagaki Robun's *Tale of Takahashi Oden the She-Devil.*

The Genesis of
Takahashi Oden yasha monogatari

When Robun went to work turning out Oden's life story in the *Kana-yomi shinbun*, he was not alone. Oden was put to death on January 31, 1879. Robun began publishing her story the very next day, but two competing tabloids were just as quick off the mark. The *E-iri shinbun* (Illustrated Paper) and the *Tōkyō shinbun* (Tokyo Paper) both began running what were to be full-length serialized accounts *(naga-monogatari)* of Oden's life.[18]

Despite the competition, Robun's account almost instantly attracted the notice of an enterprising purveyor of *gōkan* books (that is, books binding together in one volume works originally published as separate fascicles, often in serial form). Robun ran the story in his newspaper for two days (February 1 and 2) under the name "Dokufu Oden no hanashi" (The Story of Oden the Femme Fatale). He then printed a notice on February 4 explaining that he had an offer from the publishing house Tsujibumi (also known as Kinshōdō) to bring out the story as an illustrated book *(e-iri yomihon)*, the first volume to appear no later than the middle of that same month.[19] Robun broke off publication of the story in the newspaper to throw in his lot with Tsujibumi. The publisher was true to his word, and Robun kept up with the breakneck pace he dictated. The first volume of the book, brought out under the new title *Takahashi Oden yasha monogatari* (The Story of Takahashi Oden the She-Devil), was published on February 13. The eighth and last volume appeared on April 22. In accordance with the traditional layout of the *kusa-zōshi*, the book in its bound format consisted of double-page spreads that were dominated by illustrations, with the text filling in the spaces around and between the figures. According to the memoirs of Robun's protégé Nozaki Sabun, some 45,000 copies of the book were sold.

Takahashi Oden, the Woman

It has become difficult at this distance to sift the facts of Oden's life from the rumors, exaggerations, and outright fabrications that have affixed themselves to it. What lies beyond dispute in the existing accounts (and that in itself is no guarantee of truth) is precious little: that her mother was named Oharu, that she was born in the village of Shimomaki-mura in the Tone region of Kōzuke (now Gunma prefecture), that in 1872 she left the village for Tokyo together with her husband Naminosuke, that Naminosuke died en route, and that in 1876 she was arrested in Tokyo on charges of seducing, stabbing to death, and robbing a man named Gotō Kichizō who was a moneylender and used clothing dealer. For her part, Oden claimed that Gotō had tried to rape her at knifepoint and that in the ensuing struggle he fatally stabbed himself in the throat. She was not put on trial until three years after her arrest, when she was found guilty of murder and sentenced to death by beheading. The *Yūbin hōchi shinbun* (Mail and Intelligence), one of the big newspapers, ran this grisly account of Oden's death the day after she was executed:

> When the time came for her execution, [Oden] stopped the executioner.
>
> "Just a moment." As her parting poem, she murmured, "At this, the long anticipated hour when I will meet my dead husband, I am certain that he will receive me with an offering of blooming flowers." Then, when she had stretched out her neck, the executioner gave a yell and sliced down. What she was thinking as the blade came down [one cannot know], but she jerked her head from left to right, protesting she had something more to say, and so the first stroke missed and cut her in the jaw. The sword went up a second time, and, perhaps because she was chanting "Namu amida butsu" (Save me, merciful Buddha), it missed again, so that without any other recourse the executioner then cut off her head through the throat.[20]

Beyond these few items, the picture becomes even sketchier, since existing accounts are at odds. In an account published in the *Tōkyō nichi nichi shinbun* (Tokyo Daily), Oden's husband Naminosuke dies naturally, of leprosy.[21] In Robun's account, Oden strangles him as he lies helpless in his sickbed. In the account by Robun's rival Okamoto Kisen, Oden unwittingly kills Naminosuke by giving him poison that she has been tricked into believing is medicine for the leprosy.[22] There is also disagreement among the various accounts over such matters as Oden's parentage and the details of the death of Kichizō. Robun portrays Oden as the daughter of a gambler named Ariga Seikichi, with whom her mother has several trysts before she marries another man, Takahashi Kanzaemon. Okamoto Kisen's account, in contrast, portrays her as the daughter of a samurai in service to the Toki family (who were direct vassals of the shogunate). In this version, her mother Oharu marries the samurai but is then run out of the house over rumors she was involved with another man. As for the details of Kichizō's death, there is disagreement over, among other things, the fundamental question of just when it occurred. The *Tōkyō nichi nichi* account puts Kichizō's death in the afternoon of August 27 (1876), whereas Robun has the murder occurring just before dawn on the following day. More examples might be listed of the many points on which existing accounts are at variance.[23]

But the more important, related, point is that—perhaps because of the confusing variety of competing accounts in circulation—Robun's account expends considerable energy in playing up its own truth and accuracy, even as it introduces obviously sensationalized material to meet the demands of the marketplace.

The Rhetoric of Referentiality

Takahashi Oden is likely to strike any modern reader as patchy and uneven. The narrative contains several long interpolations that have only the most tenuous of connections to the main story and numerous episodes that can hardly have been based on anything more substantial than Robun's imaginings. He himself admits that he added to the account, as he puts it, "occasional embellishments made...to sharpen it, as an example of evil coming to a bad end, for the benefit of women and children."[24] But because Robun, partly inspired by newly emerging ideals of journalistic accuracy, started with the facts of Oden's life and death, the text still preserves—and indeed deliberately plays up to a striking degree—its relation to actual events.

Even after Robun truncated the newspaper account and began publishing Oden's story in the *gōkan* edition, Robun continued to invoke reminders of the account's beginnings in the newspaper, presumably as a sign of the account's factuality. For example, in his interpolations into the account in his own voice, Robun refers to himself not as "Robun" or "the author" *(sakusha)* but as "the reporter" *(kisha).*[25] He ends the introduction to the first installment of the book version by signing it "Kanagaki Robun, at the offices of the Kanayomi Newspaper" *(Kanayomi Shinbun-sha ni oite)* (p. 4), as if to give the imprimatur of the newspaper company to the account. As subsequent installments are introduced, Robun signs them with the somewhat more ambiguous notation *Kanagaki Robun hotetsu,* or "supplemented by Kanagaki Robun." Although this notation implies a certain license has been taken where gaps in the account needed filling in, it also underlines the account's basic grounding in a factual record that exists independently of Robun's narration.

But the most significant reminder of the *gōkan* version's origin in the newspaper comes in the introduction to the first installment, which both invites the reader to compare Robun's account with those that have appeared in competing newspapers and promises that *Takahashi Oden yasha monogatari* is the most accurate version available:

Judging that [Oden's] deposition was enough to understand the course of her whole career, the reporters at a number of newspapers

have taken up their brushes to write multi-installment features based
on it. But...the deposition consists of nothing but the lies and connivances of an evil woman; it is actually an attempt to pull the wool over
the eyes of an upstanding court, and in the end it does not bring one
to the truth *(sono jitsu o tsuguru ni itarazu)*....What has been printed
in the various newspapers, being based on the fictions of the evil woman's wily tongue, does not convey the facts. When the various reporters
discovered this, they printed addenda promising without fail to publish, at some future date, further reports based on certain information.
This account has sought to come as near as possible to approximating
the truth, with occasional embellishments made only to sharpen it, as
an example of evil coming to a bad end, for the benefit of women and
children. (Pp. 3–4)

This emphasis on the connections between the text and the real world—
even though it is yoked uneasily together with mention of embellishments
and moral examples—would continue in the translations of detective stories turned out by Kuroiwa Ruikō in the coming decades.

Another way that Robun's account implicitly asserts its own truth is in
its concern with the correct dating of the events in Oden's life. Each installment of *Takahashi Oden* begins with a preface. In these prefaces, Robun
mentions more than once the cross-checking he has performed on the
chronologies of his sources. This labor has resulted in a liberal sprinkling
of exact dates throughout the account. Robun even goes so far as to correct these dates in subsequent installments when misprints creep in. In the
preface to the fifth installment, he writes: "In the first volume, in the biographical sketch of Seikichi [Oden's alleged father], where it says Bunsei 2
[1819], that is a mistake for Kōka 2 [1845]; in addition, where Oden's year
of birth is given as Kaei 3 [1850], that is a mistake for Kaei 1 [1848]. I offer
in this installment my apologies" (p. 15).[26] By correcting the dates in this
way, Robun's text implicitly enforces its claims of referentiality to a real
world beyond itself in which things happen in a particular, unchanging
sequence, regardless of any act of narration (or misnarration).

The Incorporation of Legal Documents

Another significant element of referentiality in Robun's text is its incorporation of two actual legal documents—documents that would not have been
publicly available under the old Tokugawa regime. The first of these documents is the court's verdict in Oden's case, which is quoted in its entirety
in the introductory installment. The second document appears near the
close of the narrative, making a mismatched pair with the terse verdict: it

is an extended excerpt from Oden's long court deposition, cast in the stiff cadences of officialdom known as *sōrō bun*. Neither of these documents can have been fabricated by Robun for his account, since they both duplicate versions of the same documents printed in the *Yūbin hōchi shinbun* on February 1, 1879, the day after Oden's execution.[27]

Oden's deposition was printed in its entirety in the *Yūbin hōchi shinbun,* in the four days immediately following her execution (February 1 to February 4, 1879).[28] The document's use of the stiff *sōrō bun* style, with its admixture of *hentai kanbun* (Chinese-Japanese hybrid constructions), indicates that it is not a verbatim transcription of Oden's own words. Rather, it is a formal summation of her testimony, elicited in the course of interrogation, that nonetheless retains the first-person voice. In her deposition, Oden claimed that she had accompanied her alleged victim, Gotō Kichizō, to the inn where he died in the hope of recovering from him a sword that used to belong to her supposed half sister. She further claimed that Gotō had brought about his own death when he slipped and accidentally stabbed himself in an attempt to rape her at knifepoint. The deposition described the pair's arrival at the inn this way:

> Because Kichizō knew someone there, we went to a place run by an Ōtani Sanshirō, I think it was, in Asakusa Kuramae Katamachi. I didn't know the name at the time, but it was an inn called Marutake that we went into. It was already dusk and I was a bit suspicious, but Kichizō went directly up to the second floor, and I followed him. In a little while one of the serving women asked whether they should bring us sake and something to eat, but I said I didn't feel well and went off to the toilet. When I came back the sake and snacks had arrived. Kichizō repeatedly pressed them upon me, but since I felt ill I had none, except for a bit of pear when he offered that to me. When Kichizō had finished drinking and dinner was served, I also refused that, but Kichizō kept insisting, so I had one bowl of rice. After that about an hour went by, but since there was still no word from the other party [from whom Kichizō has promised to obtain a sword that used to belong to Oden's supposed half sister], I told Kichizō what I was doing and went outside for a walk to cool off, returning, as I remember it, at about twelve midnight. Kichizō was lying there in bed.[29]

In Robun's account, things unfold quite differently. Oden persuades Kichizō to go to an Asakusa teahouse in order to meet an associate who would like to borrow money from him at interest. When the man does not arrive on schedule, Oden proposes that Kichizō spend the night with her at a nearby inn and then meet the would-be borrower the next morning:

With her usual artfulness of tongue and seductiveness of word, she coaxed [Kichizō] from the teahouse to the Inn Marutake, which is in Katamachi in the same part [of Asakusa as the teahouse] and owned by Ōtani Sanshirō. She led him up to an eight-mat room on the second floor and then went back down to the front desk herself and ordered sake and something to eat with it. In the guest register she signed them in as "Uchiyama Sennosuke, 38, tea seller, and Omatsu, 25, wife of same, from Shinshuku in Kumagae station, Ōsato district, Musashi province, Kumagae prefecture." They took turns going to the bath and then went up to the second floor and cooled themselves off in the breeze blowing in through the lattice window. They had not waited long when the food and drink were brought up from below. Oden relaxed her obi so that the coquettishness with which she poured the sake was matched by the looseness of her appearance. Kichizō was being led where his inclinations pushed him anyway, so he was soon more than drunk, and when he keeled over, Oden had the maid hang the mosquito netting and wrestled him onto a futon. . . . Oden satisfied herself from the sound of his breathing that [Kichizō] was asleep. Rather than put her own head to her pillow, she began to turn her scheme over in her mind. . . . She sharpened the razor she had secretly taken when she left Shishikura's house and then blew out the lamp. Still listening intently to Kichizō's breathing, she pulled back the thin top cover and made as if to get in bed with him. Allowing herself to be pulled in by the arm that Kichizō reached toward her in his sleep, she cuddled her left hand around behind his neck. With the razor she held in her right, she stabbed him full force through the windpipe. Using a hand to smother the dying yelp that came from his mouth, she twisted [the blade] around with all her strength. (Pp. 57–58)

In Robun's version there is no mention of Oden's feeling ill. Robun has Oden going downstairs to order the sake and snacks herself, whereas she says the offer of drink and food came unsolicited. In Robun's version, Oden pours sake for Kichizō, whereas in the deposition he apparently pours it for himself. In Robun's version Oden cools off in the breeze from the window; Oden says she cooled off by going for a walk. In Robun's version Oden wrestles the drunk Kichizō into his bed and then kills him; in Oden's version she returns from her walk to find him in bed already.

Robun's framing narrative resolves the contradictions between Oden's deposition and its own version of her life (which was premised on the notion that Oden was a "poisonous woman") by claiming that the deposition was "a lie that made not the slightest bit of sense" (p. 61). But by including this real-world document in the account in order to fulfill (however imperfectly) newly emerging ideals of journalistic accuracy and completeness,

Robun's indictment of Oden was ultimately rendered less convincing than seventeenth- and eighteenth-century courtroom narratives' indictments of their criminals had been. The difficulty the narrative has in reconciling the competing accounts of Oden's identity was, as we will see later in this chapter, a sign of the transformations in class identity occurring during the early Meiji period.

In one crucial respect, however, Oden's deposition and Robun's account are strikingly similar: in their recording of the order of the principals' comings and goings, of who ate what, and the fact that it was necessary to cool off, both have *something* to say about what happened at this level of seemingly inconsequential detail. Robun's use of such detail in his account was another important by-product of his access, as a journalist, to court documents that would have been kept secret under the Tokugawa regime. His use of such seemingly inconsequential details heightens the reader's sense of connection between text and reality.[30] This not only set a precedent for Kuroiwa Ruikō's later characteristic bridging of fiction and fact; it also accustomed readers to the task of digesting realistic detail in the reconstruction of suspects' movements. Such painstakingly thorough reconstructions had no precedent in the native Japanese tradition of courtroom narrative, but they would play a central role in the translated detective literature introduced in the following decade.

Both Robun's account and Oden's deposition also supply considerable detail about the locale in which the alleged murder occurred. We learn just which neighborhood of Asakusa the Marutake stands in as well as its owner's name. We learn that the front desk and the bath are on the first floor, and Oden and Kichizō's room is on the second. We are given the size of the room (the floor area is that of eight standard tatami mats), and told that it has a window. We even know that the window is covered by a lattice.

As far as plot requirements go, there is very little necessity behind the details. In contrast to Edgar Allan Poe's "Murders in the Rue Morgue" (1841), in which an orangutan enters a second story room by swinging on a shutter, the construction of the window in the Marutake turns out not to matter particularly. But because these details do not matter in the way they do in Poe, they matter in another way. Mention of such details concerning the environment heightens the reader's sense that they have been relayed by the narrator simply because that is the way things really were at the scene of the crime.

Roland Barthes has pointed to just such an effect (which he has called "the reality effect") in Gustave Flaubert's story "A Simple Heart." In this story Flaubert mentions a piano, telling the reader that it has on top of it, "under a barometer, a pyramidal heap of boxes and cartons." Barthes singles out the barometer as a "futile" detail, since it has no necessary connection with the story. Precisely because of its "resistance to meaning," its failure to be an intelligible (or telling) detail, the barometer's presence creates for Barthes a sense of reality.[31] Details, in other words, whose place in the design of the narrative is obvious or that are readily translatable into a running metanarrative, reek of artifice for Barthes. Those that puzzle us, that do not yield up a meaning simply, more closely reflect what Barthes takes to be our normal experience of living a life that has no apparent metanarrative.

In the passage from *Takahashi Oden* quoted above, Robun supplies some details that are read very easily but also a number that are not. Oden's giving of false names in the guest register and her loosening of her obi, for example, are easily read as signs of Oden's wiliness and her allure, which are themselves subsumed beneath the rubric of *dokufu,* or femme fatale. But how is one to read such things as the names themselves, the trip to the bath, the cooling off before the lattice window, the upstairs location of the room, the name of the inn, and the name of its owner? One can imagine reading the details of the inn's architecture, say, as a sign of the characters' socioeconomic class (they are people who frequent places appointed in such a way), or one might read the pair's sharing of the room as a sign of their increasing intimacy. But as a group these details tend to resist, in the same way that Flaubert's barometer does, yielding a ready meaning.

The deposition presumably includes such details because they are the lifeblood of interrogation in criminal cases. Details that may turn out to be insignificant are, after all, a staple of legal testimony. It is by building up the densest possible accounting for every movement of a suspect that the detective or prosecutor hopes to reveal some inconsistency that will undermine an alibi. There is no such thing as an obviously irrelevant detail in legal testimony, since there is no telling what trifling thing may unravel an entire case. That is why legal systems the world over have long provided written records of testimony for later consultation and why the reader of a mystery novel turns back the pages to reread what he thought he had already taken in.

Robun apparently included these details in his account because they were present in the deposition that remained his main source of information about the events in question, despite his need to negate most of the document's substance in order to make Oden into the unrepentant femme fatale that he had promised his public. As far as the requirements of his plot are concerned, it does not matter where the Marutake is, or how many stories it has, or that Oden and Kichizō went to the bath, or that they did so before Kichizō began drinking rather than after, or that they waited only a short time before the drinks came, or that they cooled themselves in the breeze during that interval. But precisely because the mention of these actions leading up to the murder is unmotivated by the needs of the plot, the remarking of them gives Robun's account an aura of journalistic accuracy and seeming referentiality seldom if ever duplicated by *gesaku* artists working before the rise of the tabloid. As noted above, this element of referentiality in crime writing would remain a distinguishing feature when the age of translation began, and writers such as Kuroiwa Ruikō began turning out adaptations for the Japanese audience of Western works of detective fiction.

Takahashi Oden as a Registrar of Social Anxieties

Takahashi Oden's quality of referentiality was not limited to its literal incorporation of the facts required by a journalistic biography. It also had a more abstract connection to its social and cultural milieu, thanks to its treatment of the themes of personal identity and social mobility.

Among the many momentous social changes that occurred in the early Meiji period, the dismantling of the feudal status system was perhaps the most far-reaching in its implications. With the demise of the pre-Meiji status system, opportunities for social mobility increased, and traditional notions about the link between birth and personal identity came into question. Huge masses of commoners thus found themselves in transition between two schemes of identity: the old one, under which social origin closely circumscribed a person's life course, and the new one, under which a person was free to present himself to the world as he chose, regardless of social origin.

At the same time, the Meiji Restoration increased geographic mobility, both for people and for goods. The new government abolished the official checkpoints *(sekisho)* that the Tokugawa had installed along the main roads leading to Edo. With the concurrent abolition of the old domainal tariff barriers and tolls, the population now enjoyed the freedom to travel at will, to obtain employment wherever they desired, and to transport goods freely. The rickshaw, invented in 1869, also did its part to ease travel. The first railroads, although they were only modest in scale, had been built by the end of the 1870s. The Shinagawa-to-Yokohama line was finished in 1872, and the Kobe-to-Osaka line in 1874. Other, more ambitious, railroad lines would soon follow.

These changes offered new chances for people to go where they pleased and to make of themselves what they would. The Meiji government was eventually to be the most centralized and far-reaching system of state control Japan had yet seen. But while it was finding its feet, this new free-

dom meant that one's local reputation was suddenly no longer the control-
ling force it had formerly been. At least until the nationwide telegraph system was completed in 1878, a criminal with pluck could outrun his name.
Thanks to the absence of checkpoints and the spottiness of police records,
one could escape one's past by moving to a new place and presenting one-
self to the world afresh.

It was to just such possibilities that Takahashi Oden owed her career in
crime. She was thus nearly ready-made for Kanagaki Robun as a distillate of
the cultural anxieties touched off by the radical social changes of the early
Meiji period. What is more, Robun's means of storytelling—hybridizing as
they did the traditions of *gesaku* writing and a newly emerging journalism—
all but guaranteed that Oden the literary character would also be a transitional figure between old and new schemes of identity.

On the one hand, Robun's account seemingly fixes the limits of Oden's
character in its very opening sentence, by referring to her as *dokufu Takahashi Oden,* "the femme fatale Takahashi Oden." The label *dokufu* announces
Oden as a predictable character type familiar from Kabuki drama and
other *dokufu-mono* (poison woman stories). In its presentation of a known
type, *Takahashi Oden* also had roots in the Edo period *katagi-mono* (character sketches, or character sketch collections) of writers such as Ejima Kiseki
(1666–1735), whose *Seken musuko katagi* (The Character of Society's Sons,
1715) and *Seken musume katagi* (The Character of Society's Daughters, 1717)
take as their organizing premise the notion that society is nothing other
than a constellation of recognizable types.

But on the other hand, the journalistic specificity with which portions
of Oden's career are described brings her to life with remarkable individu-
ality that sets her apart from the characters in the *katagi-mono*. Because the
story so persistently connects itself to a particular woman who was put to
death on a particular morning and because Robun's portrait is so full—
including such varied details as Oden's childhood penchant for fighting
tops, the precise addresses where she stayed in Tokyo, and the poem she
spoke before her beheading—it requires a certain willfulness to look upon
Oden as being "just like all the others." We know too many ways in which
she is unique.

And, paradoxically, even as Oden's identity is delimited by her casting as a *dokufu,* she is at the same time freed to be magnificently protean.
Masquerade and self-refashioning of all sorts become the very stuff of her
existence. As she moves from place to place, duping her victims under varied guises, ever able to outsmart or outrun her pursuers, her life takes on
a seeming open-endedness of possibility that mirrors the promise of early
Meiji social reforms. But with her capture, imprisonment, and execution,

these freedoms are ultimately curtailed. The figure of the *dokufu* itself,
then, is torn between two competing schemes of identity: one scheme in
which human character is reducible to a type that is ruled by an unchanging, essential nature and a second scheme in which identity is potentially
open-ended and remakable, something one assumes, a matter more than
anything of disguises worn and stories told rather than of a continuing and
fixed essence. The tension between these two schemes of identity continually crops up in Robun's biography.

As biography, an account such as *Takahashi Oden* bears responsibility
for shedding light on the secrets of personality and the motives for human
action. How, the reader of such an account wonders (and this is surely one
reason for the success of popular criminal biography offered for sale following an execution), did this fellow human being come to the point of
being executed for her deeds? This question is with Robun from the very
beginning of his account, where he takes up, after his own fashion, the sort
of issues concerning gender, nature, and nurture that have long divided
behavioral scientists:

> The difference in sex between males and females, and the fact of there
> being a distinction between their qualities, is a device of the creator. It
> is nothing other than an ingenious means of multiplying the human
> seed. In anatomy there are no more than minute differences. But in
> the matter of the goodness or badness of the soul *(reikon no zen'aku)*,
> those who, despite being female, surpass men [in either extreme] are
> born out of a confusion between what is known in Western thought
> as the male and female principles. Added to this, rather like the color
> with which one dyes a white yarn, is the intimacy or distance of the
> nurture given by mother and father. But it is impossible to lump every-
> one together under the notion that those who have a saintlike beauty
> on the outside are always she-devils at heart *(gemen no bosatsu naishin
> kanarazu yasha no gotoshi)*. There are beautiful women who have done
> good deeds and hags who have done bad ones. (P. 4)

This is a relatively evenhanded discussion, but as the narrative unfolds this
beginning is overshadowed by Robun's continual editorializing, which
persistently returns us to the idea that Oden is ruled by her unchanging
essence. Oden is a *dokufu*, Robun repeatedly reminds us, and that, it seems,
is all one need know to explain her behavior.

An example of Robun's harping on the explanatory power of Oden's
essential nature can be found in the episode that occurs soon after Oden
and Naminosuke run away from Shimomaki-mura. They meet Kawabe Yasuemon, a generous parishioner of Kōshōji temple in the village of Fujikawa-

mura. He hires Oden as a seamstress and scullery maid and then loans the couple enough money to go to Kai in search of a doctor to treat the leprosy with which Naminosuke has been stricken. We are told that Oden, "because she was Oden, malevolent by nature *(moto yori akui no Oden nareba)*, set her eye on Yasuemon's wealth and...began contemplating how she might involve herself with him sufficiently to charm him with her allure *(iro)*" (p. 27). Her later decision to strangle the bedridden Naminosuke likewise arises from an inherent malice that renders her motives thoroughly suspect: "'He will have to make the journey to the world beyond sooner or later; rather than allow his pain to continue at length, wouldn't it be kindest to be done with it once and for all?' To have such malicious thoughts is in the nature of the femme fatale *(isso no koto ni hito omoi to ukamu akui wa dokufu no honshō)*; that night she stole to his pillow [and killed him]" (p. 37). Robun again ascribes Oden's conniving tendencies to her evil-heartedness when she later meets Kurokawa Nakazō, a wealthy dealer in curios: "Learning that his business dealings were wide of scope and that he had big-spending clients, her habitual maliciousness of heart suddenly issued forth *(rei no akushin niwaka ni hasshi)*. She asked herself how she might swindle him" (p. 53). And at the start of the nineteenth installment, in a short interlude in which Robun pauses to cast a backward glance over the story up to that point, he again refers to Oden's fundamental intractability even as he acknowledges the mystery of human character: "We cannot know from whence spring good and evil in human nature.... How is the common man to judge such matters? In any case, Takahashi Oden was unable to tame her evil-natured self *(sono sei no aku naru mizukara o kyōiku suru atawazu)*, and the poison of her malice seeped further and further into her brain *(kandoku masu masu nō ni shimi)*" (p. 48).

This mention of Oden's brain, with its hint of physiological causes for evildoing, anticipates the account's final, striking insistence on a determinate identity that rules Oden from within. After Oden was executed, we are informed, her body was sent to the Number Five Police Hospital (Keishi dai go byōin), in Asakusa, for four days of careful autopsy.[32] The resultant, vaguely prurient, doctors' report weirdly combines Western medicine with essentialism: "It was discovered that she was amply endowed both with brains and with fatty tissue, and also that her lust was deep *(jōyoku fukaki mo shirareshi to zo)*" (p. 61). All the chief elements of Oden's identity—her cunning, her curviness, and her libido—are located here in the determinate physicality of the body. By studying that body, and by cutting it open, the doctors are ostensibly able to lay bare the essence contained within.

The idea that Oden's essence is both fixed and knowable thus officially dominates the account. The biography's force as propaganda justifying

Oden's execution depends in part on her unrepentance, on the utter impossibility of reform, and on the obviousness of that impossibility.

But *Takahashi Oden* incorporates a countervailing trend as well. It contains many passages that present the opposite view, that personal identity is not fixed but malleable. One of the most intriguing things about *Takahashi Oden* is the way that it implicitly puts to the reader the proposition that identity depends not on one's essential nature or even one's upbringing so much as it depends on the power of narrative, whether in the form of the stories that Oden tells about herself or in the form of the verdict of the court (which is, needless to say, diametrically opposed to Oden's own story).

The rhythm of meetings and partings that make up Robun's narrative of the road creates numerous occasions for Oden to tell her story to other characters. We repeatedly see Oden exercising her skill in creative autobiography, omitting important details about her recent activities whenever they might prove awkward.[33] The outstanding example of Oden's self-accounting, however, is the elaborate story she tells in her deposition when she is taken into custody for the murder of Gotō Kichizō. Robun incorporates into his account an extended verbatim quotation of the deposition, only to dismiss it as a clever fabrication. But there is room to wonder whether this is entirely so.

Unlike the stories we see Oden telling as she gives her all-too-partial updates to the men in her life, her deposition goes well beyond a simple accounting for her actions. It is a story as well of her origins, a bold attempt to remake her identity by the sheer force of narrative. In her deposition, Oden claims to be the daughter not of Seikichi the gambling ruffian, but of Hirose Han'emon, chief retainer to the prominent Numata clan, by whom her mother was impregnated while in service at Hirose's household. She explains that she had a half sister named Okane, also Hirose's daughter, whom she suspected had been killed by Gotō Kichizō. She also claims that she arranged various meetings with Gotō in the hope of avenging her sister but that he repeatedly put her off. He at last met with her only to attempt the rape at knifepoint, and in the ensuing struggle slipped and fatally stabbed himself in the throat. Finally, Oden claims that when she realized her revenge for Okane's murder had been accomplished (albeit by unexpected means), she left a note to that effect with the corpse.

The uncertainty that haunted the actual Oden's paternity lends a certain plausibility to the self-making in her deposition. This uncertainty lingers in Robun's account despite his obvious efforts to dispel it. When Oden is born, Kanzaemon, then the husband of Oden's mother Oharu, believes he is the father. But later his second wife, having heard rumors that the child is actually the gambler Ariga Seikichi's, convinces him otherwise. The couple put Oden up for adoption when she is four. Oden herself, however, knows nothing of Seikichi until he turns up much later (after having been in prison), claiming to be her father.

Once the account has introduced the theme of uncertainty about paternity, it is then compelled to dispel that uncertainty once and for all, and to do so at any cost. As a story of an irremediably evil woman justly punished, it cannot countenance the possibility that Oden is the daughter of Hirose Han'emon, as she claims in her deposition. The great degree to which this alternative story poses a threat to the biography's premises is obvious in Robun's narration of a scene in which Oden is reunited with Seikichi after his prison term. The episode seems to be staged for no purpose other than to inoculate the reader against Oden's claim to be the daughter of the Numatas' retainer Hirose Han'emon. In the scene, Seikichi shows Oden that their freshly drawn blood blends together and claims this as proof of actual consanguinity. A rival gang of gambling hoodlums has raided the house where Oden and Naminosuke live, and with the aid of Seikichi, the couple have killed their enemies in a sword and gun fight:

> In the scuffle Seikichi had taken a stray bullet in his right arm. Oden, too, when she drew near to Naminosuke's side while he was fighting Hatasaku, had felt the touch of Hatasaku's spearpoint in her left arm. When things quieted down and she had a look, she found that the blood was trickling steadily. It was nothing serious, however, and as she was looking here and there for some medicine to stanch the bleeding, Seikichi stopped her. "Just a moment." He brought a plate from the kitchen and collected Oden's blood in it. To the suspicious couple he said, "…I have been thinking to tell you who I am for some time, but since I had no proof I have kept my silence up until now. I am Oden's biological father. I'll explain it all to you later. But first, the proof that we are parent and child. It was lucky that we were both injured on the arm. Watch closely and you will see we have an undeniable blood tie." Onto the plate where Oden's blood had dripped, he squeezed fresh blood from his own arm. Before their eyes the pool of blood seethed and churned, and then suddenly settled *(ugomeki uchimajiri tachima-chi kuwa seshi)*. Husband and wife watched raptly, without so much as blinking…. [Oden] had known for some time of people's saying that such a blending of blood was irrefutable [proof of relationship]. (P. 16)

We are meant to take this entire scene—including the seething and churning of the blended blood—as having no less reality than anything else the narration offers up. It is a memorable and revealing moment, one that was singled out in later editions of the book for illustration. It shows the narrative's great investment in undermining Oden's own story of her paternity at all costs—even to the point of risking its own credibility. And, even more important, it shows the degree to which *Takahashi Oden* is not a single, unified story so much as a contest between competing stories that is played out before the reader's eyes.

In the world Robun portrays, the idea is always kept alive that Oden's criminal nature is a matter of bad blood, that it arises from her being the illicit child of a gambler and a woman with morals as loose as Oharu's. Her tomboyishness, for instance, which Robun sets up as an early sign of her deviance, is mentioned in the same breath as her parentage: "Perhaps because she had inherited the ne'er-do-well Seikichi's qualities *(warumono Seikichi no shitsu o ukeshi ka)*, Oden's nature *(saga)*, like her mother's, engaged her in nothing but the roughest sort of unfeminine play. At New Year's she gave not so much as a glance to badminton, preferring to launch a kite on the wind with the boys or play at battling tops" (p. 11). Her penchant for gambling (which starts her down the road to her other crimes) is also linked to her father, in a remark of the friend to whom Seikichi turns when he has been released from prison and is attempting to locate Oden: "True to form as the heir to your blood" *(aniki no chisuji dake)*, the friend tells him, "she has loved gambling since she was thirteen or fourteen" (p. 12).

The deposition is such a strong threat to this theory of heredity-based character development precisely because it provides Oden with an alternative heredity. If the story Oden tells in her deposition were true, she would have in her not the blood of a gambling ruffian but of a high-ranking samurai. This would at a stroke clear her of the genetic influences that allegedly led her to a life of crime as well as transform the murder itself into a semblance of a vendetta killing, a practice that had been legal as recently as 1873.[34]

The struggle in *Takahashi Oden* to establish Oden's identity by means of narrative is heightened by Robun's invocation of yet another version of Oden's life story, that contained in the court verdict quoted in the introduction to the tale. The verdict pronounces Oden guilty of attempting to "use her charms to deceive Kichizō and take his possessions and, when that failed, stealing his money after killing [him] by means of a razor wielded with premeditated murderous intent" (p. 4). To support its denial of Oden's claim that Kichizō accidentally killed himself, the court enumerates the evidence against Oden:

> First, [there is] the note left at the scene claiming responsibility for the murder of the aforementioned Gotō Kichizō, along with the deposition made on August 10 of Meiji 10 [1877] under interrogation at

the police commissioner's station in these offices; second, the results of the coroner's examination; third, the testimony of Imamiya Hidetarō; fourth, the testimony of the innkeeper Ōtani Sanshirō; fifth, the testimony of Shishikura Sashichirō. From this multitude of evidence we rule that it is clear the death was not self-inflicted. However, [the defendant] claims to be the illicit offspring of a certain Hirose and also that she was carrying out a vendetta on behalf of her half sister. Again, there is no creditable evidence, in spite of her designation of Sutō Tamejirō as a witness to it, of such a sister's actual existence. (P. 4)

The court's discounting of Oden's claims as false and its affirmation of those of other witnesses as true produces an official version of Oden's story, an interpretation of events that also fixes Oden's identity as a murderer. The court, in other words, does what all criminal courts do when rendering a guilty verdict. It settles on an account of what happened at a certain time and place, and envelops the story of the defendant in its story.

And yet as Robun presents the case, the critical reader has little reason to believe the court's story is truer than Oden's. Of the evidence referred to in the verdict, we are shown only the note left at the scene and an excerpt from Oden's deposition. The court presumably brings them forward as evidence against Oden because they establish Oden's presence at Gotō's death and her satisfaction with it. But they also offer up the alternative scenario of Gotō's attempted rape of Oden at knifepoint and his accidental stabbing of himself. This scenario may sound unlikely, but it is not completely implausible in and of itself. The burden of disproving it falls on the other testimony mentioned, and yet Robun neglects to give us any access to this testimony. We are left to take Oden's guilt on the authority of the court and on the authority of Robun's own narrative. Indeed, one crucial difference between the narrative structure of *Takahashi Oden* and later Western-influenced crime writing is that in Robun, the investigation of the crime and the pursuit of the criminal—far from being the center of interest—are disposed of in some three or four brief lines near the end (p. 59). The voice of the narrator does not at any time recognize uncertainty about Oden's identity as the culprit; nor does any character within the narrative (apart, of course, from Oden herself). Instead, the identity of the culprit in the crime that will later be narrated is preestablished by the focus on Oden from the time of her birth. If her guilt had not already been announced by the court's verdict quoted in the preface, this focusing of the narrative on Oden would in itself insist "she is the one."

But since so little is offered in the way of justification for that insistence, one is, in the end, left only with competing narratives and their competing claims to be telling the truth. And since we are left without means of adjudicating among these competing stories, narrative becomes not, as the court and Robun would have it, a way of fixing identity, but rather a way of putting it into a state of flux. Oden was and is a story not only in the sense that she was a newsworthy person, but also in a deeper sense: her identity—who she was—depends even to this day on the stories that have been told and written about her. It is thus highly fitting that her name should be "Den" (the "O" is a detachable prefix), which can mean "a life story." Indeed, the subtitle of Okamoto Kisen's version of Oden's life makes a pun on just this sense of the name.[35] Kisen's version was called *Sono na mo Takahashi dokufu no Oden: Tōkyō kibun,* which might be translated as *Her Very Name a Brief Life Story: The Femme Fatale Takahashi Oden, a Strange Tale of Tokyo.*

The narrative's official premise, then, is that Oden's identity as unrepentant femme fatale was fixed almost from the moment of her birth. But at the same time it is constantly showing us how heavily identity depends on narrative. We are shown scenes in which Oden remakes herself by making calculated omissions when she retells parts of her life story to other characters. And we see, staged before us, a contest between the autobiography of Oden's deposition, on the one hand, and the narratives of the court verdict and the framing narrative by Robun, on the other. Although Robun heavy-handedly resolves this struggle in favor of the court and against Oden, the text's inadvertent staging of this competition between versions of Oden's story directly reflects the signal transition through which early Meiji society was passing at the time.

Social Mobility and
Social Identity in *Takahashi Oden*

The figure of Oden distilled with startling purity the anxieties stirred up by this transition. Oden's geographic mobility and her continual acts of self-remaking—not to mention her brazen assumption of quasi-samurai status in her story about being the daughter of Hirose Han'emon—captured in symbolic form the potential energies of the newly mobile mass of commoners in early Meiji.

Part of Oden's symbolic power derives from her constant habit of movement. When her mother dies, the rumors that she is the daughter of the gambler Seikichi prompt Kanzaemon to put Oden up for adoption, beginning her career of roaming at age four. After her tomboyish childhood (spent under the care of Kanzaemon's brother Takahashi Kyūemon), she marries Naminosuke, the two discover for themselves the attractions of gambling, and before long they are involved in two fatal fights with underworld hoodlums. Rather than report the incidents and risk an interrogation, in which the details of their illegal gambling activities would certainly come out, they flee under the cover of night.

From this point on, Oden spends her entire life on the lam. She gets out of scrape after scrape by the simple expedient of relocation, and her repeated escapes (the emphasis falls more heavily on her departures than on her arrivals) become a central organizing principle of the narrative. Her exit from Kawabe Yasuemon's house after stealing money from his daughter is characteristic: "Since all eyes had turned to Oden as the culprit, she could not afford to linger; making use of the dark of night, she fled, heading nowhere in particular *(izuko to mo naku nigesari-keri)*" (p. 47).

The route she travels in the course of the narrative is thus highly unpredictable and often takes her overland. Moreover, being dictated by little more than moment-to-moment expediency, it is remarkably circuitous. Having left the village of Shimomaki-mura with Naminosuke, Oden travels first through pathless mountain terrain to the village of Fujikawa, then southwest to Kōfu (in Kai), then east to Yokohama; from there she escapes with Ichiyakko (a pickpocket who becomes her lover) by boat to Yokosuka in order to evade the police. From Yokosuka they take another boat to Shimoda (to the southwest, on the Izu peninsula) and then turn north again, traveling overland to cross the Tōkaidō at Mishima. They then continue across Kai and Shinano into Kōzuke and back to Oden's home village of Shimomaki. There she steals money from her adoptive father and returns to Fujikawa, where she steals more money and again flees in order to avoid capture. Continuing now in a southerly direction along mountain paths until reaching the Naka-sendō somewhere east of Kōfu, she then follows the main road to the east until she eventually makes her way to Tokyo. But she has not been there long before she finds it necessary first to move from one house to another and then to return to her village in Kōzuke in order to elude a man she has spurned and robbed. Having claimed her inheritance, she once again returns to Tokyo to try her hand at sundry business ventures, and it is in various neighborhoods of the city (most notably Kōjimachi and Asakusa) that the story's remainder unfolds. By the latter half of the story, Oden's departures have been described with such frequency that the verbs *nigesaru* (to take fleeing leave), *nogaru* (to escape or slip away), and *sugae o nasu* (to pull up stakes [literally, "to make a change of nests"]) have become almost numbingly familiar.

Robun's handling of space and time in the narrative further emphasizes Oden's mobility. When he describes Oden's movements, he does not minutely account for the passage of time as he does in his narration of the events leading up to the murder of Kichizō. Whenever Oden must cover the distance between two places, Robun in fact dispenses with all detail, obviously telescoping his account of the time her travel takes. For a narrative that depends so heavily on the motifs of travel and escape, we see Oden on the road surprisingly little. When she and Naminosuke first run away from Shimomaki-mura, their daylong journey to the next village is covered by the cursory "they made their way over mountain after mountain, and at nightfall they arrived in Fujikawa-mura" (p. 26). The usual ratio of words to minutes of story time shrinks here, with the time spent traveling reduced to a mere place-holding repetition *(yama yori yama ni wakeirete)* reminiscent of the conventions of the folktale. The next leg of the journey (from Fujikawa-mura to Kōfu) likewise relies on glaringly empty repetition to fill what little narrative time is devoted to it: "Counting on the assistance of some few acquaintances, they set out for Kai, Naminosuke in a palanquin and Oden walking alongside. In this way Oden, having set out in the direction of Kōfu with Naminosuke in a palanquin, very soon arrived there" (p. 31). The effect is equally prominent when Oden and Ichiyakko, with the police on their trail, catch the boat for Yokosuka. After carefully evoking the tension the couple feel waiting to go aboard, the narrative abruptly shifts to an account of the trip itself that could not be more abbreviated:

> When they heard that evening that the boat to Yokosuka set sail at six in the morning, it seemed a gift from heaven. In Miyakobashi, which was just a stone's throw away, they got onto a lighter and concealed themselves to wait. There they waited on tenterhooks for dawn, the minutes passing like years, unable even to sit down in their fear that the sound of every lapping wave might be their pursuers. With dawn they shifted to the main boat and for the first time felt they were alive. A bit after noon that day they landed in Yokosuka. (Pp. 39–40)

Once Robun has gotten the pair onto the main boat, he allots not even a word to their actual travel between Miyakobashi and Yokosuka. Since Robun so rarely shows Oden en route, and since he devotes so little narrative time to her travel, Oden seems able to cover large distances with little effort and to pop up almost anywhere without warning. This heightens her power as a symbol of the possibilities and dangers associated with the new geographic mobility of early Meiji society.

Takahashi Oden also tapped into anxieties surrounding the new socioeconomic mobility of early Meiji society. Legislation passed in the early and mid-1870s ended the prohibition against marriage between *shizoku* (people of samurai descent) and commoners; it also ended the *shizoku*'s monopoly over military office (by instituting a system of universal conscription) and their exclusive privilege of wearing *haori* jackets and *hakama* trousers. In 1876 a ban on sword-wearing removed the *shizoku*'s last badge of distinction, and no outward sign remained by which one could unfailingly tell samurai from those of common ancestry. At the opposite end of the social spectrum, former criminals, too, were made harder to distinguish by the Meiji government's banning of the tattoos on the forearm (or, depending on local custom, the forehead) with which they had formerly been branded.[36]

The significance of personal names also changed. A law allowing commoners to take surnames was enacted in 1870, and another requiring them to do so was enacted five years later. Until the scramble precipitated by this second law, one could depend on surnames to convey useful information about their bearers. The mere fact of a person's having a surname at all generally suggested samurai status. Those others who had unofficial, de facto surnames had usually derived them from their place of residence or occupation. But in 1875 large numbers of names had to be generated in short order. Hard-pressed to come up with sufficient numbers of unique names for their citizens, Toyoda Takeshi reports, town officials resorted to such devices as running through brands of teas (Aoyagi, Kisen, Takazume, Uji) or even names with such aristocratic associations as those of the four chief retainers *(shitennō)* to the Tokugawa (Honda, Sakai, Ii, Sakakibara).[37] Some among the lower classes who lacked names simply borrowed that of the village headman.[38] By introducing this element of caprice, the law requiring universal adoption of surnames paradoxically conferred a new anonymity on the names' recipients. Names no longer automatically marked people as coming from a particular place or belonging to a particular social class.

The old economic order was upset as well. The economic security of the samurai was undermined by the conversion of *shizoku* stipends into government bonds and onetime cash payments. Faced for the first time with the management of a nest egg, many either squandered their wealth at teahouses, restaurants, and theaters, or lost it outright by making ill-advised investments.[39]

A further source of change was the general financial disorder that plagued Japan throughout the 1870s. Not only did over two hundred different currencies (each issued by a different former domain) remain in circulation until the end of the decade; the yen, which had been issued as a national currency in 1871, was subject to monumental inflations and deflations (most notably in connection with the Seinan civil war in 1877).[40] The same volatility of financial markets that wiped out the fortunes of so many naive former samurai could also make anyone suddenly rich, no matter what his or her class origins. Speculative fevers came and went in waves and with them a variety of fraudulent financial schemes.

With the erasure of traditional socioeconomic class markers had come
an entirely new set of possibilities for self-making and self-presentation, and
with them new possibilities for deception and misrepresentation. As a character capable of adroit metamorphosis and shameless duplicity, the figure
of Oden distilled all the potentially angst-inducing aspects of this new social
reality.

Oden's use of multiple names is one obvious manifestation of her ready
assumption of new identities. In the course of the story she goes by not only
"Oden," but also "Hanayama" and "Omatsu" as well as using the surname
"Hirose" (in keeping with the story of her origins that she recounts in her
deposition). And Robun tells us in an authorial interjection that there are
reports of her having given out her name as "Okatsu."

Oden also assumes new identities by changing her appearance. We see
this clearly in an episode in which Oden goes to a temple called Mantokuin
to take refuge from the unwelcome and violent advances of one Suzuki
Hamajirō. At the temple she meets a young, sheltered nun who wants to
see something of the world. Oden hits easily upon the use of disguise and
a new class identity as the best way to help her escape from the compound.
Oden sneaks into the samurai quarters one night and steals a *haori* jacket
and *hakama* trousers for the nun as well as clothes that she herself wears
to play attendant to the nun's samurai. The two break through the hedge
surrounding the compound and make for the river, where, thwarted by the
unresponsiveness of the ferryman sleeping on the opposite bank, they are
soon caught by their pursuers. The disguises here do not actually fool the
pursuers, but the episode is nonetheless emblematic of Oden's protean
instincts. The great variety of occupations that Oden undertakes is another
sign of this proteanism: in the course of her picaresque existence, Oden
spends time as a gambler, a thief, a seamstress, a laundry woman, a scullery
maid, a prostitute, a speculator, and a flimflam artist.

Oden is a consummate manipulator of trust as well as of appearances.
She constantly watches for chances to rob blind anyone who has shown her
kindness. After Naminosuke dies, for example, Oden returns to her village
of Shimomaki-mura and to Kuzaemon, her adoptive father. When he hears
Oden's tearful narrative of her sufferings (omitting mention of her strangling of Naminosuke), Kuzaemon takes her in again. Oden, however, as is
her wont, grows restless for change. She has no money of her own with which
to travel, but this is a small obstacle, since Kuzaemon proves an easy mark:

> She prepared to run away from her adoptive home for a second time.
> As she was waiting for a chance to give the slip to Kuzaemon and his
> old eyes, it happened that one night her father was invited to a cel-

ebratory banquet in the neighborhood. Having had pressed upon him more liquor than he could handle, he staggered home on unsteady legs. He went right to bed, and no sooner had he done so than he was snoring away loudly in complete oblivion. Seeing her chance, Oden sought out the key she had previously made mental note of. Opening the drawer of the dresser, she stealthily took twenty-four yen in gold and silver that Kuzaemon had saved, and then, like receding surf, she disappeared into the night without a trace. (P. 46)

From her village Oden returns to the house of Kawabe Yasuemon, who had been kind enough to loan Oden and Naminosuke money when they needed to travel in search of a cure for Naminosuke's leprosy. Again she is quick to take advantage of her benefactor, first by attempting to climb into bed with him in the hope that he will allow her to take the place of his late wife. When he resists her advances and decides she must leave the household, Oden then sneaks into his fifteen-year-old daughter's room while she is asleep and steals "fourteen or fifteen yen" before again leaving by night (p. 47).

But it is with the murder of Gotō Kichizō that Oden's story and her duplicity reach their climax. It is in this crime that Robun displays to greatest effect Oden's capacity for elaborately manipulating appearances. Oden meets Gotō Kichizō during one of her stints as a prostitute. Having discerned that her client's "wallet is not light" and having devoted some time to gaining his confidence, Oden tells Kichizō that she has a business prospect for him. She knows, she tells him, a man by the name of Tanakaya Jinzaburō who would like to borrow two hundred yen, and who will put up a bolt of raw silk and thirty obis as collateral. Kichizō agrees to the transaction, which sets the stage for Oden:

> On the twenty-seventh, which was the appointed day, Oden...went to the bath in the morning and gave herself a thorough scrubbing. She put up her hair and hung her favorite coral beads from the back of it. She dressed with special care. In the afternoon she left Shintomi-chō for the appointed place, a soba shop in Minami-hatchōbori. Arriving there, she asked whether [Kichizō] had come yet and was told that he was on the second floor expecting her impatiently. She went up to a private room and found that Kichizō, unable to wait for her, had started drinking by himself. When Oden came in, however, he gazed intently at her, thinking how her looks had improved and how refined she had become since he last saw her. Kichizō, drunk with her new grace...watered at the mouth. "Come here now, come here."...He pulled her close to his side. "I've brought the money I promised— see?—it's right here. As long as everything is in order with the other

party, we can take care of our transaction without delay, so relax and
have a drink." Even the way Oden playfully resisted the sake cup was
coquettish.

After a time, the two left the soba shop in a double rickshaw, heading for Kuramae-dōri. "[Tanakaya] never was very bright—he is bringing the collateral to Asakusa," said Oden. This was a shameless lie,
but the quick-witted Oden had them dropped in front of a certain
teahouse that she knew [in Asakusa] and asked there, "Has such-and-
such a person showed up yet?" The woman running the teahouse said,
"No, no customer meeting that description is here." Oden did not miss
a beat. "He should have been here ages ago. How strange. But come,
Mr. Kichizō, let's go up," she said, leading Kichizō to a small room
inside, which they took over for themselves. While they were having
a smoke, Oden stood up and said, "Since he is so very late in coming,
I'm going to go over to an inn up the way and find out what is going
on. Will you wait here?"

Leaving Kichizō by himself, she went out in front of the teahouse
and waited a while before going back inside. "He gave his solemn
word he would be here, but there was a message saying that something had come up and that he would like to carry out the transaction tomorrow morning.... But it really would be too much to ask you
to make another special trip early tomorrow, so [the other party] has
asked specially that you be put up for the night... at an inn near here
called the Marutake.... Would you be willing to go along with that?"
(Pp. 56–57)

Kichizō assents, and Oden's trap snaps shut. In this scene we see her not
only taking in Kichizō, but also slyly making the woman at the teahouse
into an unwitting accomplice when the two have the conversation about
Tanakaya (who plainly does not exist) in front of Kichizō. Oden's surprise
at her fictitious associate's failure to show up, her pretended trip up the
street to the inn for a message, and the promise of a meeting in the morning are all carefully planned to build the illusion that she is representing
Tanakaya. Her game is, needless to say, a success. It is only a matter of hours
before Kichizō is awakened by the stab of Oden's razor at his throat.

To understand the significance of Takahashi Oden as a character and
the degree to which she embodied the cultural energies of early Meiji, it is
helpful to remember just how fully the idea of social advancement (risshin
shusse) had by then captured the imaginations of Japanese. The best evidence of this is the great popularity of Nakamura Keiu's book Saikoku
risshi hen (Stories of Western Success, 1870). Nakamura's book, a loose
translation of Samuel Smiles' Self Help (1859), introduced the reader to
several dozen Westerners, ranging from Isaac Newton and James Watt to

Benvenuto Cellini and Francis Xavier, who had, despite their humble origins, climbed the ladder of success and enriched public life. Although Nakamura's translation would probably have been too difficult for most readers of the *Kana-yomi shinbun* or the *gōkan* edition of Takahashi Oden, its ideas would have been familiar to them in other forms. The appearance of plays based on the work, of excerpts in ethics textbooks, and of a host of imitations ensured that it had thoroughly permeated Meiji culture within a decade following its initial run.[41] Nakamura's blueprint for social advancement would have been available to *shizoku* and commoner alike.

Takahashi Oden can be read as a figure who carries out a nightmarish distortion of Nakamura's program of social advancement. If individuals had the power to remake themselves at will, regardless of their origins, Oden took the fullest possible advantage of that power. Her story presented the reader with the specter of a society in which, in the absence of traditional markers of identity, no one was what he or she appeared to be, and everyone was always on the lookout for the main chance.[42] In fact as Robun portrays her, Oden is uncannily well qualified as a sort of evil doppelgänger to Nakamura's self-made man. Her pluck and resourcefulness—and especially her dismissiveness toward what the world takes to be the facts of her low birth—match exactly the qualities of the men Nakamura portrayed in his book. Yet her femaleness immediately marks her as something other, and that otherness is borne out by the tenor of her career. Far from serving her nation, she gambles, steals, cons, and murders for selfish and personal gain. If post-Restoration society offered commoners new possibilities for self-making, new possibilities for a self-centered individualism were their necessary concomitant. Oden's story thus stood as an implied critique of the paradigm contained in Nakamura Keiu's book.

Conclusion: A Fragile Justice

It should now be clear that many of the salient features of *Takahashi Oden yasha monogatari* are related in some way to Japan's experience of Western contact. The rise of the Japanese newspaper industry and the spread of a rhetoric for reportage that would win the reader's belief in the link between text and reality, both inspired by the example of Western newspapers, left unmistakable marks on *Takahashi Oden*.[43] The new openness of the post-Restoration court system, which afforded journalists such as Robun access to the recorded testimony of those on trial and to official court verdicts, also had profound effects on the production of the text. And—perhaps most dramatic of all—the social changes brought about by the new Meiji government's policy of dismantling the status system (undertaken to accord with

Western ideals of democracy) fomented in the popular imagination fears
that found a natural outlet in Robun's depiction of his central character.

But it should also be clear that in its basic attitude toward the authority
of the justice system, Robun's tale was a throwback to the courtroom narratives of the seventeenth and eighteenth centuries. Robun's tale attempts to
establish the infallibility of the court and its rulings at the very outset, by dis-
missing Oden's deposition as "the lies and connivances of an evil woman,"
by praising the court for its clear-sightedness, and by calling the evidence
supporting its judgment "unmistakable."[44] Even though the tale has, in a
gesture toward journalistic completeness, included part of Oden's own testimony, and even though this inclusion allows into the story the alternative scenario of Oden's innocence, the framing narrative's commitment to
Oden's guilt and to the justness of the verdict against her never wavers.

After reproducing the verdict verbatim, the narrative then launches
into its cradle-to-grave cataloging of Oden's exploits, the sheer exhaustive-
ness of which is clearly meant to obviate any doubt about her guilt well
before the reader arrives at the scene of her execution in the final installment. The narrative pattern here is not identical to that seen in *Ōoka's Rulings*, since we are presented with the court's verdict at the beginning of the
narrative rather than at its culmination. But its overall effect is the same.
The execution scene at the end of *The Tale of Takahashi Oden* displays a meting out of justice that is meant to square completely with the knowledge of
the criminal's guilt that we have had instilled in us by the preceding narrative. Like its Tokugawa period predecessors, then, *The Tale of Takahashi
Oden* uses a pattern of narrative that is meant to reinforce the reader's sense
that justice has been served and whose ultimate ideological goal is to but-
tress the legitimacy and the authority of the legal system's operations. The
narrative admits—or at least it means to admit—no doubt about the events
leading to Gotō Kichizō's death or about the identity of his killer.

And yet all of these texts, Saikaku's courtroom narratives, *Ōoka's Rulings*,
and *Takahashi Oden* included, show signs of strain when it comes to their
banishing of doubts about the legitimacy of the justice system. This strain is
least readily apparent in Saikaku's stories, which present His Lordship as so
consistently infallible as to banish any doubts about him from the page. But
this utter banishment of all doubt in Saikaku's stories is problematic, given
the historical realities of the system he was writing about. Doubt becomes
conspicuous in Saikaku's stories by its absence. *Ōoka's Rulings* confronts the
possibility of judicial error much more directly than does Saikaku, even
making it into an explicit theme. But this theme is introduced only for the
purpose of then exorcising it, by means that can stretch credulity, as when
Ōoka is granted the ability, seemingly through raw instinct, to recognize

Hikobei's false confession in "Hikobei the Haberdasher." In the case of Robun's text, the doubts about the legitimacy of the court arise as an unintended by-product of the hastily assembled account's patchy hybridizing of *gesaku* conventions with newly emerging notions of journalistic accuracy. In spite of the framing narrative's energetic dismissal of the alternative scenario of guilt and innocence contained in Oden's deposition, the tale finally fails to present the critical reader with all of the evidence that would be necessary to come to a dispassionate agreement with the court's verdict. So with Robun the celebratory tone of the conclusion, in which Oden is beheaded, simply falls flat, since one cannot be sure that the court has been so clear-sighted as Robun's tale claims.

The tensions in the Japanese legal system—and indeed any judicial process—would become more visible in the 1880s, when Kuroiwa Ruikō began translating detective stories into Japanese. When the detective novel arrived in Japan, its chief marker as a new literary technology was its narrative structure. That structure, which required the delay of the solution until the denouement, set the stage for a representation of the justice system in the popular imagination that was radically different from the authoritarian one embodied in premodern and early Meiji forms of crime literature. The detective novel, by presenting ambiguous evidence and enacting plausible but mistaken interpretations of that evidence along the way to the final solution, carried an obvious potential to highlight the fragility of the justice system. Although such narratives, at least in their most classic form, end on a note of poetic justice, that ending is generally attained at the cost of close calls with miscarriages of justice along the way. Since it is not only the agents of the law in the text but the reader as well who is by turns convinced of the guilt of the wrong people, the detective story was particularly suited as a genre for putting the authority of the justice system itself on trial. This is precisely what Kuroiwa Ruikō would use it to do.

Borrowing the Detective Novel

Kuroiwa Ruikō and
the Uses of Translation

Although early Meiji period criminal biographies such as *Takahashi Oden* often contained numerous flashbacks and digressions, their account of the events leading up to and including the crimes they narrated was essentially linear. They might, as *Takahashi Oden* did, inadvertently activate story lines that came into competition with the official one they presented, but these biographies' basic narrative strategy was to follow the life of the criminal from cradle to grave, and the process of reconstruction necessary to recounting that life was either kept at the margins or rendered invisible. These biographies did not place their retrospective reconstruction of events on display for the reader in the way that the Western post-Poe detective story characteristically did.

But even as the "poisonous woman" stories were enjoying their vogue in the 1870s and 1880s, Japanese literary culture was beginning to take in Western influences ranging from the novels of Bulwer-Lytton to the Bible. The detective novel was a part of this cross-cultural literary flow. In 1887 there appeared the first partial translations into Japanese of detective novels following the pattern of backwards reconstruction that distinguished Poe's "Murders in the Rue Morgue." *XYZ: A Detective Story*, by the American writer Anna Katharine Green, was translated into Japanese as *Nisegane tsukai* (The Counterfeiter) by Tsubouchi Shōyō.[1] Poe's story itself appeared the same year in a partial translation by Aeba Kōson (1855–1922).[2] By the following year, Kuroiwa Ruikō (1862–1920), who would become the most prolific and influential Meiji period translator of detective stories, had begun translating into Japanese works of popular French writers such as Émile Gaboriau and Fortuné du Boisgobey; English writers such as Bertha Clay,

58

Marie Corelli, and Hugh Conway; and additional works by the American Anna Katharine Green. Of the eleven crime stories and novels translated into Japanese in 1888, Ruikō translated six. Of the twenty-nine translated in 1889, Ruikō was responsible for twenty-two. And in 1890 he did fourteen out of the seventeen translations of detective novels into Japanese.[3] Indeed, Ruikō's translations may well have been, apart from newspaper accounts of actual trials, the chief textual representations of criminal justice in the popular imagination during the mid–Meiji period, at least in Tokyo.[4]

Ruikō was entirely aware of the detective novel's retrospectively reconstructed narrative as a new literary technology. In an essay titled "Yo ga shinbun ni kokorozashita dōki" (My Motives for Going into Newspapers), Ruikō recounts an episode that occurred when he first had the idea of publishing an adaptation of an English whodunit that kept the identity of the culprit a secret until the end. He writes, with evident scorn, that he recruited for the task a fellow writer on the staff at his newspaper, who "botched the job by writing the story in the conventional chronological order *(jūrai no hennentai)*, telling from the start who the good and bad characters were."[5]

One also sees this awareness in the pains that Ruikō took to educate his readers in the enjoyment of the new narrative structure. For example, in his preface to his translation of Anna Katharine Green's novel *The Leavenworth Case,* which he translated as *Utter Darkness (Makkura,* 1889), Ruikō made this announcement: "*Utter Darkness* is a tunnel-like novel. You will not see what is what until you have passed through its darkness. Since you will not at first understand [what is going on], it may well strike you as dull.... *Utter Darkness* does not yield up its pleasures from the very beginning. *Utter Darkness* leaves you completely in the dark until you have finished reading.... Let me just say this much by way of advance warning."[6] Ruikō's choice of title for this translation *(Utter Darkness)* seems to have been meant reassuringly, as a way of sanctioning his readers' potentially uncomfortable confusion. He also places into the narrator's mouth, apparently with the same intention, various expressions of puzzlement not uttered by the narrator in Green's original: "What was the truth, then?" Ruikō's narrator will say. "They were in utter darkness after all!"[7]

The foreword to another of Ruikō's translations (Fortuné du Boisgobey's *Suites d'un duel,* or *Consequences of a Duel)* indicates the breathless enthusiasm with which this innovative narrative structure was sold:

> Conventional Japanese novels *(zairai no nihon shōsetsu)* are all the same.... If you read half of one, you know the whole plot. But there comes now onto the Japanese literary scene—which, having indolently settled itself into limited [traditional] forms, is ignorant of countless

other sorts of excellent novels—there comes now something that with
its epoch-making originality of conception will set up new standards,
stirring into a windy maelstrom all our withered leaves, chasing away
the conventional, vapid novel: [that something is] the Western novel
(*seiyō shōsetsu*). There is no dearth of people who have eyes for books
with sideways writing, but few can read them all; thankfully we have
Ruikō Shōshi [one of Ruikō's pen names]. He seeks out the interesting and the unusual ones and assiduously translates them. The public
at large has, thanks to his work, come to the point where it can taste
the true flavor of Western novels, duly enjoying the surprise of their
novelties and their marvels. They toss away the many vapid works they
have at hand, hurrying and fighting to get the Western ones that have
enjoyed such tremendous sales; now no house is without its copy of a
translated novel on the desk. That this is owing to their unparalleled
plotting, readers no longer have any doubt. This *Kettō no hate*, like anything Ruikō sets his skilled brush to, is of course outstanding in its plotting, and the strength of the writing goes without saying. When it comes
to strong winds that will blow away the old leaves, it has no equal.[8]

Although this foreword indulges in the hyperbole endemic to advertising
copy, it nonetheless provides us with the elements of a possible paradigm for
understanding cross-cultural literary influence. On the one hand, it presents a vision of the Western novel as a thing endowed with its own agency,
invading the field of literary consumption with the force of a violent storm,
blowing away the "old leaves" of traditional literature (the pun on tree leaves
and printed pages is nearly identical in Japanese and English) by dint of its
sheer superiority. On the other hand, it also presents a vision of an eager
Japanese reading public willingly embracing the new form. Understood in
the context of contemporary postcolonial theory, these visions are easily
reconciled as complementary rather than contradictory. The pliancy of the
reading public, its seemingly voluntary cultivation of a taste for the flavor of
Western literature, becomes a troubling sign, a by-product of the threats of
actual violence (metaphorically displaced in the foreword as the violence
of the storm) that underwrote Japan's economic and legal subordination
to the "superior" Western powers with which it concluded the unequal treaties. Viewed through such a lens, this episode in Western-Japanese relations
becomes a minor but clear example of cultural imperialism, one that is
perhaps all the more pernicious because the seeming innocuousness of the
replacement of *gesaku* by detective fiction so effectively obscures the larger
international inequality in power that enabled it.

The unequal relationship between Japan and the West almost certainly
influenced the market for translations and, by extension, the decisions of

translators and publishers about what was most worth publishing. But when one examines the details of a case such as Kuroiwa Ruikō's more closely, one finds a number of other crucial factors influencing literary production and consumption, quite apart from this basic fact of international inequality. An admiration of the Western detective novel, and of Western culture in general, provided some of the impetus for Ruikō's translations, to be sure, but his output is much more than a mere residue of this admiration.

The popularity of Ruikō's prolific output of translated detective novels with Japanese readers had as much to do with qualities that became manifest when the form was relocated in his own cultural context as it did with the inherent attractions of the form itself. The sales of such translations were likely helped along considerably by a rising tide of interest in the gathering and interpretation of physical evidence for use in criminal trials, an interest that stemmed from legal reforms (such as the abolition of judicial torture and the opening of courtrooms to the public) that were specific to the cultural milieu of early and mid-Meiji Japan. But perhaps more important in influencing the Japanese production of the detective novel at this time was Kuroiwa Ruikō's own use of the form to further his efforts as a muckraking journalist pursuing an agenda of Japanese national enlightenment.

Ruikō's agenda had several related components. For one thing, Ruikō's translations consistently suggest that he saw detective novels as a way to open his readers' eyes to the wider world, particularly to European and American life. They often show a decidedly anthropological interest in recording and explaining foreign customs, laws, mores, material culture, and social phenomena, and in mapping these foreign things onto Japanese experience in a way that will render them more readily comprehensible. European and American culture, and European legal systems in particular, become in Ruikō's translations important touchstones for gauging Japan's national progress. In addition, his translations consistently show the awareness of the detective novel's novelty apparent in the texts quoted above. Evidently, the detective form itself was one more aspect of non-Japanese culture that Ruikō felt his readers ought to be acquainted with as they expanded their knowledge of the world beyond their country's shores. The translations also show signs of a deeper purpose beyond the mere broadening of his readership's taste or experience. Ruikō seems to have been bent on cultivating in his readers, through exposure to the detection in his translations, a mental habit of active and skeptical critical inquiry, a habit that was fundamental in his eyes to the creation of an enlightened, postfeudal society. One sees evidence of this intent, for example, in Ruikō's occasional insertion of admonishments, directed at his readers, to reread if some important logical connection beneath the surface narrative has escaped them.

But perhaps the single most distinctive aspect of Ruikō's translations is his deployment of them to serve political purposes that could never have been anticipated by the authors he was translating. He accomplished this through a variety of methods, including adding didactic prefaces, inserting direct addresses to the reader, grafting in wholly new material, and—in the pages of the tabloid newspaper he founded—juxtaposing against his translations news coverage that had an obvious thematic connection to them. The results usually betrayed their hybrid origins—sometimes comically so—but at the same time they could function as uniquely trenchant and accessible critiques of the lingering feudalism and the corruption Ruikō saw in mid-Meiji society, critiques with political implications that extended well beyond the confines of their pages.

Kuroiwa Ruikō's Career

Ruikō's early run-ins with authority, his political involvements, and his first publications all shed light on his later activities as a muckraker and translator.[9] Ruikō, whose real name was Kuroiwa Shūroku, was born in Tosa, which was soon to become famous as the hotbed of the liberal Freedom and People's Rights Movement. Ruikō moved often during his school years. He began his studies as a child at his father's own school, in what is now the city of Aki in Kōchi prefecture. When his father died, however, he spent time in two other schools (leaving the second of these, Takamatsu Toshio records, partly because of a heated dispute with a teacher about the meaning of a passage in Chinese) before entering the Osaka School of English in 1878.[10] He was sixteen at the time. Later he attended Keiō gijuku (now Keiō University). As the Freedom and People's Rights Movement gathered steam, however, he devoted increasing amounts of time to writing and speaking, eventually dropping out of the university.

Ruikō's early itinerancy exacted no great toll on his literacy or his intellect, which was varied and precocious. While at school in Osaka he wrote and had printed several letters to the editor of the *Ōsaka nippō* (Osaka Daily) newspaper; he also trounced older students regularly in the school's weekly speech contests. At twenty, just before starting at Keiō, he launched his career in muckraking with an article titled "On the Sales of a Hokkaidō Colonization Bureau Official."[11] The article attacked the bureau's director, Kuroda Kiyotaka, for selling Hokkaidō properties to his cronies in Satsuma and Chōshū at prices far beneath their market value. Ruikō's name-calling landed him in prison briefly on charges of abusing a public official. Nevertheless, his article along with similar attacks by others eventually prompted an end to the scheme.

The same year that his article on Kuroda appeared, Ruikō also published his first book translated and adapted from English, *Yūben biji-hō* (The Rhetoric of Oratory, 1882). The book, which was based on George Payn Quackenbos' *Advanced Course of Composition and Rhetoric* (1855), instructed readers in, among other things, making speeches that were attuned to the contemporary reforms of literary Japanese (the *genbun-itchi* movement). It was a stroke of genius to put out the book at a moment when, thanks to the Freedom and People's Rights Movement, public oratory was flourishing as never before. *Yūben biji-hō* became a best-seller. With this book, which transformed a Western model in order to meet a demand that his fellow Japanese had not yet fully recognized, Ruikō established the pattern for his later success with literary adaptations.

But it was as a newspaper editor that Ruikō was to come truly into his own. His contributions to newspaper letters columns proved numerous and skillful enough to lead directly to editorships, first at the *Dōmei kaishin shinbun* (Newspaper of the Alliance for Reform and Progress) and then at the *Nihon taimusu* (Japan Times). When the latter failed, in part because of continual shutdowns by government censors, Ruikō found work as a reporter and later an editor at the *E-iri jiyū shinbun* (Illustrated Free Newspaper). There he covered the dramatic Normanton Trial of 1883, dispatching daily front-page updates directly from the courtroom. On trial was the British captain of the ship *Normanton,* which had sunk, drowning all Japanese passengers aboard. He and his British crew, in contrast, came through unharmed. The following year, perhaps inspired in part by the drama of this trial, Ruikō began experimenting with serialized adaptations of foreign courtroom and crime novels, running *Hōtei no bijin* (The Courtroom Beauty) and *Hito ka oni ka* (Man or Devil?) in the *Konnichi shinbun* (Today's Newspaper), where he had occasionally had columns published. There followed over seventy-five more serialized adaptations of foreign novels not only in these two papers, but also in the *Miyako shinbun* (Newspaper of the Capital, a later incarnation of the *Konnichi,* of which Ruikō became editor in 1885), the *Tōzai shinbun* (The East-West Newspaper), the *Edo shinbun* (The Edo Newspaper), and *Miyako no hana* (Flower of the Capital). The circulation of the *Miyako shinbun* tripled when Ruikō joined the staff, and he was by then reputed to have a faithful readership of his serials that numbered ten thousand strong.[12] By 1888, when the paper was bought out and Ruikō again lost his job, he was confident that as long as he ran his adaptations, he could start a paper of his own without worry about circulation figures.

In 1892 he founded *Yorozu chōhō* (Morning Report for the Masses, but with a pun on the phrase "Ten Thousand Treasures"), the tabloid paper

with which he is most closely associated. Ruikō continued his success with
serialized foreign novels in the new tabloid, and its circulation climbed to
fifty thousand by 1894. Before long Ruikō's adaptations of foreign novels
were themselves being adapted for the Kabuki stage.[13] During the next fifteen years, Ruikō serialized over thirty foreign works in *Yorozu chōhō*, including the two for which he is best remembered today, Alexandre Dumas' *Comte
de Monte Cristo* (as *Gankutsu-ō* [The Cavern King]) and Hugo's *Les misérables*
(as *Aa, mujō.*)[14] Almost every one of these was issued in book form shortly
after its run in the newspaper. By 1902, when *Les misérables* ran, *Yorozu chōhō*
was the biggest newspaper in Tokyo, with a circulation of about 120,000
copies daily.[15]

In the years after the Sino-Japanese War, he assembled at the paper
a stable of progressive intellectuals that included the Christian leader
Uchimura Kanzō (whose duties at the paper included writing a newly begun
English-language column); the socialists Kōtoku Shūsui, Taoka Reiun, Sakai
Toshihiko (Kosen), and Ishikawa Sanshirō; the satirist Saitō Ryoku-u; and
the historian of China Naitō Konan.[16] For these men, the chance to reach
Ruikō's audience seems to have outweighed any reservations they might
have had about being associated with a paper of *Yorozu chōhō*'s reputation.
"The reason I have connections with no other newspaper besides *Yorozu
chōhō*," Uchimura Kanzō explained, "is because the *Chōhō* is read by legions
of farmers, craftsmen, laborers, and the like, the so-called lower echelon
of society."[17] Ruikō gave Uchimura and the others complete freedom in
their writing so that although the news coverage remained sensational in
tone, it was now balanced with serious social commentary. In 1901 Ruikō
founded a nationwide reform organization called the Risōdan, or "Ideals
Group," with the newspaper's own writers at its center. Among the varied
activities the organization sponsored was a tour of inspection at the Ashio
Copper Mine that the writer Shiga Naoya's father famously forbade him
from joining. The paper thus had a unique niche, combining both popular
entertainment and a social mission.

The outbreak of the Russo-Japanese War in 1904 ended the paper's
golden era. Uchimura, Kosen, Ishikawa, and Kōtoku, all of whom were
doves, resigned more or less en masse over their differences with the hawkish
Ruikō. *Yorozu chōhō* survived, but after that Ruikō seemed to lose his touch.
He backed the cabinet of Ōkuma Shigenobu throughout the election scandal of 1915 (in which the home minister had allegedly bribed Diet members) and called for troops to be sent to Europe during World War I; both
positions hurt the paper's popularity. In 1920, the year of Ruikō's death,
the paper's circulation lagged far behind its competitors.[18] It was taken
over a decade later by the *Tōkyō maiyū shinbun* (Tokyo Evening News).

Ruikō's Methods and Aims

In retrospect, Ruikō's decisions about what to translate can seem decidedly idiosyncratic. About Émile Gaboriau, for example, translations of whom number second only to those of Du Boisgobey in Ruikō's output, the judicious Howard Haycraft writes: "Few modern readers would have the patience to abide the tawdry puppetry, the fustian, the cheap sensationalism, the dull and irrelevant digressions, the dreary and artificial verbiage that are the feuilletonist at his too-frequent worst, in order to get at the few grains of highly competent detection." Of Du Boisgobey himself, Haycraft says only that he was "a lesser Gaboriau."[19]

Ruikō's decisions about what to translate were partly governed by the purely practical consideration of what he could lay hands on. He relied heavily on two cheap American subscription libraries, the Seaside Library and the Lovell Library, both of which frequently included works translated from French into English.[20] Ruikō did not read French, so his own translations of Hugo, Dumas, Gaboriau, and Du Boisgobey were themselves based on the English translations published in these libraries. The commercial success of Ruikō's translations depended in part on the lack of an international copyright agreement at the time. It was an indication of Japan's status as an outsider to the club of Western nations that it was not a signatory to such an agreement until 1899; the United States, Belgium, France, Germany, Italy, Spain, Switzerland, Tunisia, and the United Kingdom were all parties to the Berne Convention for the Protection of Literary and Artistic Works, signed in Paris in 1887.[21]

The Japanese into which Ruikō rendered these works retained many of the inflections of the classical, literary-style Japanese used by *gesaku* writers (*-nari* for the copula, *-ki* or *-ri* to indicate the perfective, *-aba* for the conditional, *-eba* to indicate causality, *-zu* for the negative). Nevertheless, because he was translating from English, his prose took on distinctive rhythms that distinguished it from his predecessors'. His sentences have a journalistic crispness. They are generally shorter than those of *gesaku* writers, and they never engage in *gesaku*-style word play. They also make somewhat greater use of first-person pronouns *(ware, sessha, yo)* than one would expect to find in a nontranslated text, although Ruikō is by no means slavish about providing an equivalent for every occurrence of the word "I" in the English original.

Ruikō's earliest literary translation was of Hugh Conway's novel *Dark Days*. Like most of Ruikō's translations, it was published first in serial form in a tabloid newspaper (in 1886, in the *Konnichi shinbun*) and then brought out as a book the following year. In his preface to the book, which he called

Hōtei no bijin (The Courtroom Beauty), Ruikō describes his method of translation:

> To translate *Dark Days* as *The Courtroom Beauty* is exceedingly unjust.
> Or rather, it is presumptuous. Yet I have been far more presumptuous
> still when it comes to the text itself. Having read it one time, I took up
> my brush and freely strung the characters together according to what
> I retained in my memory, not looking so much as once more at the
> original after I had begun the manuscript. Since I left the original in
> my study and did the writing in the editors' office at the newspaper, it
> went without saying that [the result] would deviate from the sentences
> of the original as it does and that even the plot would differ from the
> original one. It is quite improper to call this a translation, but then
> again if I were to say it is *not* a translation, I could hardly escape the
> charge of plagiarism and the disdain in which imitators are held. That
> is why I have made the stretch of calling it a translation. Since the text
> itself is what it is [i.e., so far from the original], one should not direct
> censure or blame at the title's difference from that of the original. Call
> it improper if you will; accuse me of plagiarism if you will; I make no
> pretension to being a translator.[22]

Comparing any of Ruikō's translations to the texts on which they are based
reveals that he did in fact exercise great license in condensing or expanding certain passages, cutting out others completely, or grafting in entirely
new material that he seems to have invented from whole cloth. Ruikō's
practices were by no means unusual in the Meiji period. Although there
was a long-standing tradition in Japan of translation (from Chinese, most
notably, and, during the Tokugawa period, from Dutch), increased Western
contact after 1870 touched off a new flurry of experimentation at a time
when the notion of translation itself was still in considerable flux. Ruikō's
works were part of a large body of Japanese literary adaptations, or *hon'an*,
that often preserved only certain elements in their originals, exercising
striking freedom in their treatment of the remainder.[23]

    In the serialized crime novels that he ran in various tabloids in the
mid–Meiji period, Ruikō had a system of discourse about the law, the legal
system, and criminal justice that was at once appealing to a mass audience
and also conveniently adaptable to achieve his political aims, including the
sowing of discontent with the Meiji legal system's vulnerability to error and
corruption. In its melding of fiction and reality, such a political use of the
detective novel was reminiscent of Robun's *Takahashi Oden*, but there was
one important difference: Robun began with fact and then added fictitious
embellishment, where Ruikō began with an imported fictional narrative and

added material that gave that fiction a relevance to his Japanese readers' actual political world. This pattern is especially striking in three of Ruikō's translations: *Man or Devil?* (*Hito ka oni ka*, 1888–1889), *People's Luck* (*Hito no un*, 1894), and *Consequences of a Duel*, the preface to which made such memorable mention of the maelstromlike power of Western novels.

Man or Devil? is a translation of Émile Gaboriau's novel *L'Affaire Lerouge* (The Lerouge Affair, 1866).[24] Ruikō published the translation in serial form in the Tokyo tabloid *Konnichi shinbun* between December 1888 and March 1889.[25] The source of *People's Luck* is not known, but there is no doubt that it is in fact based on the work of some other writer—the byline published at the head of each installment reads "translated by Ruikō Shōshi" (one of Ruikō's numerous pen names).[26] The translation's source, whatever it may be, is thoroughly steeped in the conventions of the same tradition of melodramatic nineteenth-century European crime literature of which Émile Gaboriau himself was the outstanding exemplar. It has a murder, of course, but there is also a large inheritance, a will, sinister legal machinations, the discovery of hidden blood relationships, and a climactic trial. *Consequences of a Duel* (based on Fortuné du Boisgobey's *Les suites d'un duel*) tells the story of a wily woman's scheme to alter the result of a pistol duel in order to secure the fortune of one of the combatants. Although all three works are broadly consonant in their aim of increasing the political awareness of their audience, *Consequences of a Duel* achieves its aim by somewhat different means from the other two and is treated separately below.

Overview of
Man or Devil? and *People's Luck*

In both *Man or Devil?* and *People's Luck*—thanks to their use of the imported whodunit form and to Ruikō's own manipulations of the texts—the justice system that Ruikō puts before his readers differs considerably from that portrayed in the older tradition of Tokugawa era courtroom literature and from earlier Meiji period crime literature as well. In contrast to these earlier forms' portrayal of the justice system as virtually infallible, *Man or Devil?* and *People's Luck*, by emphasizing the difficulty of identifying the true criminal, became part of a new Meiji period discourse about the fragility of justice, the haunting possibilities for its miscarriage, and the consequent need for respecting human rights.

Ruikō's techniques of translation placed the action of these works in an interstitial world that readers were invited to view as a virtual Japan. The herky-jerky hybrids conjured up by Ruikō's translations can seem absurd when taken literally. His novels are full of Parisian gentlemen named Ōtani and Honda whose wallets are thick with yen-denominated notes. But by partially Japanizing the novels' foreign settings and characters with his domestication of proper names and other markers of cultural identity, Ruikō authorized a mapping of the legal systems portrayed in each novel (the French one in *Man or Devil?* and the English one in *People's Luck*) onto Japan's own legal system. In *Man or Devil?* it is the potential for judicial error—particularly in cases involving capital offenses—that Ruikō invites the reader to see in the Japanese legal system. In *People's Luck*, Ruikō uses a mapping of the novel's judicial doings onto the Japanese justice system in order to underline the latter's vulnerability to bribery and corruption.

Ruikō's manipulation of both texts shows how very free a hand he exercised as a cultural borrower. In these translations of whodunits, Ruikō is far from being a mere mimic or the passive relayer of a Western cultural form. He readily adapts the whodunit to suit his own purposes as a gadfly and political agitator. In his translation of *Man or Devil?* he grafts an entirely new ending onto the novel. This ending creates an imaginary political space and installs the reader in it as a political being opposed to capital punishment, though Émile Gaboriau's original did neither of these things. With *People's Luck*, Ruikō turned a novel originally written for an English audience into an exposé of the corruption that he saw in a real-world murder trial (known as the Sōma Affair) that was then unfolding in Tokyo. In both texts, "translation" came to mean considerably more than the rendering of one language into another; it also meant finding original ways to use the foreign to talk about the domestic. Ruikō's works are thus instructive examples of the way that the act of translation can, by resituating popular cultural forms in new contexts, allow them to take on new and unexpected meanings.[27]

Meiji Period Legal Reforms

By the time Kuroiwa Ruikō began translating in the mid-1880s, the old Japanese legal system of the Tokugawa era had undergone a sea change. Not only were a new Department of Justice and a system of higher and lower courts with accompanying cadres of professional judges, legal bureaucrats, and police put in place.[28] A new criminal code was enacted in 1882, based on a draft by the Frenchman Gustave Boissonade (1825–1910). The language of the law was completely rewritten; Japanese translators invented countless new character compounds to accommodate the terminology of Western law.[29] Criminal courts were opened to the press, and advocates were for the first time allowed to represent the interests of the accused. The dismantling of the status system that had endowed Takahashi Oden with such symbolic power was also reflected in new legal practices: punishments for identical crimes no longer varied by class, as they still had even under the criminal code of 1871 (the *Shinritsu kōryō*).[30] Appeals were now possible. The visibly Confucian stratification of the courtroom itself was also revised. Those appearing before the magistrate's raised dais no longer had to approach on hands and knees or kneel on the white sands of the *shirasu*.[31]

And yet even as these reforms were introduced—perhaps because the law and the courts had been demystified and almost certainly because the severity of censorship declined—public discourse about the justice system became considerably more critical. Justice and the law were no longer seen as one and the same, as Saikaku's courtroom narratives, *Ōoka seidan*, or *The Tale of Takahashi Oden* had made them out to be. As the fad for poison-woman stories began to pass, it was translations of Western crime stories that took their place, and the changes that Westernization induced in Japanese discourse about the legal system were clearly reflected in these translations.

The Detective Novel in Japanese

In his preface to *Man or Devil?* Ruikō, in typical fashion, warned readers who might still be unused to the double structure characteristic of the post-Poe detective story that they should expect something new and different: "People who are used to reading the conventional narratives of our country *(wa ga kuni jūrai no shōsetsu)* will no doubt frequently feel fatigue *(ken'en)* in the midst of this one. But it is always the case in mystery narratives *(gigoku shōsetsu)* that things are doubtful at the beginning and that the clouds clear and the mists disperse afterwards."[32]

This difference between the narrative structure of *Takahashi Oden* and *Man or Devil?* is in evidence from their opening pages. Where *Takahashi Oden* begins with the certitude of the court's verdict against Oden, *Man or Devil?* opens with doubt and suspicion:

> In the village of Sonchō [Jonchère], at the edge of Bōkiba [Bougival], which is only a little way from Paris, in France, there was a woman of about fifty-seven or eight, by the name of Oden [Claudine in the original; "Oden" was a common name, and Ruikō implies no connection with Takahashi Oden], who lived by herself. These events happened on about March 5 of last year. Since morning Oden's door had been locked up tightly, and the villagers began to suspect that something might have happened to her.... When it was still locked up on the next day, the sixth, a neighbor, no longer able to repress his suspicions, went to the Bōkiba police.[33]

The locked door with which the story begins removes the house's interior from the eyes of the neighborhood and from the eyes of the reader as well. It is both the sign that something is amiss and the screen that prevents us from seeing what has happened. When the police enter, they discover Oden lying dead on the floor of her kitchen and the cupboards and closets spilling their contents through the house. The remainder of the novel is devoted to figuring out what happened inside the locked room; it remains locked in this sense until the detective's final revelations.

Any worries Ruikō might have harbored about confusing or fatiguing his audience seem to have been overridden by the attractions for him of the whodunit form—attractions that were more than anything a matter of its suitability for his special political purposes. The whodunit subjects the reader to the vicissitudes of an unfolding investigation in which what seem to be convincing readings of the evidence are carefully set up only to be proven false and discarded, and to have alternative readings of the same evidence set up in their place. The form of the whodunit therefore had a new potential to emphasize the ambiguity of evidence and the fragility of justice that was only latent in pre-Meiji forms such as Saikaku's *Cases* and *Ōoka's Rulings*.

Ruikō played up this potential in his translation of *Man or Devil?* In his preface to the work, Ruikō introduces the story as one containing "a case without precedent...in the doubtfulness of its particulars and in the difficulty of assigning guilt to the criminal" (p. 169). "The reason I translated this piece," he tells us, "is to let those in this world who are employed as detectives know the difficulty of their charge and to make the judges of this world see that they should render their verdicts with the greatest of care; in short, I want to show the value of human rights *(jinken)* and to show that the law should not be used lightly *(hōritsu no karogaroshiku mochiyu bekarazaru o shimesan ga tame)*" (p. 169). This is not an exceptional preface in Ruikō's oeuvre. He shows himself to be equally attentive to the didactic potential of the detective novel in, for example, the preface to his translation of Gaboriau's *La corde au cou* (Rope around His Neck, 1873), which he called *Yūzai muzai* (Guilty or Innocent, 1888):[34]

> This story is one that records the tracing of a certain crime from its discovery to its cause; it is, in other words, of the type that in the West is called a detective novel. Its main point is simply to indicate the difficulty of human justice and the error of those who, using the law carelessly, would attempt to fix guilt on a person too easily. Jurists have regarded as evidence things that should not necessarily be called evidence, and it has frequently happened that the innocent have been

found guilty. Nothing would make the translator happier than if the readers of this book would reflect for themselves and see that the law should not be lightly used and that people's guilt should not be lightly decided.[35]

Man or Devil? is not, by the standards of Agatha Christie, especially befuddling in its offering up of potential suspects (there are only two main ones), but it does cleverly shift the strongest motive for murder between them as the evidence is brought forward. The two main suspects in *Man or Devil?* are near doubles: they are half brothers of exactly the same age, the two sons of a rich count—one, Komori, is son by the count's lawful wife and the other, Minoru, is son by his mistress. The victim of the murder is the woman who nursed these two sons as infants. The novel opens in the village of Bougival (or Bōkiba, in Ruikō's translation) with the discovery of the nurse's corpse. The main plot hinges on that recurrent motif in nineteenth-century European melodrama, a switching of babies that may or may not have been carried out. For most of the novel, we believe that the nurse did switch the babies and that Komori, who has grown up as his father's heir, has the strongest motive for the murder of the nurse, since he would lose his inheritance if the switch were ever revealed. Damning footprints and cigarette butts, a missing umbrella, witness reports of having seen a man with a black mustache (like Komori's) on the train from Bougival, and a coat found on the train all seem to point convincingly to Komori's guilt. When a surprise witness near the novel's end establishes that the switch of babies was never carried out, Komori's half brother Minoru confesses to killing the nurse himself and attempting to frame Komori in order to usurp his place as the legitimate heir. But in the meantime Komori is nearly put to death.

This close call with judicial error is made all the more palpable by the book's melodramatic portrayal of the representatives of the law, which dwells on their human frailty. Taburo, the judge of inquiry in the novel, is a former rival of Komori in love. In one flashback we see him first lying drunk and lovesick in the gutter, and then trying to shoot Komori with a pistol; his lingering resentment toward Komori colors his analysis of the case and is partly responsible for his false confidence in Komori's guilt. And Chirakura, the amateur detective in the novel, is given to nightmares in which the scenario of erroneous execution figures ominously: "First [Chirakura] saw Komori being placed on the scaffold; he glared accusingly at [Chirakura] with a terrible look on his face. The next moment police had surrounded [Chirakura] on four sides and arrested him. 'You, Chirakura—it is through your error that the guilt has been placed on the innocent Komori,' they said, and then he himself was being dragged to the scaffold" (p. 328).

At the novel's end, Minoru not only confesses to his crime but also takes his own life, so any mystery about the true culprit is by the closing page completely dispelled. Thanks to the novel's whodunit structure, however, this ending is achieved only at the cost of considerable angst along the way and only after subjecting the reader himself or herself to genuine puzzlement about the true identity of the murderer.

An Interstitial World

But would Ruikō's readers have connected the novel's portrayal of a fragile and all-too-human justice with the Japanese legal system? The novel openly invites just such connections. For one thing, it would have been difficult to dismiss *Man or Devil?* as a novel about the French legal system alone, given that major parts of the Japanese legal system were closely based on the French one. Etō Shinpei (1834–1874), Japan's first minister of justice, is on record as having suggested in 1869 that the legal translator Mitsukuri Rinshō "merely translate the French civil code verbatim, call it the 'Japanese Civil Code,' and promulgate it immediately."[36] In the event, the process of legal translation and of grafting the new system onto the old was not quite so cavalier as this for either the civil or the criminal codes, but the system drawn up by Gustave Boissonade and enacted in 1882 duplicated the French one in most important respects.[37]

More significant still was the way that Ruikō's translation reimagined and partially Japanized the France of Gaboriau's original. Ruikō's translation locates the action in "Furansu" in its opening line, even though the English version mentions only the place names "Jonchère" and "Bougival." But the text's very juxtaposition of the phonetic *katakana* script for the word "Furansu" against *kanji* characters that would normally be read "Futsukoku" (the native Japanese word for "France") suggests the tension between domestication and foreignization that will run throughout the translation, a tension that will ultimately render France only dimly recognizable as such.

It is not just the proper name of France but all of the proper names in the novel that pose a problem. In deference to his Japanese audience, Ruikō feels compelled not only to transliterate them into the Japanese sound system but to assign them *ateji*, or Chinese characters that approximate their sounds. As he says in his preface, "Things like place names and names of persons, since they differ from those commonly used in our country *(wa ga kuni)*, are especially difficult to remember." Thus, he explains, Commarin, the legitimate son, will be referred to as "Komori." Noel becomes Minoru, Claudine becomes Oden, Claire becomes Kuretake, Daburon becomes Taburo, Titauclaire becomes Chirakura, and so forth. But in keeping with the book's general pattern of a Japanization that is never more than partial, the reader is not allowed to remain oblivious of the characters' original French names. Immediately following the preface, they are all laid out in a full-page table of equivalences with the characters' new Japanese names (p. 172).[38]

The illustrations of the characters in the translation can also have a distinctly hybrid feel, since they give some of the characters Japanese make-overs, even as they leave them clothed in French styles. The young Parisian woman Kuretake, for example, is depicted as having unmistakably Japanese features beneath her very Parisian bonnet.[39] The mention of Western architectural features, furniture, clothing, and currency all force decisions upon Ruikō about how much to domesticate foreign things, and he chooses in nearly every case to do so as much as possible, even as he stops short of resetting the entire novel in Japan. He converts parlors into tatami rooms (*zashiki*), cupboards into closets (*oshi-ire*), dresses into split pleated skirts (*naga-bakama*), and francs into yen. The largest omission in his translation is of a lengthy discussion by Gaboriau's narrator of the jury system (and of the difficulty it poses to prosecutors seeking the death sentence).[40] Presumably it is missing because the one glaring difference between the two countries' legal systems arose from the Japanese decision not to adopt the jury system at the time Boissonade's reforms were instituted. Every one of these elisions and transformations subtly shifts the world of France slightly closer to Japan, even as we continue to be aware that the overlap with Japan is not entirely complete.

What is more, Ruikō occasionally makes interpolations into the narrative that explicitly invite readers to map the world of the novel onto their own, Japanese, experience. For example, in one episode Chirakura, the amateur detective in the novel, reconstructs the movements of the murderer on the night of the crime. In the course of the exercise, he realizes that the clever culprit must have thrown the police off the scent by staying on the train from Paris until he reached the next station beyond the one nearest the nurse's house and then walking back overland to kill the nurse. Ruikō tells his readers, in an interpolated parenthetical explanation, that this would be "the same as, for example, going from Tokyo to Shinagawa by deliberately taking the train as far as Ōmori, getting off there, and then backtracking to Shinagawa on foot" (p. 391). This explanation has the effect—as do all of these several moments where the translatedness of the text is highlighted—of converting Gaboriau's France into "Furansu," an interstitial world that is no longer purely France and no longer completely foreign, a place that hovers near Japan, separate from it but always commensurate enough so that the legal lessons it has to teach are applicable to the Japanese reader's world.

Ruikō's New Ending:
Politicizing and Internationalizing the Reader

The two changes that Ruikō makes to the ending of *Man or Devil?* are the
most dramatic examples of deliberate recontextualization in the entire
novel. The first of these changes is to rewrite the character of the murderer's mistress (Juliette in the English and French versions) to alter the note
of poetic justice on which the novel ends. At the end of Gaboriau's version,
Noel realizes the police have trapped him inside Juliette's apartment:

> "There must be some escape!" [Juliette] cried, fiercely.
> "Yes," replied Noel, "one way."... They will pick the lock. Bolt all
> the doors, and make them break them down; it will gain time for me."
> Juliette...sprang forward to do this. Noel leaning against the
> mantel took out his revolver, and placed it against his breast.
> But Juliette,...perceiving the movement, threw herself headlong
> upon her lover to prevent his purpose, but so violently that the pistol
> was discharged. The shot took effect, the ball passing through Noel's
> stomach. He gave a terrible cry.
> Juliette had made his death a terrible punishment; she had only
> prolonged his agony.
> He staggered but did not fall, supporting himself by the mantel,
> while the blood flowed copiously.
> "You shall not kill yourself," she cried, "you shall not. You are mine;
> I love you."[41]

Ruikō completely alters this scene for his Japanese audience. In Ruikō's version Juliette is renamed Rie, and Noel is renamed Minoru, but that is the
least of his changes:

> ...[R]un with me to America!" [Minoru said.] The young woman,
> completely overcome, could not even muster a tear. She was silent for
> a time, her head bowed, but then seemed to make up her mind.
> "I misjudged you badly. A man should not talk about running at
> a time like this, when everything is in shambles. Please...take your
> life gracefully here and now, and say you are mine. If you kill yourself
> gracefully, my love will never change. I will die together with you. If
> after hearing me say this, you still say you are unsure and that you want
> to escape, I will shoot you right now.... Well—which is it to be? Will you
> die together with me? Or will you be killed by my hand? Based on your
> answer I will become either your wife forever or your enemy."
> ..."Forgive me, Rie. I am yours forever."

"Together then?"
"A graceful suicide."
"I could not be gladder."[42]

In the Japanese version, Rie not only insists on her lover's suicide despite his ambivalence, but also insists on killing herself along with him. The two write notes to posterity before carrying out a Japanese-style love suicide reminiscent of the works of Chikamatsu Monzaemon (best known for his 1703 play *Sonezaki shinjū,* or "The Love Suicides at Sonezaki"), even though the couple use Minoru's revolver to accomplish it.

But more striking still is Ruikō's expansion of the closing lines of the original, which tell us only that the amateur detective Titauclaire, in a mood of resignation about the difficulty of arriving at the truth in criminal cases, "circulated a petition for the abolition of capital punishment, and organized a society for aiding the poor and innocent accused."[43] Ruikō takes from these lines the idea of the abolition of capital punishment and the idea of the organizing of a society and joins them together in three pages' worth of extraordinary material that he adds to the novel's end.

Ruikō has his murderer Minoru hastily scrawl two separate testaments as the police are beating on the door of his apartment just before he and Rie take their own lives. In one of these he confesses his guilt in the murder of his nurse and urges the release of his innocent half brother, Komori. (This corresponds in the English version to Noel's signing of a confession that the police place in his hands as he lies dying from his self-inflicted gunshot wound.) In the second testament, which has no counterpart in the original, Ruikō has him leave all his money to found an international society for the abolition of capital punishment. "There is nothing in this world so prone to error as a court of law," Minoru writes in this second testament, "and it frequently occurs that, without anyone realizing it, innocent people are put to death. Once they have been put to death, since the dead do not speak, there is no way to know the error. If [the error] is discovered, there is no way to make restitution of the lost life; so I beg that all people who champion the cause of justice *(gi ni isamu hitobito)* should without delay form an international society for the abolition of capital punishment *(bankoku shikei haishi kyōkai)*" (p. 415).

The particular argument against capital punishment that Ruikō here puts into Minoru's mouth—one grounded on the danger of judicial error—had been circulated in Japan at least since the beginning of the Meiji period, perhaps most vocally by the Meirokusha Society member Tsuda Mamichi (1829–1903).[44] When the new penal code was adopted in 1882, the number of crimes for which one could be put to death in Japan was considerably reduced, and the means of execution were limited to nonpublic hanging (under the *Shinritsu kōryō* code of 1871 decapitation—Takahashi Oden's fate—and display of the severed head had still been allowed).[45] Predictably, the sheer number of executions had also dropped in comparison to what they had been in the early 1870s. In 1873 there were 961 executions, and in 1874 there were 452. Two years before Ruikō's translation appeared, in 1886, there had been 131 executions; one year before there had been 97.[46] But while these numbers show a relative drop in the frequency of executions, they still represent a rate of between two and three per week; clearly capital punishment continued to figure in the national imagination with a prominence sufficient to inspire a discourse on its abolition.

Ruikō does not stop at putting this argument against capital punishment into his character Minoru's mouth. He goes on to provide further details, all of his own devising, of the founding of the society to abolish capital punishment, and he does so in a way that seems calculated to move common readers to political action, or at least to imagine themselves as political beings.

After reproducing the initial subscription list for the society (indicating—in yen—the amounts that each character in the novel has contributed), he explains that the first thing the newly formed society did was to put together a pamphlet describing its aims. Included in the pamphlet as an appendix, he says, was the very story that we have just finished reading. "Your translator Ruikō got hold of one of these pamphlets," he tells us, "and this is how he came to publish [the story] at such length in the *Konnichi* newspaper" (p. 418). At the novel's end, then, Ruikō invents a provenance for it that is wholly fictional yet seems to ground the text in real events and a real political movement. Robun's criminal biography of Takahashi Oden had begun with the real event of Oden's decapitation and then fabricated a life story based as much on imagination as on fact. Ruikō's text similarly attempted to straddle the worlds of fact and fiction, but it worked in the opposite way, starting with a fiction and then introducing into it an apparent grounding in real-world events. One can imagine Ruikō's readers thinking, however fleetingly, "If the story is in my hands, then the society described here must actually exist."

Ruikō next tells his readers that recent French newspapers report that two characters who appear in the novel (Chirakura and Taburo, the amateur detective and the judge of inquiry) are launching a round-the-world speaking tour to advance the cause of the society. "They say Mr. Taburo is heading west for North and South America, and Mr. Chirakura is heading east for Asia. So it should come to pass within two or three years that we, together with the reader *(ware-ra ga dokusha to tomo ni)*, will listen in the Public Welfare Building to an impassioned address by the balding old man himself" (p. 418). The use of the word "we" *(ware-ra)* here seems a strategic one. (It is the only time it is used this way in the novel—Ruikō otherwise refers to himself as simply "Ruikō," or "your translator.") With the word *ware-ra* Ruikō projects for the reader an imagined community of like-minded readers gathering together in the manifestly political space of the Public Welfare Building *(kōsei-kan)* that is conjured up by the text. These readers are, in the first instance, Japanese who have read the account in its translated form. But the very fact that the text is a translation, a text that has come into the reader's hands by crossing international boundaries, also guarantees a link between the reader-listeners present at the imagined lecture tour's stop in Japan, on the one hand, and a larger international movement with a shared, translatable view of the need for reform, on the other.

The foreign origin of the text and its status as a translation thus enhanced its seeming power as evidence of an international movement that the reader could join and by so doing bring about change in the Japanese legal system. (Ultimately, the fact that the particular society described in the book is fictitious does not matter so much since, as Ruikō surely realized, the book could play a role in creating such a society after the fact, just as he himself had invented it after the fact of his translation.) But Ruikō's situation was quite different from that of the writer who writes in a foreign genre simply because he perceives it to be better in some absolute sense than the genres constituting the domestic literary tradition. Despite Ruikō's declaration (quoted in the previous chapter) that Japanese "readers were tiring a bit of the Robunesque stuff," his radical—and indeed creative—manipulation of Gaboriau's text suggests that subordinating *Man or Devil?* to his own political purposes was more important to him than any act of transplantation or imitation carried off for its own sake.

Yorozu chōhō and *People's Luck*

Ruikō's interest in putting translated texts to new, political, purposes that were unique to his local, Japanese context is even clearer in the tabloid serial *People's Luck*, which he published in 1894. By 1892 Ruikō had scraped together enough capital to found his own newspaper, *Yorozu chōhō*. On the first page of the first issue, Ruikō described the formula and the intended audience for the tabloid that was to become, by 1902, the most widely circulating newspaper in Tokyo:

Objective: For what purpose has *Yorozu chōhō* begun publication? For none other than that the mass of ordinary citizens might have a convenient way of knowing at a glance what is going on in the world. Accordingly, we will do everything possible to keep the price low, the page size small, and the writing plain. We will, moreover, be independent.

Price: In recent years the newsprint market has steadily gone up so that nowadays even the cheapest papers have come to exceed one and a half *sen*. In Japanese society today, one and a half *sen* is a lot of money. It is more than the daily essential of admission to the bathhouse, and it is more than the cost of that priceless treasure the postcard. . . . When a newspaper is so dearly priced, it confers no benefit upon the general public. . . .

Page size: It is our ideal that articles should be as concise as possible. Long articles are a waste of time. Reading them only causes fatigue. By day they interfere with your errands and by night they expend lamp oil excessively. . . . Because the articles will be short, there will likewise be no need for the pages to be large. It will be as if, in other words, the newspaper were a guest: anyone who has suffered the annoyance of one who overstays his welcome will see the advantages of a newspaper that is short and sweet.

The writing: . . . When the writing in a newspaper is high-flown, very likely only the master of the house—the one with the most learning—will enjoy it. But if you make it plain and colloquial, so that anyone can understand it, then after the master his wife will read it, and then the head clerk will read it, the shop boys will read it, and the servant men and women will read it, too. In short, because for the price of one *sen* the entire household benefits, there can be nothing cheaper. . . .

Independence: These days every newspaper, like a prostitute who refuses to work without having a secret lover, is the mouthpiece of some behind-the-scenes gallant. . . . The government, the political parties, the ambitious private kingmakers, the moneyed bigwigs of the business world—they all have some newspaper they are in bed with. If ordinary citizens rely on such newspapers, they will learn precious little in the way of true facts and hear little in the way of fair debate. Our company, for better or for worse, goes it alone, independently. . . . If you want twisted arguments or warped articles—well, read some other paper![47]

The reputation of *Yorozu chōhō* was less than gentlemanly. Ruikō built up the paper's circulation not only with his serialized foreign fiction, but also with scandalmongering that was sufficiently frequent to earn him the nickname "Mamushi no Shūroku," or "Shūroku the Viper." Testimony to the newspaper's commanding presence in the early days of mass journalism can be found in its permanent contributions to the Japanese language.

It is Ruikō's paper, which had a pinkish tone to its pages, that is behind the Japanese phrase *aka-shinbun* (literally, "red newspaper"), which signifies a newspaper engaged in sensational, or yellow, journalism. And it is to Ruikō's placement of the most scandalous of his reports on the third page of the paper that Japanese owes the phrase *sanmen-kiji* ("human interest story" or "chronique scandaleuse" but literally, "page-three article"). The paper would reach its nadir in this regard in 1898 with the notorious column "Chikushō no jitsurei," or "True Cases of Kept Women."[48] Using his network of investigative reporters to follow the nighttime movements of public figures secretly, Ruikō discovered the names and addresses of their mistresses. He then published the information in the newspaper along with other pertinent facts he could glean about the couples' relations. His dozens of targets included some of the most distinguished men of the day, Mori Ōgai and Itō Hirobumi among them.[49]

It was on the pages of *Yorozu chōhō* that Ruikō's translation of *People's Luck* appeared, and it is by reading it in the context of those pages that we can best understand the implications it had for its audience. Such a contextualized reading suggests that Ruikō, as he had with *Man or Devil?* saw that a strategy of partial Japanizing in translation could bring the legal system portrayed in the novel into proximity with the Japanese legal system and by so doing could underline the inadequacies of the latter. With *People's Luck*, however, it is not that the Japanese legal system is so closely akin to the foreign one as to share its shortcomings. Rather, the point is that the transgressions of highly placed people, including judges, have corrupted the Japanese system so that it is incapable of meting out justice in the way that the foreign legal system in *People's Luck* so neatly and satisfyingly does. As we shall see, the plot of *People's Luck* was nearly made to order for Ruikō as a match for the "plot" of the most sensational and closely followed murder trial of the mid–Meiji period, which came to be known as the Sōma Affair (Sōma jiken). In the trial, certain members of the household of the prominent Sōma family of Fukushima prefecture were accused of having murdered the family head in order to gain control of the vast Sōma fortune. They were in the end found innocent, and the death of the family head was assigned to natural causes. But Ruikō was convinced this verdict was the result of bribery, and he devoted enormous space in *Yorozu chōhō* to blasting the Sōma family's abuses of wealth and privilege. *People's Luck* also centered on a murder carried out to gain control of a large fortune, with the difference that the trial contained in the novel yielded a verdict of guilty. Ruikō's publishing of the translated novel alongside his coverage of the trial invited readers to read the two side by side and had the effect of turning *People's Luck* into a critical commentary on the corruption of the mid-Meiji legal system—an effect that could hardly have been present in its original English version.

The Sōma Affair

The Sōma Affair made Japanese headlines off and on for a full ten years, from 1884 to 1894. It was, especially in 1893 and 1894, the focus of great public attention. It inspired woodblock prints *(nishiki-e)* and plays portraying its events. Large betting pools rode on its outcome.[50] The colorful list of dramatis personae in the affair included Viscount Sōma Tomotane, the young head of the family, who, it seems likely in retrospect, suffered from schizophrenia; Tomotane's retainer, Nishigōri Takekiyo; the house steward, Shiga Naomichi (who was the grandfather of the well-known writer Shiga Naoya); Yoritane, Tomotane's putative half brother by their father's mistress but actually the son of the mistress and the steward Shiga; and Hidetane, Tomotane's son by one of the maids in the house.[51]

The dispute began in 1879, when a faction of the household led by Shiga declared Tomotane insane and had him locked away and then hospitalized, installing Shiga's own son Yoritane in his place as household head. The retainer Nishigōri, declaring that this was a ruse to gain control over the fortune, made various attempts to restore Tomotane to his former position, including, in 1887, a one-man raid on a Tokyo mental hospital to spring his master and whisk him into hiding. Things came to a head late in 1892, when Tomotane, by now back in the hands of the Shiga faction, suddenly vomited blood and died. Nishigōri accused Shiga, Yoritane, and the rest of their faction of murder by poisoning. The following summer and fall (in 1893) there ensued the murder trial of these parties, which culminated in the exhumation and autopsy of Tomotane's corpse. At the same time the members of the Shiga faction parried with a suit of their own, accusing Nishigōri of knowingly bringing false charges against them.

As the scholar Itō Hideo has pointed out, this scandal matched the most sensational story that Ruikō could have found in the cheap paperback libraries he combed for likely looking crime novels to translate: it involved murder, money, bastardy, insanity, forensic medicine, and the reputation of an aristocratic family, all focused into the drama of a courtroom confrontation. Ruikō's coverage of the affair was relentlessly thorough, and the story dominated all else in *Yorozu chōhō* for a period of about eleven months. Starting in July of 1893, when Nishigōri formally filed his accusation of murder, Ruikō ran almost daily updates on developments in the case under a front-page headline ("Sōma-ke dokusatsu sōdō," or "Sōma Family Poison Murder Scandal") set in oversized type. He carried the complete text of all the important motions filed and decisions handed down. He published interviews with everyone from experts on poisoning and autopsy to childhood friends of the principals in the trial and the personal physician of Tomotane's wife (whose inability to produce an heir was, Nishigōri claimed, also the result of a nefarious plot by the Shiga faction). And of course he ran numerous editorials commenting on the unfolding drama. Only in May of 1894, when the second trial (that of Nishigōri) came to an end, did his coverage taper off. No reader who had seen the paper in the months before *People's Luck* began running could have been unaware of the Sōma Affair.

Looking back on his career in newspapers, Ruikō was to say about *Yorozu chōhō:* "We stuck firmly to the following editorial policy...: (1) be simple, (2) be clear, and (3) be entertaining."[52] Ruikō's reporting of the Sōma trials was true to that policy. He offered his readership a narrative that transformed the ambiguities of the trial into a familiar and easily recognized contest of good versus evil with a dose of class antagonism thrown in. In an editorial titled "Chūshin to kanbutsu," or "Faithful Retainers and Villains," he compared the scandal to the infamous *oiesōdō*, or protracted family disputes, of the Edo period—the Date Sōdō and the Kuroda Sōdō. "The great inheritance disputes of the past," he wrote, "have had in them without exception a faithful retainer and a villain."

> They glower at one another, each looking for a weakness in his opponent, as if in some Titanic struggle *(ryūko no aiarasou ni nitaru mono ari)....* The well-known Sōma poisoning affair is a Meiji *oiesōdō,* the cause célèbre of our time.... [But] even if we provisionally take Nishigōri as the faithful retainer, who from the Sōma side should we take as the villain? Taking as the villains those whom Nishigōri has accused somehow does not feel entirely satisfactory *(nan to naku kuita-ranu kokochi suru),* and Nishigōri, unfortunately, lacks weight and seriousness as the faithful retainer.[53]

This particular editorial stops short of casting Nishigōri as the hero and Shiga as the villain, but Ruikō's tentative use here of the *oiesōdō* as a narrative template signals the direction that his coverage was to take. By invoking the paradigm of hero and villain already made familiar by popular retellings of these famous disputes, Ruikō was beginning to turn the Sōma case into a modern version of them, in spite of the resistance offered by the material he had to work with. About the necessity of filling the roles of hero and villain there never seems to have been doubt, and in fact this editorial was the last to mention any qualms about the fitness of Nishigōri and Shiga to do so.

The narrative that Ruikō had set in motion began to gather a momentum of its own. It was not long before the paper unambiguously took up the cause of Nishigōri, turning him into a righteous underdog attempting to wrest justice from a legal system lubricated by money. The Shiga faction, in contrast, was rich, powerful, and so corrupt as to go to any length to hang onto its ill-gotten position, including widespread bribery and tampering with evidence. Shortly after Nishigōri filed his formal accusation, for example, Ruikō ran this note in his regular column of trial updates: "Vial of Blood Missing—The vial that contained the blood from Viscount Seiin's [Tomotane's] mouth and nose, which is the most important evidence in the poisoning incident, was recently stolen from police custody by some party. Stranger than strange that it should have been lost without a trace!"[54]

Ruikō ran editorials criticizing the authorities for moving with inordinate sluggishness in arresting the parties accused by Nishigōri.[55] He published a series of attacks (sometimes in the form of "letters" to the paper almost certainly written by Ruikō himself) on the coverage in other newspapers, suggesting that they were accepting bribes to slant their coverage in favor of Shiga.[56] When the autopsy of Tomotane's body turned up no signs of poison and the court declared the Sōma house innocent of the murder charges, Ruikō's report of the decision struck a pose of dumbfoundedness: "This is on a par with grain raining down from the heavens or horses growing horns," he wrote.[57] The following day he ran the first installment of an innuendo-filled editorial titled "Trial by Law and Trial by Society," which dwelled at length on the fallibility of judges.[58] "What are judges?" Ruikō asked. "They are nothing but ordinary people.... They have in their power of judgment... their vision, their knowledge, their desires, and their morals all the usual shortcomings of ordinary people."[59] He went on to invoke the name of Ōoka Echizen, the magistrate from *Ōoka's Rulings,* as a standard all but impossible to live up to: "[Judges] make mistakes in their judgments, and their vision can be corrupted *(shikiken no fuhai suru ari);* perhaps if one could get someone as knowledgeable and insightful as Ōoka Echizen, one could minimize error *(ayamachi no sukunaki o uru),* but barring that, one cannot hope that errors will be few. No matter what country one looks to for examples, one is apt to find judges leaving blots on their robes."[60]

The tone of Ruikō's trial coverage by itself suggests the degree to which the range of popular attitudes toward the justice system, at least as it was expressed in print, had broadened and changed since Saikaku's *Cases, Ōoka's Rulings,* and *The Tale of Takahashi Oden.* But equally striking is Ruikō's continued deployment of translated crime fiction in this period as a vehicle for criticism of the justice system. *People's Luck* began running in the newspaper in March 1894, five months after the Shiga faction had been found innocent but simultaneously with the beginning of the trial of Nishigōri. The outlines of the novel are so similar to those of the Sōma Affair as to suggest that Ruikō was inviting his audience to read the two as a mutually illuminating pair.

The Plot of *People's Luck*

The first section of *People's Luck* introduces two young couples. Just as he did in *Man or Devil?* (and, indeed, in most of his translations), Ruikō gives his characters Japanese names. We meet at the novel's outset Fudei Kiyoshi, who we are told is one of the richest men in England. He falls in love with Enoki Kaede, a poor itinerant actress, when he is traveling through a village in the English countryside called "Eborushamu" (presumably Eversham). We also learn that Kiyoshi has a cousin, Awashi, who is in love with a woman named Matsuko. He cannot marry her because he does not, as a struggling literary critic, have enough money to ensure her future.

Kiyoshi asks the actress Kaede to marry him, and is accepted, but is then almost immediately shot to death on a dark back road. This murder sets up the chief questions of the novel: who killed Kiyoshi, and who will control the Fudei family fortune? As is usual in novels with an inheritance plot, the rules for answering the second question have been set forth in a will, that of Kiyoshi's dead grandfather. He had three sons named Fukashi, Kiyoshi, and Awashi. Each of these men in turn had one son, to whom he gave his own name. The grandfather's will stipulated that the fortune would pass first down the line of his oldest son and then in turn down those of each of his younger sons should a prior line die out. At the novel's opening, the fathers Fukashi, Kiyoshi, and Awashi are all dead. (They are not so much characters as nodes in a tree of legal relationships.) Fukashi Jr., who was a soldier, is also dead, having been killed in battle, apparently unmarried and without issue. Hence the Fudei fortune was in Kiyoshi Jr.'s hands at the time of his murder. According to the terms of the will, upon Kiyoshi's death the fortune should pass first to his offspring. But he has none, so the money goes to his poor cousin Awashi, the literary critic. Thanks to his newfound wealth, Awashi can now marry Matsuko. He does so, moves onto the large estate vacated by his dead cousin, and takes over his seat in the House of Lords.

The detective in the novel is Kurita, a close friend of the murdered Kiyoshi. After discovering that he is himself the police's chief suspect in the case, he resolves to find the true murderer. At the same time, he begins looking into the background of the distraught Kaede, whom he has taken it upon himself to console after the murder of her betrothed. After a good deal of legwork, he puts together proof that, unbeknownst to her, Kaede is actually the long lost daughter of Fukashi Jr., who had in fact secretly married before his death in the war. Her mother, he realizes, is Ryūko, an insane woman who (true to the English crime novel's gothic antecedents) lurks in the upper story of the house where Kurita has been boarding while in Eversham. Kurita deduces that she lost her wits during her pregnancy, when she received news of Fukashi's death and had to go into hiding to give birth and then to give up her child for adoption. All of this means that Kaede has a claim to the Fudei fortune that is stronger than Awashi's, since she is descended from the grandfather's first son, and Awashi is only descended from his third.

Awashi, whose motives become more and more suspect, disputes her claim, casting doubts from every angle upon Kaede's legitimacy: he questions whether the secret marriage ever took place, whether Ryūko might have become pregnant by another man, and whether the fortune can legally pass through a bloodline sullied by insanity. In the last, climactic section of the novel, Kurita wages a court battle on Kaede's behalf in order to take the fortune from the usurper Awashi. At the same time, his investigation of Kiyoshi's death leads him, by means of a bloody (and conveniently monogrammed) handkerchief found at the scene of the crime, to the suspicion that Awashi is the murderer. The latter, now becoming desperate, hires a crooked lawyer named Sujigawa to help him keep his apparently ill-gotten fortune. Sujigawa and a henchman abduct Kaede in order to drown her, and Sujigawa satisfies Awashi that he has done so.

Kaede's disappearance only deepens Kurita's resolve to bring down Awashi, and he eventually induces Awashi to confess in court by confronting him with the bloody handkerchief. Awashi is convicted of killing his cousin. He goes to prison, where he falls ill and dies. Sujigawa also goes to prison under a life sentence. Kaede, mirabile dictu, has not actually been drowned. Sujigawa, we learn, had planned to use the threat of her reappearance to extort half the Fudei fortune from his client. The actress is recognized, to her surprise and delight, as the legitimate heir to the fortune. For good measure, she and Kurita are married. Her mother, as the novel closes, is beginning to regain her sanity, thanks to the loving attention of the newly married couple.

Parallels between *People's Luck* and Ruikō's Coverage of the Sōma Affair

People's Luck, as has already been suggested, had significant parallels with Ruikō's newspaper coverage of the Sōma Affair. There was an inherent similarity between the characters and the plot of *People's Luck* and the characters and plot of the Sōma Affair, at least as Ruikō presented it in *Yorozu chōhō*. There was also a more general similarity between the suspense of the whodunit form itself and that of the unfolding coverage of the trial. Just as important, Ruikō's particular handling of the translated serial placed special emphasis on these parallels between fiction and reality. Not only his timing of the serial to follow closely upon the trial coverage, but also his partial Japanization of the serial's characters and setting and his interpolations into it in the voice of the translator transformed *People's Luck* from mere entertainment into a gloss on the real-world trial and the miscarriage of justice that Ruikō saw in it.

The cast of characters in the real-life scandal—as Ruikō read it—matches that of the novel with great exactness. Nishigōri, the loyal retainer to the dead victim and the motive force behind the prosecution of the Shiga faction, has his fictional counterpart in Kurita, the loyal friend who carries on his own investigation; Tomotane, the household head who dies under suspicious circumstances, has his in the murdered Kiyoshi; Tomotane's son Hidetane, whom Nishigōri insisted was the rightful heir, corresponds to Kaede, true heir to the Fudei fortune; Shiga Naomichi, the steward and scheming usurper, corresponds to Awashi, ultimately exposed in *People's Luck* as the murderer. Even Shiga's lawyer, Hoshi Tōru, whose ethics had come under attack in Ruikō's paper, had a counterpart in the crooked lawyer Sujigawa. The two plots also follow each other closely: the launching of events with the death of the holder of the family fortune, the subsequent investigation, the motive for murder that arises from a particular network of blood relationships, the climactic courtroom scenes, and even the similarity between the central pieces of physical evidence (a vial of blood, on the one hand, and a bloody handkerchief, on the other) all tie the events of the serialized novel closely to those of the actual trial.

The parallels between reportage and serialized fiction also extended to matters of form and feel. In the same way that the trial had its near-daily update, always in the same position on the page and always under the same title, so too did the novel have its regular daily installment. Each update on the Sōma case brought with it new evidence and testimony, and the sense that one was moving closer to the legal truth that would eventually be spoken in the form of the verdict. Likewise, each daily installment of *People's Luck* brought fresh complications that at the same time advanced the reader one step closer to the public unmasking of the true murderer. The whodunit's generic requirement that this most crucial ritual be delayed until the novel's end ensured that *People's Luck*'s unfolding would mimic that of the trial reportage.

As with *Man or Devil?* Ruikō's partial Japanization of the serial's setting also brought the world of the novel closer to Japan than other imaginable strategies for translation would have. The peculiarity of giving all of the characters Japanese names has already been mentioned. Ruikō does not, in *People's Luck,* come up with *kanji* characters for English place names—he simply renders them in the phonetic *katakana* script, so one's sense that the action is unfolding in some liminal space is perhaps not quite so powerful in *People's Luck.* These characters do, however, use yen as their currency, the *shaku* as their unit of length, and *zashiki* rooms as their parlors.

But Ruikō drew his most explicit connection between the world of the novel and the world of his Japanese readers in an interpolation that came between the novel's eighty-sixth and eighty-seventh installments. Pleading illness and lack of time to translate because of the outbreak of the Sino-Japanese War, Ruikō left Kurita's fictional investigation hanging for four days while he ran a four-part account of still another inheritance dispute that had taken place in Tokyo the previous year. He gave this account the same headline he customarily used for the novel—*People's Luck*—and he placed it in the same space on the page where the novel's daily installment usually appeared.

This real-life inheritance dispute centered on the twenty-thousand-yen fortune of an Asakusa woman named Hirasawa Shina and broke out when she was poisoned to death without leaving any obvious heir. Despite competing claims from several impostors, one Takejirō, a poor rickshaw man from Jōshū (now Gunma prefecture), was eventually able to establish his identity as the nearest relative of the woman and thus to inherit the fortune. In order to make certain the parallels between this real-life dispute and the plot of his novel were clear, Ruikō wove references to the characters of *People's Luck* into the account. "When all manner of people were coming forward to claim the fortune as the woman's relatives," he wrote, "this rickshaw man...suddenly appeared with his [irrefutable] claim; he was met with an astonishment even greater than that of Fudei Awashi toward Kaede."[61] And at the end of the last installment, Ruikō connected the episode with his novel by echoing its title in the narration itself: "[The court decided] that Takejirō should inherit the dead Hirasawa's property, and the twenty thousand yen passed to the hands of the...rickshaw man. Yesterday a rickshaw man, today a rich man—there is no telling how people's luck *(hito no un)* will play itself out."[62]

Admittedly, the suggestion that Ruikō wanted his readers to connect the events of the serialized novel specifically with the Sōma trial—in which luck seemed to him to be suspiciously on the side of the wealthy—would be even more compelling if Ruikō had inserted in his translation some explicit reference to the Sōma Affair. There is no such explicit reference. But Ruikō's interpolation of the story of the rickshaw man demonstrates his sensitivity to exactly the sort of similarity of plot that the Sōma Affair had with *People's Luck*—even when perceiving it required straddling the divide between real events and a fictional text. In this case Ruikō provided no didactic preface explaining how he meant *People's Luck* to be read, but its unmistakable similarity to the events of the Sōma Affair strongly suggests that he intended *People's Luck* as the portrayal of an ideal that the Japanese justice system had, in the Sōma Affair, failed to live up to. *People's Luck* ends happily; its legal system serves up justice in spite of the machinations of the crooked lawyer Sujigawa and his henchmen. The outcome of the Sōma Affair, in contrast, was a miscarriage of justice that would have become all the starker when viewed alongside the fictional ideal represented in *People's Luck*. So in its offering of a corrective and alternative vision of the workings of justice and in the critique of the existing justice system implied by such a gesture, *People's Luck* was wholly of a piece with the earlier *Man or Devil?*

The Consequences of a Duel

Although *Man or Devil?* and *People's Luck* both use the French and English legal systems (or at least imagined versions of them) as touchstones for exposing lingering feudalism and corruption in the Japanese legal system, Ruikō did not always make his comparisons with European culture in ways calculated to expose Japanese shortcomings. Ruikō's translation of Du Boisgobey's novel *Les suites d'un duel* (Consequences of a Duel), is similar to *Man or Devil?* and *People's Luck* in that it promotes an agenda of Japanese legal reform in keeping with Ruikō's characteristic vision. But it is considerably more subtle than *Man or Devil?* and *People's Luck* about doing so, and it sets up a relationship between the native and European legal systems that differs from the ones found in Ruikō's earlier works. *Consequences of a Duel* aligns France with pre-Restoration and early Meiji Japan in order to underline the positive progress Japan has made in comparison to its former feudal self. In this translation France, rather than being held up as a model to be emulated, becomes an object of almost purely anthropological interest, a curiosity that self-respecting cosmopolites ought to have some knowledge of and that merits study primarily on that ground. Ruikō's translation thus strikes an attitude of ethnographic mastery, a mastery that it achieves by mapping France onto Japan's past, both in order to render France comprehensible and in order to define Japan's present as a distinct improvement over that past.

In thus aligning France with Japan's feudal past, the work subtly asserts that—thanks to the legal reforms Japan has made since the Meiji Restoration—Japan is superior to the France portrayed in the translation. Where *Man or Devil?* looks forward to a hoped-for future abolition of capital punishment and *People's Luck* directs an accusing finger at corruption in the present, *Consequences of a Duel* invites the reader to fix a rearward gaze on what Japan has left behind. *Consequences of a Duel* thus differs from the other two texts in the way it configures European culture as an intermediary for Japanese self-scrutiny. Nonetheless, *Consequences of a Duel*'s cultivation in the reader of a national consciousness and a sense of progress made (and, by implication, of the further progress possible) ultimately makes it, too, wholly consonant with the vision of Japanese enlightenment contained in Ruikō's other works.

In addition, the translation offers evidence of Ruikō's apparent belief that the detective novel could be a tool for cultivating a healthy skepticism in his readers. The translation faithfully preserves both the intricacy of the original's plot and the narrative pattern of gradual revelation characteristic of the detective novel. When, on the final page, Ruikō introduces another interpolation, this time exhorting the reader to clear up any doubtful points by rereading the whole from the start, it suggests that he saw the detective novel as a means of instilling in his readers the same relentlessly critical mind-set that Ruikō himself embodied and that he believed was such an important trait of an enlightened Japanese citizenry.

Translation as Ethnography

Ruikō's translation of *Consequences of a Duel* projects for itself a reader with an unmistakably cosmopolitan curiosity. In this regard it is typical of much of Ruikō's output. His translations nearly always catered in some way to the Meiji reader's understandable hunger for knowledge about the Western countries with which Japan had so recently begun interchange. Unlike some other Meiji period literary adapters (such as Tokuda Shūsei), Ruikō never relocated foreign works to Japan. His portrayals of foreign countries—once he had finished substituting Japanese yen for French francs or Japanese surnames for English ones—may turn them into oddly hybridized places, but their unvarying official premise is that they are set in some actual foreign locale. It is telling that so many of his translations begin by announcing the name of that locale (Paris, say, or London, or New York) in their very first sentence, even when the original omits or delays this information. These settings contained an implicit promise to acquaint the reader with the foreign lives, customs, and material cultures that had become newly accessible only since the Restoration. In his translation *Makkura* (Utter Darkness), for example, he inserts an explanation of that device of monumental importance to the Western detective novel, the key-operated lock. "Western locks can be locked from either the inside or the outside," he informs his reader. "The same key that works the lock can also be used to open the door itself [i.e., by continuing to turn it]. Usually the key is left in its hole."[63]

But in *Consequences of a Duel* the stoking and satisfaction of the reader's anthropological interest in the world beyond Japan is even more conspicuous than usual. Much of this interest centers on the distinction in the French legal system between rightful and wrongful killings as they are carried out on the dueling ground and in the bedroom. Ruikō's interpolations into the translation have about them a consistently ethnographic tone that encourages his readers to view French laws and customs as oddities. This tone is apparent from the translation's beginning, where Ruikō has inserted introductory remarks in his own voice. "In our country," the translation begins, "before the Restoration dueling was an established custom...; but the place where it thrives most is France. If there is a difference of opinion [in France], they immediately duel; if there is some dispute, they immediately duel. There is probably no French gentleman who goes through his entire life without once sampling the taste of a duel."[64] Ruikō goes on to explain how elaborate and strict the rules for French dueling are and then implicitly underlines these rules' curiosity by saying how much on his mind it has been to spread knowledge of them to a wider public in Japan: "Since I take pleasure in reading English and French books," he writes, "and because I know virtually all the rules of dueling for that reason, I have planned many times to take up my brush to do a translation in order to make these rules known to our country." Later in the same introductory remarks, Ruikō enlarges the scope of the reader's imagined fascination beyond the controlled violence of dueling, introducing a hint of voyeurism and a whiff of the boudoir. The readers of his translation will, Ruikō promises, "not only become acquainted with dueling in its authentic form, but will also be able to penetrate the secrets of the society of the ladies and gentlemen of that country [i.e., France]."[65]

The story that follows Ruikō's remarks makes good on his promise. As the story opens, three Frenchmen (whom Ruikō, as usual, has given Japanese names) are riding in a carriage through the countryside outside Paris in order to keep an appointment for a duel. One of these three— Kuwayagi—is a principal in the duel, and the other two are his seconds. Kuwayagi has been challenged to the duel by a fellow member of his club named Honda, whom Kuwayagi struck during a card game. From conversation between Kuwayagi and his friends, we soon learn that Kuwayagi's

betrothed, the alluring Mademoiselle Moriyama, has been the object of
unwelcome advances by Honda and that Kuwayagi struck Honda to provoke a duel between them without bringing Mademoiselle Moriyama's
name into the matter.

Skilled with the pistol, Kuwayagi faces the duel with calm. But his bullet unexpectedly misses its mark and he is shot dead by his rival. Ōtani, one
of Kuwayagi's seconds, suspects foul play when he discovers on the dueling
ground a bullet fashioned of wood and covered in lead-colored paper. Much
of the detection in the novel is given over to deducing how the wooden bullet was substituted for the real one that should have gone into Kuwayagi's pistol, how the subsequent drawing of the pistols was rigged, and who is responsible for this ploy that turned the duel into an outright murder. The result of
these investigations is surprising: acting on clues gleaned at an antiques auction and a night at the Paris opera, Ōtani and Kobayashi (Kuwayagi's other
second) establish that the wooden bullet was fashioned by Kuwayagi's fiancée
herself—the innocent-seeming Mademoiselle Moriyama—and substituted
for the real bullet by Honda's second, Furuyama. It comes out that Mademoiselle Moriyama has been Honda's lover all along, that she plotted the
death of Kuwayagi, and that she agreed to marry him only out of greed for
his money, which she is due to inherit under the terms of a will that Kuwayagi
drew up shortly before the duel.

Ōtani now plans a revenge killing that, much like Moriyama and Honda's own plot, will use a loophole in the law in order to commit a murder
under the guise of legality. Relying on Mademoiselle Moriyama's greed for
his money, Ōtani proposes marriage to her, and she accepts. Ōtani then
searches out the rented house where Mademoiselle Moriyama and Honda
have their assignations, with the idea of surprising the two together in bed
and then killing them both. As Ruikō explains in another of his ethnographic
interpolations addressed to the Japanese reader, under the infamous article
324 of the Napoleonic Code, a husband was granted the legal right to kill his
wife and her lover on the spot if he caught them committing adultery:[66]

> The reason Ōtani made Mademoiselle Moriyama his wife was in order
> to kill her and Honda, and to be able to act as Moriyama's husband
> when he did so. Under French law, a husband is given the right to kill
> his wife and her paramour. If he discovers the wife and her paramour
> at the site of an assignation, it is within his discretion to kill them on
> the spot. Ōtani, settling his matrimonial union with Moriyama and tak-
> ing this law as his shield, planned to watch for the chance when Mori-
> yama and Honda would have a rendezvous and then come storming
> in to kill them both. This was a dangerous scheme.... The letter of the

law stipulates that even if the man is the lawful husband of the woman, if he has deliberately planned to conceal himself in order to wait for his wife and her lover's assignation, then he is no longer adjudged innocent and will be subject to a prison sentence of ten years.[67]

In the event, there is a deus ex machina that saves Ōtani from sullying his hands with this killing. His friend Kobayashi rushes to the house where Honda and Moriyama are known to meet, intending to stop Ōtani from carrying out his risky plan. When Kobayashi arrives there, he first thinks he is too late. Moriyama lies dead on the staircase, and he finds the corpse of Honda in an upstairs bedroom. But in what amounts to a miniature detective-story-within-a-detective-story, Kobayashi deduces that the two were coincidentally killed by thieves who forced their way into the house and that Ōtani must still be on his way there. Returning to the street outside, he indeed finds Ōtani just arriving, gives him the news of Moriyama's and Honda's deaths, and hustles his friend away from the crime scene lest they be implicated.

The fascinating thing about Ruikō's focus on the finer points of French law in the novel, and indeed about his selection of *Les suites d'un duel* for translation in the first place, is how closely the crucial French codes mirror those of pre-Restoration and early Meiji Japan. When Ruikō's translation first appeared in 1889, Japanese legal codes had only recently been revised as part of the new Meiji government's program of *bunmei-kaika* (civilization and enlightenment) to reserve the right of execution for the state. Under the old Tokugawa regime, vendetta killings *(ada-uchi)* had been perquisites of the samurai class, and they were not outlawed until 1873.[68] Tokugawa law had also allowed the killing of adulterous wives by their husbands in cases where they were caught flagrante delicto. This practice was outlawed just three years before vendettas, in 1870, when the *Shinritsu kōryō* (Outline of the New Criminal Law) was enacted.[69] Duels to the death *(hatashiai)* and their abetting were officially outlawed in 1889, the very year that Ruikō first published *Kettō no hate,* when an offense designated *kettō-zai* (dueling crime) was added to the books.[70] Ruikō's introduction to the novel in fact capitalizes on this element of topical interest in the story, noting that "in our country...there has recently been renewed discussion of dueling."[71]

The French legal codes spotlighted in the novel, then, have suggestive, built-in similarities to those of Tokugawa and early Meiji Japan. Ruikō's translation, however, frames these similarities in a way that encourages his readers' belief in a narrative of Japanese national progress. This framing begins in the very first line of the translation, where Ruikō says, "In our country the custom of dueling existed before the Restoration."[72] This opening line sets up an implicit binary opposition between pre- and post-Restoration Japan, and it associates dueling with a past that Japan has put behind it. Ruikō then contrasts the binary difference in the Japanese case with the supposed situation in France, where the narrative of progress apparently is not so clear. As Ruikō explains things, in France dueling to the death is now "forbidden by law, but since it is a custom of such long standing, the courts do not reproach [duelers] very strongly . . . and if honest means are used in an honest fight, [a duel] actually redounds to the honor of the victor."[73] This observation, and indeed the entire subsequent novel's preoccupation with French dueling and the murder of adulterous wives, has the effect of aligning contemporary France (the story is set, in both the English and the Japanese versions, "last year") with the retrospectively constructed otherness of pre-Restoration Japan. Ruikō's translation does not openly say that dueling or wife killing is barbaric, nor does he directly state that Japan is more advanced than France because it has outlawed these practices. (Indeed, to say so would have involved Ruikō in some extremely awkward sleight of hand, since the list of legal reforms that the Meiji government carried out was inspired in large measure by the example of French law.)[74] But the translation's attitude of ethnographic fascination, when taken in combination with the binary opposition set up in its first sentence, clearly implies as much.

The translation's combination of ethnographic fascination and temporal displacement of France into Japan's past is perhaps most apparent in an interpolation that Ruikō makes near the novel's end. The English version of the novel concludes by telling the fates of several minor characters (including a Madame Fresnay, an actress named Delphine, and the mother of the evil fiancée). Ruikō omits most of this section, substituting for it a meditation upon Mademoiselle Moriyama:[75]

> It is said that all Parisian women habitually live for today without a thought for tomorrow; but even among this group there is occasionally one who stands out, one who horrifies by the sheer magnitude of her desires or the deftness of her scheming. Perhaps she aims to hold a powerful politician in the palm of her hand, or perhaps she wants to marry a billionaire; Mademoiselle Moriyama was one of this type, the sort of femme fatale *(kyōfujin)* that is perhaps found only in Paris and not in any other country. No one discoursing today upon the theme of "poisonous women" *(dokufu)*, who present the outer appearance of ladies but contain inner demons, fails to borrow his first example from [Moriyama].[76]

Most of this interpolation emphasizes the otherness of Mademoiselle Moriyama, an emphasis that is particularly apparent in its suggestion that her type is "perhaps found only in Paris." This underlining of Moriyama's otherness is, moreover, made in the context of a broader cataloging and description of her type that is consistent with the translation's basic attitude of ethnographic observation. Such a passage invites the Japanese reader to feel that he or she has understood something of the otherness of French society and the representative social phenomena peculiar to it.

And yet at the same time, in the passage's final lines, Ruikō invokes a Japanese stereotype—that of the *dokufu*, or "poisonous woman"—as the most ready means for rendering this otherness comprehensible. Ruikō's words here are in fact a variation on a bit of Buddhist misogyny that may date back as far as the Heian period (985–1192).[77] The Japanese for the phrase "present the outer appearance of ladies but contain inner demons" is *gaimen o shukujo ni shite naishin no yasha o tsutsumu.* This phrasing echoes an archaic Buddhist cliché used to describe all women, whom Buddhism has traditionally viewed as the source of male suffering: *gemen nyo bosatsu naishin nyo yasha,* or "outer appearance like a bodhisattva, heart like a demon." By echoing this archaic phrase, Ruikō renders Moriyama comprehensible for his Japanese reader by mapping her onto native Japanese traditions of thought about femininity and female deception. Ruikō's use of this phrase and of the word *dokufu* itself—which he introduces even though there is no equivalent epithet in the original—also links Moriyama's story to the early Meiji tradition of "poison woman" narratives exemplified by Robun's biography of Takahashi Oden.

Ruikō not only labels Mademoiselle Moriyama a *dokufu.* He also glosses her death at the hands of the murderous thieves—an event that might just as easily be construed as the result of bad luck—as the comeuppance for her plot to kill Kuwayagi:[78]

> The nefarious scheme of Moriyama, the confirmed poisonous woman, did not of course come to fruition. As the proverb reminds us, "to kill another is to dig your own grave" *(hito o norowaba ana futatsu);* the bullet that Honda used to kill Kuwayagi had pierced the breast of Moriyama in her photograph [which Kuwayagi had been carrying in his own breast pocket during the duel], and this proved to be an omen: Moriyama met her end in the most violent and untimely fashion.[79]

The connection between the murder Moriyama commits and her own death is tenuous, to say the least. But Ruikō compacts the narrative's significance into the moral wisdom of its concluding proverb ("to kill another is to dig your own grave") in the way typical of *dokufu* narratives and the older moralizing *gesaku* writings to which they in turn traced their lineage.

Like Ruikō's declaration in the translation's first lines that dueling was a custom that existed in Japan "before the Restoration," the recycling at its conclusion of these musty Japanese narrative conventions has the effect of subtly aligning the French world of the translation's characters with Japan's own past and with the traditional narrative forms that the translation's preface has framed as obsolescent. As if to exorcise once and for all the ghosts of that past and to reinforce the distinction the translation insists on between modern and premodern, the translation goes out of its way in this episode to make an example of its female protagonist's punishment. At least some editions of Ruikō's translation heightened the horror of her fate with a double-page drawing of Moriyama's corpse, sprawled head downward on the staircase, her blood dripping over the edges of the steps like icicles.[80]

This exorcism of the past is admittedly paradoxical, since it threatens to subvert the narrative structure of the translated detective novel itself, changing it back into a variant of the very *gesaku* (complete with the requisite pattern of *kanzen-chōaku,* or "reward of the good and punishment of the bad") it is meant to supersede. But Ruikō seems to have shown little concern for such niceties. He was a seller of newspapers first and a popularizer of the detective novel second, and the mixing of genres we see in *Consequences of a Duel* suggests that he was concerned about maintaining the stylistic purity of his translation only to a point.

More significant for our understanding of the uses of translation than the style of Ruikō's ending is its consistency with the novel's beginning. The novel's ending, like its beginning, aligns a France it represents as contemporary with Japan's outmoded past. In creating this imaginary alignment, Ruikō's translation of *Consequences of Duel* took its place alongside his other translations as a calculated stimulus to still further Japanese national progress. Even when Ruikō's works were not directly critiquing the Japanese justice system, they could still act in concert with his muckraking to cultivate a citizenry that took pride in its new cosmopolitanism, a citizenry attuned to the national project of "enlightenment." By suggesting to the reader, as *Consequences of a Duel* subtly did, that Japan's legal reforms had allowed it to surpass the very culture that had inspired those reforms, Ruikō's translation heightened the reader's awareness of Japan's national and historical trajectory, and did so in newly comparative and international terms.

But *Consequences of a Duel* seems not only to have been designed to develop its Meiji audience's cosmopolitanism and its national consciousness; Ruikō also seems to have intended that audience's encounter with the detective form itself to improve its capacity as actively engaged, thinking readers and citizens. Precisely because the story is narrated as a mystery, in which crucial plot elements are withheld from the reader and only indirectly revealed, it requires the reader to penetrate beneath the surface narrative to make inferences that are enabled but not immediately endorsed by the text.

Ruikō always preserves this basic characteristic of the original with painstaking care, even when he alters some of its details. The novel contains, for example, an episode in which Kobayashi, the murdered Kuwayagi's second, bids at an antiques auction on an ivory desk (the English version has it as an ugly ebony chiffonier). At first he does so merely to indulge the glamorous young actress accompanying him, but he soon realizes that his opponent in the bidding is none other than Furuyama, one of the men who had acted as Honda's second in the deadly duel. Furuyama, moreover, seems willing to pay a preposterously high price for the desk. His suspicion aroused, Kobayashi outbids Furuyama with the aid of a sympathetic auctioneer. It later turns out that the desk has a secret compartment in which is hidden the will of Kuwayagi, the man murdered in the duel. If the will, in which Kuwayagi bequeathed his fortune to Moriyama, were to go undiscovered, the murder under the guise of a duel would have been for naught. But both Honda and Moriyama needed to appear disinterested in the will's revelation, so they have sent Furuyama to the auction in their stead. These connections are made completely explicit only near the novel's conclusion, though they are hinted at along the way.

Ruikō's text shows a clear preoccupation with training the reader to properly assemble the disparate hints that are scattered through the narrative. For one thing, Ruikō occasionally makes these hints rather broader in the Japanese than they are in the English, as if he mistrusted that his readers, inexperienced as they were with the detective genre, would clearly see all the nuances of the text without some help. Where, for example, Ruikō has Kobayashi wondering immediately after the auction whether the desk might contain the missing will (p. 119), at that point in the English version Courtenay (the character who corresponds to Kobayashi) merely muses, "I do not know why I imagine that in that ugly thing will be found something relative to poor Salieu's assassination" (p. 90).

More tellingly still, after the final explanations have been made, Ruikō interpolates in the final pages of the novel another of his disarmingly direct addresses to the reader: "If there are points that seem doubtful to you in the plot of this story," he says, "read it again from the beginning as many times as necessary. [As the Chinese proverb says], 'Read a book a hundred times, and the meaning becomes clear of its own accord'—any doubtful points will vanish."[81] Although this proverb encapsulates a potentially problematic view of the endpoint of careful reading (as a state in which all doubt has been spontaneously resolved), it nonetheless provides an indication of the active effort Ruikō imagined his text might prompt its audience to undertake. Ruikō's encouragement of the reader to act on any lingering doubts—to tackle the text undaunted by its intricacies—suggests once again that he saw the detective novel as a means of instilling in his audience a habit of relentless skeptical inquiry about the story behind the story as well as a muckraker's spirit of critical engagement with the world, regardless of the resistance one's efforts might encounter.

Conclusion: The Uses of Translation

The examples of *Man or Devil?*, *People's Luck*, and *Consequences of a Duel* make clear how far Ruikō's translations were from being mere mimicry of a dominant Western cultural form. Not only were these translations capable of taking on entirely new meanings when relocated to a Japanese context; they also demonstrate how flexible Ruikō could be as a cultural borrower. This flexibility manifested itself in two distinct ways. First, we see it in the remarkably free hand he exercised in his adaptations themselves, in the way he modified his materials to suit his purposes. Despite Ruikō's obvious fascination with the new literary technology of the detective novel, he did not feel compelled to preserve it wholly intact; nor was he blind to its potential pitfalls. Just before the densest of the legal testimony begins in *Man or Devil?* for example, he goes so far as to insert an apology for its dullness: "Note from Ruikō: From this point on comes the record of the trial. It has a number of tedious spots, but this is where the meat of this story is, so even recognizing its tedium, I have not been able to abbreviate it. I implore you to hold back your yawns for a time and read attentively."[82] The same lack of compunction evident here also enabled Ruikō to turn *Man or Devil?* into a tract against capital punishment, *People's Luck* into a critique of the corruption of Japanese courts, and *Consequences of a Duel* into an affirmation of Japanese national progress.

Second, Ruikō's flexibility as a borrower is also evident in the variety of relationships his texts established between Japanese and European culture. All three texts examined here turn European culture, and European legal systems in particular, into catalysts of Japanese self-scrutiny. But while *Man or Devil?* and *People's Luck* implicitly recommend the emulation of certain elements in European culture (the first by imagining and endorsing a French anti–death penalty movement and the second by applauding the integrity of the English court system), *Consequences of a Duel* does not. Instead, *Consequences of a Duel* turns France into a quaint object of anthropological curiosity, an "other" that it aligns with Japan's own premodern past in order to affirm, on the one hand, Japan's break with that past and, on the other, its progress toward a modern, enlightened society in which such feudal relics as duels, revenge killings, and the murder of adulterous wives no longer have a place.

It is in some ways tempting to look at the presence of the translated whodunit in the pages of Japanese tabloids as a form of colonization by a dominant Western popular culture. But if one is properly attentive to what a writer such as Ruikō actually did with the whodunit, the picture becomes decidedly more complex. Indeed, Ruikō's translations of these three novels suggest that the concepts of "domination," "imitation," and even "resistance" are overly blunt instruments for the task of understanding what happened at the interface between Japanese and Western popular crime literature in the Meiji period. The texts that Ruikō produced were not merely imitations of Western cultural forms already in circulation—they clearly had their own inflections and their own uses. That said, these inflections seem to have had very little to do with any consistent attempt to resist Western cultural influences. Indeed, as we have seen, Ruikō's works often embraced that influence as a positive good.

Ruikō's works present a case, then, in which domination, imitation, and resistance as they are conventionally understood do not seem to be particularly useful labels for the possibilities of cross-cultural interaction. All three phenomena are so attenuated and intermixed in Ruikō's oeuvre as to render them at best only partially recognizable. What we have instead is an indication of the importance of the local context in which cultural borrowing occurs and of the particular purposes of its individual agents. Neither of these things is likely to be wholly or even mostly determined by international inequalities, whether real or perceived.

Arresting
Change

Okamoto Kidō's
Stories of Nostalgic Remembrance

B y the 1910s and 1920s, when Okamoto Kidō (1872–1939) wrote most
of the detective stories now collectively called *Hanshichi torimono-chō*
(Hanshichi's Arrest Records), disenchantment had begun to temper Japan's
early enthusiasm for foreign borrowing. Japan's deepening involvement
with the outside world had both tied its fortunes to Western countries and
increased the chances for conflict with them. A newly modernized military
had fought and won two foreign wars, the Sino-Japanese War (1894–1895)
and the Russo-Japanese War (1904–1905). But Japan had suffered, after the
first of these wars, the humiliation of the Tripartite Intervention (1895), in
which Russia, Germany, and France forced the renunciation of its terri-
torial gains. It had suffered disappointment after the second, too, when
a large anticipated indemnity failed to materialize. And after the turn of
the century, discriminatory immigration policies put in place by the United
States became a lingering source of resentment.

During World War I the pace of Japanese industrialization quickened
to keep up with wartime demands. European nations, more occupied with
conflict than with commerce, could no longer supply Asian markets, and
Japan stepped into the breach. Japan was also the beneficiary of large muni-
tions orders placed by the Allies. Increased trade stimulated the shipping
industry especially, but also the textile, construction, and chemical indus-
tries. During the war Japan's factory labor force roughly doubled, and at
its end Japan's industrial production surpassed agricultural production for
the first time.[1]

But when, at the Paris Peace Conference of 1919, the Allied leaders
rebuffed Japan's efforts to include a racial equality clause in the covenant

of the League of Nations, it became clear to many observers that Japan's modernization was as likely to be a source of friction as a source of empowerment. The country had become entwined in a network of international relationships that made political and economic life newly complicated. For Kuroiwa Ruikō the West had represented a cultural grab bag from which Japanese might draw more or less indiscriminately. As Japan became a military and economic power to be reckoned with, its foreign relations became increasingly adversarial, and its own nationalism became an increasingly significant barrier to unself-conscious borrowing.

Okamoto Kidō's stories were part of this uneasy cosmopolitanism. As far as their narrative structure is concerned, they all make use of the Western, post-Poe formula (that is, they reconstruct the story of a crime by telling the story of an investigation), particularly as it was practiced by Arthur Conan Doyle in his Sherlock Holmes stories. In an essay titled *"Hanshichi torimono-chō no omoide"* (Memories of *Hanshichi's Arrest Records*), Kidō recalls discovering his inspiration for the series while shopping at Maruzen, an emporium of imported merchandise. In 1916, he says, he "bought Sherlock Holmes' *Adventures, Memoirs,* and *Return* on a trip to Maruzen, read all three at a sitting...and became interested in writing some sort of detective stories myself."[2] The year after he read Conan Doyle, Kidō published "Ofumi no tamashii" (The Spirit of Ofumi), the first story in a series that would eventually total sixty-eight. At this story's end, Kidō explicitly acknowledged Conan Doyle's influence. "This tale [I had just heard] impressed my young mind as one of extraordinary fascination," the story's narrator says. "Yet when I reflected later, I realized that to Hanshichi"—the retired private agent who is Kidō's detective—"the investigation had surely been mere child's play and that he must have had many other risky assignments that were more exciting still. He was an unsung Sherlock Holmes of the Edo period."[3] Kidō even went so far as to gloss the Japanese ideographs for the phrase "risky assignments" *(bōken shigoto)* with the *katakana* for the English word "adventures" *(adovuenchuā),* in an echo of Conan Doyle's well-known title.[4]

Despite Kidō's obvious admiration for Conan Doyle's work, he was leery of standing too fully in Conan Doyle's shadow. This was a danger that he felt his very choice of genre forced him to confront. "When one writes modern detective stories," Kidō wrote in his essay about discovering Sherlock Holmes at Maruzen, "no matter what one does, it is easy to slip into imitating the West. [I thought that] if I were to write in a form that was pure Edo *(jun Edo-shiki),* something might come together with a different sort of flavor."[5] Much of this different flavor derived from Kidō's choice to narrate the stories as the remembrances of a retired *okappiki* (literally, a "puller on the side"; more loosely, a "thief catcher")—that is, a private agent in the unofficial employ of the old Edo police force who investigated and apprehended criminals. Hanshichi, casting his backward glance from the vantage point of old age, continually and regretfully remarks on the dramatic changes Japan has seen since his heyday. This infuses the stories with a subtly nationalistic nostalgia for the insular old world of Edo, a world that had been largely obliterated by the incursion of Western modernity. In this Kidō's stories had something in common with his contemporary Nagai Kafū's nostalgic portrayals of the Tokyo pleasure quarters, although Kafū did not usually look so far into the past as Kidō. Kidō thus placed in the borrowed form of the detective story a content that decisively separated his work from that of his Western predecessors.

Given this incongruity between form and content, Kidō's stories—like Ruikō's translations—show that what begins as imitation can end up deeply undercutting the dichotomy of original and copy. Although Kidō's stories can be read as remakes of Conan Doyle's, the remaking in this case resulted in changes that turned the supposed "copies" into stories with an entirely different ideological valence from the original. Where Holmes' penetrative reasoning became a symbol of Western, post-Enlightenment rationality and ostensibly benevolent British imperialism, Kidō's Hanshichi personified the charm of a lost but easily comprehensible and culturally pure Japan, a charm that depended heavily on that Japan's difference from the very modernity that Holmes so effectively embodied.

Okamoto Kidō's Career

In 1891, after graduating from the First Tokyo Middle School, Kidō joined the staff of the *Tōkyō nichi nichi shinbun* (Tokyo Daily) as a reporter. For roughly the next twenty years he earned his living by writing for various newspapers, and he was dispatched to Manchuria as a war correspondent during the Russo-Japanese War. But it was as the writer of a column of theater criticism and, later, as a playwright that he was to wield his greatest influence in the world of letters. In 1908 Kidō began collaborating with the young Kabuki actor Ichikawa Sadanji II, for whom he wrote such warhorses of the modern Kabuki repertoire as *Shuzenji monogatari* (A Tale of Shuzenji Temple, 1911) and *Toribeyama shinjū* (Love Suicide at Toribeyama, 1915). By the time he died in 1939, Kidō had written nearly two hundred plays and established himself as the outstanding Kabuki dramatist since the great Kawatake Mokuami (1816–1893).

Hanshichi torimono-chō benefited in at least three important ways from Kidō's work as a playwright. First, as a master of the drama, Kidō had a refined ear for lively dialogue and a knack for the delineation of character through speech, both of which he exploited fully in his detective stories. Indeed, it is the passages of dialogue that make the backbone of the typical Hanshichi story, which, in contrast to the escapes of *Takahashi Oden* or the duels and the opera-going in Ruikō's adaptations, tends to boil down to a series of interviews conducted by Hanshichi. Second, because the most successful Kabuki continued even after the turn of the century to adhere to the tradition of using historical settings, Kidō was by necessity extraordinarily knowledgeable about the history, society, and customs of pre-Meiji Japan. The vintage objects and clothing that give the Hanshichi stories their distinctive color are also the stock in trade of the dramatist restaging the past. By setting the Hanshichi stories in the Edo period, Kidō created ample opportunity to recycle the research for his plays. Kidō ironically acknowledges as much in the story "Jūgoya goyōjin" (Caution on the Night of the Fifteenth), in which a prominent role is played by *komusō,* mendicant Zen priests whose face-obscuring, basketlike headgear makes them a predictable choice in popular literature for impersonation by evildoers. The narrator begins the story by saying, "I once wrote a two-act play called *Komusō* that was performed at the Kabukiza Theater. I did some research of my own into the life and practices of the *komusō,* but for the most part I based [the play] on things that Old Hanshichi told me about them" (vol. 4, p. 118). The truth, in fact, is the reverse: the things that Old Hanshichi will tell Kidō about *komusō* in the course of the story have been based on Kidō's research for his play.

Kidō's position as a popular playwright also allowed him to keep his fingers more closely on the pulse of the public than would otherwise have been possible. The reporter and the writer work at a remove from their readers; the playwright who attends his own plays can directly and continuously monitor the level of attention and interest in the house. It is not possible to know just how much the audiences for Kidō's plays had in common with the readers of his detective stories, but the similarities between the material he deployed in each venue are striking. A great number of the murders Hanshichi investigates arise either from a desire for revenge *(katakiuchi)* or from the jealousy of a spurned lover involved in a triangular affair. Both themes are essential staples of Kabuki, and Kidō later adapted six of the Hanshichi stories for the Kabuki stage.[6]

Kidō's early stories appeared in the publisher Hakubunkan's magazine *Bungei kurabu* (Literary Club). Kidō was not new to the pages of *Bungei kurabu,* where he had also published his play *Shuzenji monogatari.* The true boom in mass market literature was not to come until 1924, the year after the Great Tokyo Earthquake, but as the evolution of *Bungei kurabu* shows, the growing market for popular literature had made its influence felt for some years before this. During the Meiji period the magazine had regularly published stories by the leading literary artists of the day, including Higuchi Ichiyō's "Nigorie" (Muddy Bay) and "Takekurabe" (Comparing Heights); Kunikida Doppo's "Gen oji" (Old Man Gen); as well as works of importance by Izumi Kyōka, Tokuda Shūsei, Yamada Bimyō, Kōda Rohan, Tayama Katai, and Shimazaki Tōson. By the time the magazine published Kidō's first Hanshichi stories in 1917, it had been transformed into one of the first magazines of popular entertainment.[7]

Kidō's Hanshichi stories would in time become hugely popular, eventually inspiring adaptations for both the large and small screens as well as his own imitators in the subgenre of Edo period detective stories, including Nomura Kodō (1882–1963), inventor of Zenigata Heiji, and Yokomizo Seishi (1902–1981), inventor of Ningyō Sashichi. Kidō's first efforts, however, attracted little attention. The circulation of *Bungei kurabu* in 1917 was limited to about five thousand copies, and Hakubunkan did not show any interest in publishing a separate collection of Hanshichi stories.[8]

Publishers' attitudes would change, however, after the Great Tokyo Earthquake of 1923. With the extensive reconstruction carried out in its aftermath, the Tokyo cityscape made a dramatic move away from its former self. The quake left roughly a quarter of a million dead and injured, doing the greatest damage to property in the lowland districts, precisely where the remnants of Edo had been most concentrated. Some new buildings, certainly, used traditional architectural forms, although this did not necessarily mean they were built using traditional materials (the Kabuki-za and the Ueno National Museum were not).[9] The Western-style buildings that went up after the earthquake, if not necessarily new in conception—the four-story department store, for example, had been around since 1911—nonetheless dominated the landscape by their sheer numbers as never before.[10] White concrete (or *konkurīto*, as it was called in Japanese, the foreignness of the name a constant reminder of the foreignness of the substance) was a favored material in the reconstruction. The author Kawabata Yasunari lamented that famous traditional sweets were being sold "from concrete shops that look like banks."[11]

A city that had relied on its crisscrossing waterways for transportation now came to rely increasingly upon the automobile and the trolley line. The city's *sakariba*, or centers of commerce and leisure, began to shift. In Edo and early Meiji they were concentrated at the intersection of water and land routes (such as Kyōbashi); by the mid–Taishō period, new centers of activity were growing up around the new trolley stops, such as the one at Ginza 4-chōme.[12] Three years after the earthquake the novelist and poet

Jō Masayuki (1904–1976) looked at the transmogrified modern city with a mixture of fascination and horror. "Behold!" he wrote. "The green and purple sparks, the reverberation of the elevated railway and the trolleys and the generators, all made possible now by machines as never before; the odor of gasoline, the race of apartment dwellers who know the sun but one hour in a day, and yes, still other, similar sensations and scenes experienced by no person before now—these form the intricate warp and woof of the modern city."[13]

The quake also ushered in the era of the café, the dance hall, the Western revue, and jazz music. In the face of these changes, the Hanshichi stories' nostalgia for Edo found a growing audience, and in 1925 the publisher Shinsakusha brought out a five-volume set of the stories Kidō had written up to that point.[14] Kidō responded in the same year to requests for more Hanshichi stories from numerous magazines put out by both Kōdansha and Hakubunkan, including *Shinseinen* (New Youth), *Shūkan asahi* (Asahi Weekly), *Sandē mainichi* (The Mainichi Sunday Magazine), *Shashin hōchi* (News in Photographs), and *Kōdan kurabu* (Kōdan Club).[15] But in 1926, with the publication in *Shinseinen*'s January issue of "Mittsu no koe" (Three Voices)—his forty-fifth Hanshichi story—Kidō brought the series to a halt. "The arrest-record stories have piled up in large numbers without my quite realizing it," he wrote in his diary that year. "Given that the author himself has already lost interest in them, I can't imagine that they are of interest any longer to readers."[16] This marked the start of a hiatus that was to last nine years. Then between 1934 and 1936 Kidō turned out twenty-three more stories after giving in to a campaign of repeated requests from Noma Seiji, who was the founding president of the publisher Kōdansha as well as a fan of Kidō's detective. Except for "Yasha jindō" (*Yaksa* Shrine), which ran in the magazine *Kingu* (King), all of these later stories came out in the magazine *Kōdan kurabu*.[17]

Historical Detail in
Hanshichi torimono-chō

In his Hanshichi stories, Kidō revels with an antiquarian's glee in historical details ranging from the structure of the Edo police force to the etiquette of bribery at the shogun's court. The painstaking care with which these details have been worked into the stories not only strengthens the illusion of time travel they provide; Kidō also consistently uses these details to turn his stories into lessons in Japanese history. In many of the stories some forgotten tidbit of Edo culture proves to hold the key to the case. The stories thus form a closed, self-validating system that rewards immersion in their

imaginary world. The more one knows about the history of Edo, the more
likely one is to have at least an inkling of the solution to the mystery in
any given case. And the more stories one reads, the more knowledge one
gains about the history of Edo. The ideological insularity manifested in the
stories' focus on Japan's pre-Meiji past is thus matched by the formal and
self-referential insularity of the series itself.

An example of the care that Kidō devoted to incorporating accurate historical detail into the stories can be seen in his portrayal of the Edo police
force. The chains of command in the police force had multiple links, and
although they are never more than peripheral to his tales, Kidō takes the
time to make them plain. The Tokugawa Shogunate divided administrative
responsibility among five primary offices: the *ōmetsuke,* or inspectors general, who oversaw the daimyo; the *wakadoshiyori,* or junior councillors, who
supervised the *hatamoto* and *gokenin* (the direct retainers of the shogun);
and three commissions known as the *san bugyō*—the *jisha-bugyō,* responsible for affairs concerning temples and shrines; the *kanjō-bugyō,* or finance
commissioners; and the *machi-bugyō,* or city commissioners, responsible for
the affairs of urban commoners.[18] The *machi-bugyō* (of whom there were
usually two, designated north and south) were charged not only with general city administration, but also with judicial and police duties.[19] Directly
beneath the city commissioners were inspectors, or *yoriki,* of whom there
were about fifty in Edo during Hanshichi's time. These inspectors oversaw
teams of *dōshin,* or police sergeants, who were responsible for making the
rounds of the neighborhood watch stations and patrolling the streets. As
Kidō explains, it was the sergeants, numbering between two hundred and
two hundred forty in the late Edo period, who would unofficially hire men
such as Hanshichi as private agents.[20]

Private agents, besides being a welcome addition of manpower to the
police force in a city of over half a million commoners, tended to be well
versed in the ways of the underworld, many of them being reformed or
semi-reformed criminals themselves. They were thus invaluable to the sergeants in gathering information and making arrests. But because the shogun had repeatedly outlawed their use, the private agents' relationship with
the commissioner's office was always kept unofficial, and pay was low. Kidō
sketches in this background in a passage typical for its conversational handling of historical detail:

> One time Old Hanshichi told me in some depth about his former posi-
> tion. For the convenience of the readers of these Edo period tales of
> detection, I'd like to pass on here some of what he said....
> "The public referred to us with a variety of terms as they saw fit:

goyō-kiki [roundsmen], *tesaki* [assistants], *okappiki* [thief catchers]. *Goyō-kiki* was a sort of term of respect, used by others to address us or by ourselves when we were trying to frighten someone. Our official designation was *komono* [literally, "small one"]. But *komono* doesn't cut much of a swath, so they came up with names like *goyō-kiki* and *meakashi* [spy]; generally speaking, however, we were known as *okappiki*. The inspectors had four or five sergeants each, and below each sergeant were two or three private agents, and each of those agents had four or five assistants below them—that was the ranking. When a private agent became more influential, he might have seven or eight or as many as ten assistants. The commissioner paid the private agents about one *bu* two *shu* a month at most and in the worst cases about one *bu*. No matter how low prices are, there is no way to get by for a month [on so little]. On top of that, you might have five or ten assistants and not so much as a *mon* for their pay from anyone....In other words it was set up from the start that there was no way to make ends meet, so there were all kinds of abuses—eventually it got so most people wouldn't want to come within ten feet of a private agent or his assistants. But most agents had some other business on the side. You'd run a bath-house under your wife's name or have a little restaurant." ("Ishi dōro" [The Stone Lantern]; vol. 1, pp. 34–35)

The presentation of such detail about the private agents' names, their salaries, and their place in the police force runs the risk of putting off the reader in search of leisure-time reading. But by putting this detail into the mouth of Hanshichi, Kidō brought Edo alive for the reader in a way few conventional histories could match.

Even more characteristic still is Kidō's penchant for placing at or near the heart of a case some detail about a defunct Edo period law or custom. This may, for example, be a law that made the stakes in perpetrating a particular crime much higher than they would have been for Kidō's readers, such as the laws meting out death as the punishment for falsely ringing the fire alarm ("Hanshō no kai" [The Fire Bell Mystery]), for counterfeiting ("Yuki-daruma" [The Snowman]), or for keeping a hawk ("Taka no yukue" [The Whereabouts of a Hawk]). The crimes in this category can look decidedly quaint from the perspective of the post-Tokugawa reader. A case in point is the story "Matsutake" (Mushrooms), which is about the shogun's express mushroom-delivery corps. The story centers on a particularly hapless member of this elite corps who, having carried a basket of mushrooms from one post station to the next at a dead run, carelessly leaves his used tobacco pipe inside. Since the basket is destined for the shogun's own dinner table, the runner fears for his life, and he concocts a blackmail scheme out of a desperate hope that he will be able to duck responsibility for his fatal lapse.

Some stories involve an attempt by the criminal to camouflage a crime by using an Edo period legal loophole or superstition. In "Aoyama no kata-kiuchi" (Revenge at Aoyama) a criminal stages, in a public place, what appears to be a revenge killing. If truly a matter of revenge, such a killing would be permitted under Edo law. Hanshichi, however, discovers that not all is as it appears, and the killing is revealed as an unlawful murder. In "Raijū to hebi" (Thunder Demons and Snakes), a criminal commits a murder during a violent thunderstorm and arranges things to look as though the killing is the doing of *raijū*, beings of old superstition that were thought to ride lightning bolts to earth. And in "Shin-kachikachiyama" (Mt. Kachi-kachi Revisited), which involves death by drowning, the solution to the case depends on knowing, as Hanshichi says, that "in the Edo period, apart from fishermen's daughters, it was extremely rare for the ordinary woman to know how to swim" (vol. 5, p. 39).

On occasion Kidō even goes so far as to play with the reader's expectation that each case will contain such a lesson about Japan's past. In "Kin no rōsoku" (The Golden Candles), for example, the mystery lies in five candle-sized golden rods, each concealed by an artfully applied layer of wax. The enigmatic objects have been recovered from the bottom of the Sumida River together with the corpse of a townswoman. Hanshichi follows a trail of clues to a metalsmith who admits to having been shown a similar rod by a moneylender named Sōbei, to whom he was at the time deeply indebted. Sōbei, we learn, offered to forgive the smith's debts entirely if the smith would help him convert the wax-covered gold rods into cash. He wanted the metalsmith to cut them into pieces small enough to avoid attention, to sell them using his professional connections, and then to bring the money to Sōbei when he was done. The metalsmith tells Hanshichi that his suspicions were naturally aroused and that he asked for an explanation of the strange candles:

> [Sōbei] said to me, "You no doubt wouldn't know this, but the wealthy [houses] in Kyoto and Osaka make these [rods] up as a precaution against theft. No matter what pack of burglars breaks in, they'll never think of looking at the candles, so this is the safest method of conceal-ment. What is more, if you have gold in the form of coins, you yourself are much more likely to be tempted to spend it, so it is the custom [in Kansai] to keep it shut away in the form of rods. They store not only the gold in the tradesmen's houses this way, but also the military funds kept in the residences of daimyo." (Vol. 6, p. 180)

For the reader who has been expectantly awaiting the story's lesson, this explanation certainly has the ring of one—especially in the final sentence, which seems to put rather more social history into the mouth of the shady Sōbei than is necessary or even plausible. But Sōbei is soon revealed to be an imaginative liar. He confesses under pressure to having killed a traveling stranger and taken the rods from him. This stranger, Old Hanshichi speculates at the story's end, was perhaps the retainer of a Kyūshū daimyo:

> The traveling man was strangled by Sōbei, so we had no information about his identity or where the candles came from. But judging from Sōbei's statement, the candles seem to have been a gift from some daimyo to an Edo official. In those days they called such gift giving *kenmon*, but it was simply a form of bribery. They couldn't very well give money openly, so they would put gold coins in the bottom of boxes of sweets, or make ornaments out of gold or silver, or use any number of other tricks. These candles were simply a new trick. Probably some daimyo from Kyūshū planned to sneak the gold bars [into Edo] under the pretense of making a gift of the candles made locally in his domain. No doubt he had a large number of samurai escorting such a treasure between there and Edo, but apparently there was a rotten one among them who knew the game. Somewhere along the way he must have stolen a box of them and run off. . . . Then he suddenly got sick at Kanaya and fell into Sōbei's hands. (Vol. 6, p. 188)

With this, the false lesson is replaced by a true one; the reader's expectations are not, in the end, disappointed. This sort of play with readerly expectation indicates how thoroughly self-referential the series form became in Kidō's hands. By this, the forty-eighth of the series, the motif of the history lesson is so familiar that it has become fair material in its own right for a metagame of misconstrued clues and red herrings that parallels that of the narrative proper.

Listening and Telling

The word *torimono* means "arrest" or "capture." The suffix *-chō* means "record book" or "accounts." *Torimono-chō* thus literally means "record of arrests," although it is often translated as "casebook" or, more loosely, "memoirs." But all of these translations slight a connotation of the word that is important to *Hanshichi torimono-chō*, that of note taking and retelling. Kidō provides us with this gloss of the term at the opening of "Ishi-dōrō" (The Stone Lantern): "'. . . When an inspector or sergeant would listen to the reports of a private agent and then report in turn to the commissioner's office, there was in the office a book rather like a temporary account register in which a clerk would make a preliminary memorandum. That register was what we called the arrest record *(torimono-chō),*' Hanshichi explained" (vol. 1, p. 34). The arrest record thus contained abbreviated transcriptions, made by a clerk for later amplification, of the reports of inspectors and sergeants, which were themselves secondhand accounts of the activities of the private agents.

This chain of rewriting and retelling is preserved in the narrative of the Hanshichi stories. The stories of Hanshichi's adventures are not committed to paper by Hanshichi himself but are rather, we are given to understand, a polished version of notes taken by the first-person narrator during his visits to the retired Hanshichi.[21] Although this first-person narrator goes unnamed, he gives enough facts about himself (including his authorship of the play *Komusō*) for us to understand that we are to equate him with the persona of the author.[22] The stories typically begin with this voice of Kidō describing the circumstances of a recent visit to Hanshichi's house. This same voice then relays, by means of direct quotation, the words with which Hanshichi begins his story. But once Hanshichi has gotten started narrating his adventure in his own voice, it is only a short while before a new voice appears, signaled by a blank space on the page and the absence of a quotation mark at the next paragraph's start. This cannot be the voice of Hanshichi himself, since it refers to him in the third person; nor can it be that of the original first-person narrator, since the story's opening has established him as the listener. This third-person narrator bears the main burden for telling Hanshichi's story.[23] At the story's end, the first-person narrator again takes over, and we return to Old Hanshichi's house for a tying up of loose ends. This use of the first-person voice at the beginning and end of each story creates the sense that the reader is listening to recollections of Edo as told by someone who knew the old city and its laws and customs firsthand, a sense that makes Hanshichi's nostalgia for this bygone world all the more affecting.

The story "Fudeya no musume" (The Writing-Brush Seller's Daughters) offers a typical example of this pattern of voice changes:

> Having seen Old Hanshichi again after such a lapse of time [the story begins], visiting him became once more a passion with me. I found myself wanting to hear his stories more than ever. Four or five days after hearing the story of "The Battle of the Butterflies," I went to Akasaka to say thank you and found the old man out on the veranda, changing the water in a goldfish bowl. The morning was a bit overcast, and the green leafy branches in the narrow garden cast dim shadows, their heads hanging low as if in expectation of the rain.

"You bring bad luck. It looks like it's going to rain on us again today." Old Hanshichi smiled.

We talked about the rainy season being the most difficult time to net goldfish. From there I gradually steered the conversation in the direction of our usual topic [Hanshichi's Edo period exploits]. Today he launched smoothly into a story of his own accord, without saying so much as "At it again, I see."

"Now when was that?" The old man closed his eyes and thought. "Ah, yes, that's right. It was the year that Tarō Inari [a shrine in Asakusa] was all the rage, so it must have been the eighth month of Keio 3 [1867], when the summer heat was still strong. . . . The daughter of the owner of a brush shop in front of Kōtoku temple mysteriously died. . . . There were two sisters in the family. The older was eighteen at the time and named Oman; the younger was sixteen and called Otoshi. Both were beautiful, with pale white skin. . . . The older one died quite suddenly, so it caused a big stir in the neighborhood."

Now comes the blank space and the change of voice to that of the third-person narrator:

It was given out that Oman had died of an acute illness, but a rumor spread that her death was unnatural. . . . Genji [one of Hanshichi's men], who was posted in the neighborhood, followed this up and found out that the circumstances of Oman's death had indeed been strange. She'd started saying she felt bad on the evening of the twenty-fifth of the seventh month. At first no one thought it was very serious . . . but by eight o'clock she was in terrible pain, and eventually she vomited blood. Everyone in the house was shocked. They called the doctor, but it was too late. She thrashed the bedclothes about wildly in her suffering and then finally died. . . .

It was not clear how they arranged things at Tōsandō [the brush shop] with the doctor, but in any case the funeral and burial were to be held the next day under the pretense of her having died of food poisoning. Genji decided to make a report to Hanshichi, who also expressed doubts. To be on the safe side, Hanshichi informed a sergeant in Hatchō-bori of the situation and, with his concurrence that there was reason for suspicion, had the funeral postponed. (Vol. 2, pp. 219–220)

Hanshichi discovers a tangled set of relationships behind the mysterious death. He realizes that Oman must have been poisoned by a woman named Omaru, who had actually meant to poison the younger sister Otoshi. Omaru, he has learned, was in love with the man Otoshi was engaged to marry. He believes Omaru applied the poison to one of the store's brushes, which she knew the sisters were in the habit of licking for their customers when they made a sale. Being less than clearheaded in her jealousy, however, she did not foresee that she might kill the wrong sister. More investigation suggests that Omaru used poison supplied to her by a man named Yonosuke, with whom she has since run off, so Hanshichi sets out with his assistant Shōta in pursuit of the two. All of these events (more than three chapters' worth) are told by the third-person narrator. But in the fifth and final chapter there is a second change of voice—back to that of the original first-person narrator—and we are returned to the scene in Old Hanshichi's garden. The transition occurs after Hanshichi has caught up with Yonosuke at a brothel on the Naka-sendō highway. Yonosuke tries to escape from the brothel by night. Hanshichi, giving chase, is led onto a tree-lined uphill path. As he runs, Hanshichi realizes that his quarry is making for the gate of a temple known to give asylum to criminals:

> Only a few feet separated the two, but Hanshichi could not for the life of him reach the other man's collar. They were already more than halfway up the long slope. The black gate...was bathed in faint starlight. The light of stone lanterns was just discernible inside it.
>
> Hanshichi was becoming desperate. Yonosuke's entire fate depended on whether he crested the hill safely or not. The closer they got to the shadow of the black gate before them, the faster Yonosuke ran. Hanshichi also rushed on. Luck was against Yonosuke. Ten yards from the gate, he tripped on a stone and fell to the ground.
>
> "I was really sweating that time," Old Hanshichi said. "The next morning my legs were all cramped up, after I had thrown myself so completely into running up that long hill. I did some more checking and gradually figured out the whole story. As I said before, this woman Omaru had a wickedness ill-matched to her beauty.... She had relations with any number of men she barely knew, to say nothing of the son of the pawnbroker's where she worked.... But then the pawnbroker's son took a liking to the girl at Tōsandō and was going to take her as his bride.... In short order she forgot her own loose behavior and was overcome with a terrible jealousy. Eventually she came up with her plan to kill the girl at Tōsandō." (Vol. 2, pp. 242–243)

In the remainder of the story, which is also narrated by the now reinstated voice of Kidō (relaying his conversation with Hanshichi), Hanshichi confirms that all of his suspicions about Omaru's plan to poison the younger sister were correct. In response to a question put by the narrator, Old Hanshichi explains that Omaru had run off with Yonosuke but then stolen his money belt and given him the slip in Kumagai. She was later found dead in the woods, having been murdered by highwaymen and robbed of all clothing and possessions. As for Yonosuke, Hanshichi says, "whether because he thought it was his only recourse or by accident in his fall, he bit off his tongue. When I collared him, he was spitting out bright red blood. I dragged him back to the brothel and did all I could for him, but he soon breathed his last. The dead don't speak, so what Omaru told him [she planned to do with] the poison I don't know" (vol. 2, p. 244).

The identity of the third-person narrator that does the bulk of the telling is never made explicit. But Kidō the first-person narrator mentions in some stories that he takes out a notebook as Old Hanshichi is beginning to speak.[24] This suggests we are meant to take the third-person voice in all the stories as that of Kidō writing sometime after his visit is over, giving us a polished version based on the notes he took while Old Hanshichi spoke. Like a long tablecloth centered on a still longer table, the third-person narrator's version covers all but the two ends of Hanshichi's own account.

This overlaying of the rewritten version on Hanshichi's "original" version has several important consequences. Kidō uses it, for one thing, to allow into the story the description of certain details that, on reflection, one realizes Hanshichi himself could not actually know about. In "The Writing-Brush Seller's Daughters," for example, there is a scene in the brothel in which a woman is bathing a wound on Yonosuke's arm. Outside the door, Hanshichi's man Shōta eavesdrops on their conversation. When he hears the woman warn Yonosuke that Hanshichi is at the same inn, he realizes he and Hanshichi have found their man. But the version of the scene that we read contains mention of details that could not be known to someone listening at the door: "'Your hands are very white, aren't they? Almost like a woman's,' Okon said *as she wiped the man's arm with a thin piece of paper*"; "The man fell silent and, *turning his pale face away from the flickering lamplight, sipped at his now cold sake*" (vol. 2, p. 240, emphasis added).

Conversely, the device of third-person narration also makes it possible to keep information from the reader and to do so without fuss. Much of the mystery in these stories comes not from the enigma presented by the original crime but from the puzzling behavior of the investigator himself. In order to preserve suspense, the narrator frequently keeps from us Hanshichi's views on the evidence he finds and his reasons for acting as he does. The story "The Fire Bell Mystery" is a typical example of Kidō's method. In the story, Hanshichi is called on to investigate a rash of false fire alarms. (As Hanshichi explains, ringing the fire bell when there was no fire was, under shogunal law, a crime punishable by death.) In Hanshichi's search for the criminal, his suspicions eventually come to rest on an abandoned house and a small

shrine. Strange noises have been reported around both. We are anticipating
a showdown at the shrine when the story takes an unexpected turn. Hanshichi has enlisted the help of a neighborhood urchin named Kentarō:

> Hanshichi brought his mouth near Kentarō's ear and whispered
> something into it, whereupon Kentarō nodded.... [The boy] stole
> to the front of the shrine and removed from his sleeve five or six
> tangerines.... He rolled them softly through one of the openings in
> the wooden latticework doors and lay flat on the ground, holding his
> breath for all he was worth.
>
> Hanshichi sat waiting for a time in the empty house, but there was
> no report from Kentarō, and he became impatient. He sneaked back
> out.
>
> "Pssst, Kenta, no luck?" he asked in a low voice. Kenta raised his
> head and shook it from side to side. Hanshichi's heart sank....
>
> "No sound came from inside the shrine? No thumps?" Hanshichi
> asked again.
>
> "Not so much as a bump. Doesn't seem like there's anything
> there."... The two went back into the empty house.
>
> "Do you still have some tangerines?"
>
> Kentarō brought out three more. Hanshichi took them and noise-
> lessly opened the sliding paper door.... Hanshichi crawled inside....
> [He could see] a tidy six-mat room with some furnishings in it. Even in
> the dimness he noticed that both the paper and the wooden ribs of the
> sliding door leading onto the veranda were badly damaged. The ribs
> were broken here and there and the paper was ripped open in a wide
> slash. Hanshichi rolled two tangerines into the middle of the six-mat
> room. Then he opened the door to the maid's room and tossed one
> into it as well. He closed the sliding door at the entrance again and
> returned to the vestibule.
>
> "Stay quiet," he cautioned Kentarō. The two waited, holding
> their breath. No sound came from inside, and Kentarō became a bit
> impatient.
>
> "Maybe there's nothing in here either."
>
> "I said to be quiet!"
>
> Just then there was a soft rustling sound in the back of the house.
> The two looked at each other. Apparently someone or something had
> come through the hole in the paper door and crawled into the six-mat
> room.... When they listened very carefully they seemed to hear the
> sound of something chewing on the tangerines Hanshichi had rolled
> in....
>
> Hanshichi signaled Kentarō with his eyes, and the two... opened
> the sliding doors together. They kicked open the next door and rushed
> in.... (Vol. 1, pp. 163–164)

By narrating the story in this way, Kidō multiplies the mysteries quickly. What is it that Hanshichi whispers to Kentarō? Why the tangerines? We do not blame the narrator for keeping us guessing about these things. For Hanshichi himself to do the narrating and keep such questions alive would, however, quickly become awkward ("I leaned close to Kentarō and whispered something in his ear").

In this story the most important information that Hanshichi uses to solve the mystery is kept from the reader, thanks to this use of the third-person narrator. After it becomes apparent that the culprit is an ape (Kidō has apparently borrowed here from Poe's "Murders in the Rue Morgue"), we are still left with the question of how Hanshichi suspected this. This part of the mystery is cleared up by Old Hanshichi after we have returned to the scene of the story's telling: "What, you ask, made me think it was an ape? You see, when I climbed up to inspect the bell tower, there were a lot of markings on the lookout ladder that had been made by the claws of some animal. They didn't seem to have been made by a cat. Suddenly it occurred to me that this just might be the prank of an ape" (vol. 1, p. 166). This is the first mention in the story of the telltale markings on the ladder. When Hanshichi visited the scene of the crime, the narrator told us only that "[Hanshichi] gazed up at the watchtower and thought for a moment but then climbed to the top of the ladder without further pause" (vol. 1, p. 150).

First-Person Narration
as a Link to the Past

Kidō's strategic omissions of crucial information may seem exasperating today, since they violate what we think of as the implicit contract of fair play between reader and writer. But the use of this technique cannot be chalked up to maladroit imitation on Kidō's part. Because the Sherlock Holmes stories are narrated from Watson's point of view, they obscure information from us in just the same way that Kidō's do. We are never privy to Holmes' complete theory about a case until a story's end. He is forever studying footprints in silence and brushing off Watson's questions by saying things like, "I should prefer to have clearer proofs before I speak." Holmes has his share of secret plans, too. The mystery in "A Scandal in Bohemia," for example, arises entirely from Holmes' silence about the details of his plan for inducing Irene Adler ("*the* woman") to reveal the whereabouts of the photograph she has threatened to use in her blackmail scheme. Likewise, the tension in the climactic scene of "The Speckled Band" arises from Watson's (and our own) ignorance of just what Holmes is waiting for as the two sit in the dark, cane and pistol at the ready. And even after the snake begins to slither down the bell-pull, Holmes can see it, but Watson cannot, and so we are still not sure what is happening. "Holmes sprang from the bed," Watson tells us, "struck a match, and lashed furiously with his cane at the bell-pull. 'You see it, Watson?' he yelled. 'You see it?' But I saw nothing. At the moment when Holmes struck the light I heard a low clear whistle, but the sudden glare flashing into my weary eyes made it impossible for me to tell what it was at which my friend lashed so savagely."[25]

Of the devices Kidō and Conan Doyle use to conceal information from the reader—switching in midstream to a third-person narrator and the use of a Watson—the second has the advantages of seamlessness and elegance. That Kidō passed up these advantages is significant. It is likely that he wanted his stories to stand apart more clearly from Conan Doyle's than they would have if he had used a Watson-like character. But Kidō also seems to have been after the illusion that Hanshichi tells his own stories—an illusion that they maintain with at least partial success, since the stories do begin and end with the scene of Hanshichi's telling. Thanks to this device, readers have a stronger sense of connection to the past, through the person of one who has known it firsthand, than they would have were the third-person narration consistently maintained. The "presence" of Old Hanshichi himself, telling about the exploits of his younger days, places the stories not merely in the past but in a past that is manifestly remembered and wistfully, nostalgically, reconstructed before the reader's eyes.

Much of the stories' sense of nostalgia derives from the interplay of disparate time frames that Kidō has built into this narrative setup. As a rule, the Hanshichi stories shuttle among three different times—the "present" moment of narration, the occasion of the author's visit to Hanshichi, and the time of Hanshichi's exploits. The opening of "The Golden Candles"— the story with the false history lesson—shows this shuttling among time frames particularly well:

> It was autumn, when the nights get long. I was visiting Old Hanshichi as usual and listening with interest to his talk of the old days, when the lights in the room suddenly went out.
> "A blackout." Hanshichi called to the maid to bring some candles. "Electric lights are certainly more convenient than lanterns and kerosene lamps, but the occasional blackouts are a bother, aren't they?"
> "But it's quite impressive the way you have candles ever at the ready," I said.
> "No, no. Nothing impressive about it. I'm just old-fashioned. Even with the spread of kerosene lamps and the invention of the electric light, I can't help feeling that a house isn't a house without candles, so I always keep some around. They come in handy on nights like tonight."

Hanshichi called himself old-fashioned every other sentence, but to use electric lights then, which was around Meiji 30 [1897], was actually ahead of the times. At my own house at the time I was still using kerosene lamps. There was something very characteristic about Hanshichi's using the new electric lights but not getting rid of his candles.

Unlike nowadays, the blackouts then were long. Sometimes part of Tokyo would be in darkness for thirty minutes or an hour, causing all sorts of trouble. The blackout on this night was one of the long ones. Host and guest sat looking at the dim candle flame flickering in the night air and went on talking. Before long, the old man, taking his cue from the conversation about candles, began a tale of old-time detection called "The Golden Candles."

"As you are perhaps aware, on the sixth night of the second month in Ansei 2 [1855], Fujioka Tōjūrō and one Tomizō, a vagrant from Yashū, conspired to break into the safe in the main keep of Edo Castle and stole four thousand *ryō* in gold pieces." (Vol. 4, pp. 154–155)

This scene of the blackout during the narrator's visit to Hanshichi is remembered and written down in a narrative "present" named by the word "nowadays" *(konnichi)*. Simply taking the story's publication date for this present would fix the year as 1934. Even if we allow for the possibility of the story's "present" being set back some years from the time of its actual publication or composition, the contrast drawn between the length of blackouts "nowadays" and those at the time of the narrator's visit to Hanshichi still suggests that the story's "present" is, at the earliest, the beginning of the Taishō period—in other words, sometime after electric lighting came into widespread use in Tokyo homes.[26] From the vantage point of this "present" are narrated the events of a visit that took place between ten and thirty years earlier. And during that visit were narrated events of more than forty years before that, retold for us in an account (Kidō's polished version) that has been written sometime *after* the visit—perhaps as recently as in the "present"— from notes made while listening to Hanshichi.

The narrative is thus something of a Chinese box. Through its alternate nesting and unnesting of present and past, of recollection within recollection, it takes us from Taishō-Shōwa, into Meiji, and then farther still, to Edo, and back again. The interplay of these time periods is made all the more apparent by the rough symbolic correspondences Kidō draws between each historical period and its characteristic technology of lighting: candles (and lanterns) represent Edo, kerosene lamps are associated with Meiji, and electric lights with Taishō-Shōwa. Hanshichi's role as a link between past and present is expressed in this code as a preference for both candles and electric lights. The first-person narrator's relative youth and his lack of direct connection to the past are apparent in the lack of candles in his own house.

In addition to such conspicuous shuttling among time frames, the stories also contain countless other, smaller indications of time's passing. They overflow with such phrases as "in contrast to the way things are now" (*ima to chigatte*), "as was the law in those days" (*kono jidai no hō to shite*), "the time being what it was" (*sono koro no koto desu kara*), "back then" (*mukashi wa*), "as was so frequently the way in those days" (*kono jidai ni shibashiba aru narai de*), and the like.

The stories also call attention to the passage of time by making dramatic and literary references. They frequently invoke the names of old Kabuki plays and dead actors, and occasionally quote ancient poetry. "Kiku ningyō no mukashi" (In the Days of the Chrysanthemum Dolls), for example, quotes the most famous poem of Ariwara Narihira (825–880). The story is about a riot during the famous Dango-zaka chrysanthemum-doll festival. The riot starts when a woman picks the pocket of a visiting foreigner, one of a small group that has come, traveling under official Japanese escort, to see the dolls. The man accuses her loudly, but the wallet is nowhere to be found. The crowd rallies to the accused woman's support, stoning the man and his companions; in the confusion, the foreigners' horses are stolen. Hanshichi eventually recovers the horses and proves that the woman passed the stolen wallet to a confederate in the crowd. It is as Old Hanshichi is wrapping up his narrative that Kidō slips in the quotation from Narihira:

> "I haven't been to Dango-zaka in some time, but from what I see in the papers...the chrysanthemum dolls are much more skillfully made than they used to be. But the people who went in the Meiji period to see the doll displays never dreamed that a little over thirty years earlier people were shouting...'Kill the foreigners (*ijin*)!' there. The world has changed completely. The very word *ijin*...has become obsolete. Whenever I hear mention of chrysanthemum dolls now I am always reminded of those events of long ago."
>
> There is an old poem that goes: "Is the moon not itself, the spring not the old spring? Only I have stayed my old self." Old Hanshichi's sentiments seemed to be something like this. And it is with that same forlorn feeling that I put down the brush with which I wrote this record. (Vol. 5, p. 219)

In Kidō's hands, the quotation of Narihira's poem becomes an especially significant marker of the passage of time. The poem itself is recognizably ancient; its grammar is that of classical Japanese. The difference between the inflections of the poem and the modern inflections of the surrounding text calls attention to the way the passage of time has left its mark on the Japanese language. The poem itself, Narihira's most famous, is on mutability, the great theme of the Japanese poetic tradition. This poetic tradition—itself insular, given to subtle variation on poems centuries old—is invoked against the change that is represented by Japan's increasing absorption of foreign influences ("the word *ijin* [foreigner]...has become obsolete," Hanshichi says). And in the final line, when the narrator says he shares Hanshichi's sentiments, the reader is invited to become the fourth sympathetic mind in a line extending backward through time from the moment of reading to Kidō's moment of writing, to Hanshichi's moment of telling, back to the imagined moment of Narihira's own poetic inspiration.

A Charmed World

In contrast to the feats of Sherlock Holmes, Hanshichi's feats of detection rely considerably more heavily on his hunches and his sixth sense than they do on scientific deduction. His consistent success, even though he applies what often seem to be haphazard methods, makes the city of Edo look like an enchanted, golden world where the clues always leapt to the eye and justice was served with a lack of ambiguity reminiscent of Saikaku's courtroom narratives. The fact that this world never actually existed does not lessen its power as an object of nostalgic longing. Indeed, as Stephen Vlastos and others have demonstrated, invented traditions have often served in Japan as especially effective rallying points for reactionary thought at times when Japanese cultural identity has come under pressure.[27]

Nothing shows the enchanted, imaginary side of Kidō's remembered past more clearly than the way Hanshichi's world smiles upon his investigations. In Hanshichi's world there are no wholly random occurrences. Coincidences are always favorable. To solve his mysteries, Hanshichi need only take a token step toward one of the many possibilities; once he has done this, everything will fall into place. This fundamental benevolence of Hanshichi's world comes conspicuously to the fore in the story "Hiroshige to Kawauso" (Hiroshige and the Otter). In the story Hanshichi is called on to handle a case involving a *hatamoto* family (one in direct service to the shogun) named Kuronuma. The dead body of a small girl, about three years old, has turned up on the rooftop of the Kuronuma mansion. Hanshichi examines the body and questions the members of the household but is unable to come to any immediate conclusion. No one recognizes the girl, and no way of identifying her presents itself.

Hanshichi then goes out walking, stopping along the way to invite his assistant Shōta to go with him to a shrine in Suna-mura, which lies in the

district of Jūman-tsubo, on the far side of the Sumida River. Shōta is puz-
zled, since the place is two hours away, and it is getting late. He tags along
all the same. At a tea shop near the shrine, Hanshichi strikes up a conversation with the proprietor and learns that there was in the shop that very day
a young woman who had come to pray at the shrine for the return of her
missing three-year-old stepdaughter. It turns out that her stepdaughter is
the very child who has turned up so mysteriously on the Kuronumas' rooftop and whom Hanshichi has set out to identify. Shōta, perhaps acting as a
surrogate for the reader, voices his astonishment at Hanshichi's ability to
advance toward a solution so quickly. Shōta asks what clue led him to the
tea shop so far from where the body turned up:

> "I wasn't completely without a clue [Hanshichi answers], but it was
> such a vague hunch, and I hated the thought of your laughing at me,
> so I've been keeping it to myself all this while, but I did have something
> to go on when I dragged you out here."
> "How did you know what direction to go in?"
> "That's what's so odd. Listen, and I'll tell you," Hanshichi said
> with a smile.
> "When I had them show me the body...at the Kuronuma mansion,
> there didn't seem to be any sort of wound on it, so at first I thought
> the girl had died of some disease and been quietly deposited on the
> roof. When I looked more closely, there were some things that looked
> like little fingernail marks faintly visible on her neck. But they were
> not human nail marks; they looked more like they had been made by
> a bird or an animal.... Wondering what in the world they could be, I
> left the mansion to go to your house, and on the way I happened to
> see a picture at a print shop. It was one of Hiroshige's of famous places
> around Edo—a scene of Jūman-tsubo in the snow.... [In the picture]
> white snow is falling, and in the wide sky there is a big eagle flying with
> its wings outspread.... Then I thought of the incident at Kuronuma's
> mansion.... [It occurred to me that] the thing that had sunk its claws
> into the girl might have been an eagle. The marks on her neck cer-
> tainly fit.... I thought we might as well take a walk in the direction of
> Jūman-tsubo.... Of course it was a bird that I was dealing with, so there
> was no particular reason to go in the direction of Jūman-tsubo. I had
> no idea whether to go toward Ōji or Ōkubu or where, so, since it was a
> picture of Jūman-tsubo that had given me the idea, I thought I might
> as well set out in that direction." (Vol. 1, pp. 258–259)

With this, the work of the detective is complete. As Old Hanshichi explains,
in a characteristic elimination of alternatives, "there didn't seem to be any

other way to explain what had happened, so we decided the girl had been snatched away by an eagle and left it at that." In this story the coincidence of having seen the Hiroshige print solves the entire case at a stroke. It not only gives Hanshichi the right idea about the girl's abductor, which would be plausible enough. But it also tells him in what direction he should set off in order to happen into the tea shop where the victim's stepmother will have happened to be earlier that day.

One could certainly accuse Kidō of laziness for using such a string of chance occurrences. But whatever Kidō's intentions, the ultimate effect of the story is to create a hand-in-glove fit between the detective and his world. In this charmed world the detective can safely trust his hunches and safely surrender himself to the whims of chance. As Hanshichi is fond—perhaps overfond—of saying, "Even a dog will come upon a stick if only he will walk" *(Inu mo arukeba, bō ni ataru)*. This deliberately unscientific, old-fashioned streak in Hanshichi's procedures is yet another marker of his difference from Sherlock Holmes, and it becomes a point of departure for his characteristic nostalgic musings. "Now that we are in the reign of Meiji," Old Hanshichi explains on one occasion, "the police's way of doing things has completely changed, and new methods of detection have also developed. But when we carried out an investigation in the old days, we would start with our hunches: a hunch that something *seemed* to be the case, or [that the criminal] *seemed* to be so-and-so. That was extremely useful, and it often happened that our suspicions would turn out to be marvelously correct."[28] A huge proportion of Hanshichi's cases in fact turn in some way on his keen sixth sense rather than on the logical deduction that one associates with Holmes.

This keen sixth sense allows Hanshichi (and, for that matter, the reader) to keep the branches of possible logical inference well pruned. "[Hanshichi] could tell by the pathetic tears flowing from the young man's eyes that there was no falsehood in his confession," we will be told, or "[Hanshichi] could see easily from his long years of experience that there was not the slightest bit of deception in the abbot's countenance or his manner of speech," the narrator will say ("Obake shishō" [The Ghost Teacher], vol. 1, p. 132; "Fudeya no musume," vol. 2, p. 228). Hanshichi is seldom if ever wrong in these judgments, and the reader quickly learns the futility of expending mental energy on the possibility that he might be. Despite the stories' focus on crime as their theme, Hanshichi's world, in contrast to Takahashi Oden's, is ultimately benevolent rather than treacherous, and Kidō's emphasis falls far more heavily on the containment of violence and evil than it does on the harm that violence and evil may inflict.

Ambivalent Signs of Anti-Westernism

Nonetheless, even stories about the containment of violence must portray in some way the violence that they contain. The Hanshichi stories present us not only with rampant simians and birds of prey, but also with poisonings, stranglings, drownings, blows with blunt instruments, and—to a markedly lesser extent—stabbings and slashings. But as a rule, the stories do not dwell on violence or the description of its effects. In fact many of the corpses that surface in the stories are oddly clean and inviolate. It is therefore striking that some of the series' most memorably violent scenes should involve violence against non-Japanese.

An example of Kidō's general propensity for populating his stories with oddly inviolate corpses can be seen in "Jūgoya goyōjin" (Caution on the Night of the Fifteenth). In the story four dead men (two priests and two monks) are discovered submerged in an old well on the grounds of a temple outside the city:

> Surprised by this sudden report, the village officials hurried to the scene. Other villagers also gathered. Discovering four bodies all at once was the sort of strange occurrence one seldom heard of even within the Edo city limits, let alone in the village, so it caused a great stir; even so, in accord with protocol a report was filed and an inquest was carried out....
>
> One [of the monks] was about forty, and he had a small scar on his left shoulder. The other was twenty-seven or -eight, a fair-skinned, neat-looking man.... The strange thing was, no sign of a wound could be found on any of the four corpses. There was no evidence of their having been strangled. They didn't even appear to have swallowed any water. Whether someone else had killed them and dumped the bodies in the old well or whether some circumstance had caused them all to commit suicide by throwing themselves in at the same time was a mystery not easily solved. (Vol. 4, pp. 123–124)

It turns out that the four men were thieves who were only posing as clerics and that a female member of their band slipped a fatal dose of morphine into their sake and then dumped the bodies into the well. Summing things up for his listener, old Hanshichi says, "Even in cases of poisoning some sign will remain that can be detected in the inquest.... There is nothing other than a narcotic that can be used to kill someone without leaving any mark at all" (vol. 4, p. 39). In this case, the very lack of a sign of violence thus becomes an important clue to the cause of death.

But inviolate or nearly inviolate bodies figure even in stories where there is no such direct link to Hanshichi's unraveling of the case. In "The Golden Candles," for instance, when the corpse of a young woman is recovered from the Sumida River, she is described to Hanshichi as "a nicely turned-out married woman" who "had swallowed water" but "had no sign of a wound on her body" (vol. 4, p. 157). Rather than being a homocide victim, she is found to have committed suicide by jumping off the Ryōgoku Bridge. In "Neko sōdō" (Cat Troubles), when an old woman is found dead in her house, the coroner examines her and finds that "there was nothing amiss with her body," and even though "there was discernible just in front of the crown of her head something that looked like the mark of a blow," he is "unable to conclude with certainty whether she had been hit by someone else or whether she had hit her own head against something in a fall" (vol. 1, p. 312). The coroner ultimately decides that the woman collapsed when she suffered a stroke, and it is only after Hanshichi investigates further that the seemingly incidental wound on her head (the result, he learns, of a blow dealt by her dull-witted son) is determined to have killed her. These corpses are elements in a puzzle rather than outlets for violent fantasy, and they disturb the harmony of Kidō's imaginary past no more than is necessary to create a premise for Hanshichi's investigations.

Because of this unwritten rule, those stories that break with the general pattern of minimizing violence stand out dramatically. And it is all the more striking that some of the most conspicuous exceptions to the pattern should involve descriptions of violence directed against Westerners. It would be possible to make too much of these exceptions. But given the stories' insistent return to the theme of nostalgic remembrance, it is hard to escape completely the idea that the descriptions of violence in these stories indirectly fed nationalistic impulses, either in Kidō himself or in his readers.

The description of the stoning of the foreigners in "In the Days of the Chrysanthemum Dolls," for example, lavishes an attention unusual in Kidō's oeuvre upon the violence of the mob and upon the wounds suffered by its victims. When the pickpocketed foreigner accuses the woman he takes for the culprit, she yells at the crowd in protest:

> This foreigner is trying to pick a fight, saying I took something I didn't! He's trying to make me out to be a thief. Come on everyone, give me a hand!" she bawled out.
> It was an era in which foreigners were hated, so no one could let this cry go unheeded. "Damned barbarian *(ketōjin-me),* he's got a lot of

nerve!" "Saying she took something she didn't, trying to treat a Japanese like a thief!" This was unforgivable, so two or three hot-headed men came running up to throw punches at the foreigners. Now things were at a crisis. In a moment a large mob had gathered and started a commotion, roundly beating the three foreigners.... Soon some were throwing stones at them.... One of the foreign men was struck hard on the left cheek by a stone, and his blood began to flow.... The foreigners started running.... The mob raised a war cry and chased after them. More people joined in as if possessed, thinking if foreigners were involved, they would let them have it, without even knowing any of the details.... Some climbed to the rooftops and threw down roofing tiles. Rocks, bamboo sticks, pieces of firewood—people were throwing whatever came to hand, so it was impossible to defend against it all. All three foreigners and their escort were wounded in some way, and they fled covered in blood.... Having lost their hats and canes, their blood-soaked hair a bedraggled mess, they were unsightly indeed. (Vol. 5, pp. 191–192)

The battle lines between Japanese and foreigners could hardly be drawn more clearly. The use of the epithet *ketōjin-me* (damned barbarians), the offense taken at the attempt to treat "a Japanese" as a thief, and the seeming willingness of the mob to attack on any pretext make this a scene of almost pure ethnic violence. This violence is made all the more raw by Kidō's relatively rare mention of blood, here flowing from the foreigners' wounds into their hair and (in the case of the man struck by the stone) over their faces.

The image of hair matted with blood—probably the most gruesome in all of Kidō's idealized world—makes a repeat appearance in "Ijin no kubi" (The Foreigner's Head), a story about a band of samurai engaged in the systematic assassination of foreigners. Near the beginning of the story the men, wearing masks and swords, arrive by night at a pawnshop, force their way in to the attached house, and demand money to finance their mission. As collateral to pawn, they offer the chief shop clerk and the other assembled assistants a mysterious parcel wrapped in cloth:

From within the cloth appeared something wrapped in blood-stained oilpaper. When they removed the oilpaper, there emerged a severed head. The clerk was aghast. No one breathed.

What shocked them so was not just that it was a human head but that it did not seem to be the head of a Japanese. When it dawned on them that it was the red-haired, red-bearded head of a foreigner, everyone was twice as frightened. The samurai pushed the head toward the clerk, saying: "Once you've seen this, there shouldn't be any need for elaborate explanations. We are loyalists to the cause of barbarian erad-

ication, and tonight as a ceremonial sacrifice we have sliced off the
head of this foreigner."...

The foreigner's head, still soaked in fresh blood, sat there firmly
on the oilpaper. (Vol. 3, pp. 313–314)

The clerk cannot turn away patriots who are so committed and so threatening, and he gives in to their demand for money, though he begs them to
take the head away rather than leave it as collateral.

As in the previous story, the theme of ethnic violence comes unmistakably to the fore in this encounter. The head's function as the token of that
violence is overdetermined; not only is it a bloody, freshly severed head,
cut off with the traditional weapon of the samurai; its hair is red, the color,
from the Japanese perspective, of ultimate racial otherness. And as if to
emphasize this token quality of the bloody head even more, Kidō uses the
character for "crimson" or "blood red" (readable as *kurenai* as well as *akai*)
to describe the color of its hair rather than the more usual "red" (readable
only as *akai*). The redness of the hair is thus ambiguously double, standing both for its otherness and for the bloody violence that its otherness
provokes.

Both of these stories thus seem contrived at least in part to explore fantasies of resentful violence against non-Japanese during a period (the stories were written in 1935 and 1923, respectively) when relations between
Japan and the West were becoming increasingly strained. And yet in neither
story are the fantasies given completely free rein. In the first story ("In the
Days of the Chrysanthemum Dolls"), the woman accused as a pickpocket
by the foreigner is ultimately proven guilty, at least partially undercutting
any impulse the reader might feel to sympathize with her rallying of the
crowd to her cause. The narration also elicits sympathy for the foreign victims by portraying the mob's wrath as so utterly indiscriminate. In the second story ("The Foreigner's Head"), this reining in of fantasy is even more
pronounced. Hanshichi, mystified that no foreigner has been recently
reported murdered or even missing, investigates the band of barbarian
assassins and reveals them as frauds and small-time extortionists. The severed head of the foreigner, it turns out, is only a convincing fake made
of wax.

Such turns in Kidō's stories suggest that his relationship to the West
was tinged with an ambivalence not felt by Kuroiwa Ruikō, or at least not
in evidence in his translations. Despite Kidō's painstaking re-creation of
the lost world of Edo, his stories are premised on an act of borrowing from
Conan Doyle that threatens to compromise the very fantasy of premodern cultural purity the stories so intently pursue. As a result they contain

contrary impulses. On the one hand they are a repository of resentment against the incursion of Western modernity onto Japanese soil, and on the other hand they cannot wholeheartedly endorse a retaliation—not even an imaginary one—against that incursion because they owe to it their very existence. Perhaps this is why the violence against foreigners in these stories is also staged with such evident ambivalence. It is some of the messiest, most impassioned, and bloody violence in Kidō's entire oeuvre, and yet the stories either forestall the reader from wholeheartedly endorsing the violence, as in "In the Days of the Chrysanthemum Dolls," or else they sanitize it, ultimately reducing it to a game of make-believe, even within the already imaginary realm of Hanshichi's world, as occurs in "The Foreigner's Head."

Rituals of Repetition
in *Hanshichi torimono-chō*

Revealing as the stories' ambivalent episodes of violence against foreigners are, the stories' main preoccupation lies elsewhere, in their more gently accomplished mission of nostalgically turning back the clock. The staging of Hanshichi's remembrance in an implied first-person narrative is, as we have seen, an important means to this end, as is the stories' didactic rehearsal of Edo history. A third important element in the stories' generation of nostalgia is their formal structure, which uses recurring stock motifs to turn the experience of reading itself into a ritual of remembrance.

As one might expect in a series that runs to sixty-eight stories, Kidō makes frequent use of stock situations and motifs. Indeed, the bulk of his stories are reducible to variations on a single master plot. This does not mean that nothing unexpected ever happens. Surprises occur in every story. But the unexpected always takes its place in a pattern that dictates the sorts of surprises that must occur and when. Once one has read enough stories in the series to be familiar with the master plot (probably three or four), the stories point almost as insistently at the reader's past experience of the series itself as they do at the historical past they have invented for Japan. As a result, the stories rather ingeniously meld their rhetoric with their ideology. The stories' recovery of their own past, through their ritualized repetition of stock situations and motifs, subtly encourages the reader's belief in the possibility of recovering the insularity and the self-sufficiency of Japan's historical past.

Although Kidō carries this ritualistic repetition to lengths not seen in Conan Doyle, his use of stock situations and motifs will be familiar to readers of works in the Sherlock Holmes series. Those readers know, for example, that the story will follow the fundamental formula *mystery—investigation—solution*. They know that the client will usually appear, in distress, in Holmes'

Baker Street rooms to request his aid and that almost before the client can speak, Holmes will deduce and announce the client's circumstances with seemingly impossible exactness. If the case has been written up in the papers, Watson will provide a précis of what he has learned from them. If it involves a crime, Holmes will visit its scene and reconstruct its events by means of a minute and expert attention to the distribution of footprints and tobacco ash. If long hours of thought are required to arrive at the solution to the mystery, Holmes will stare vacantly and smoke his pipe as he cogitates.

The Holmes stories form a series not only because, as Conan Doyle himself put it, "each retain[s] a connecting link with the one before and the one that [is] to come by means of its leading characters," but also because the leading characters trail along with them an assortment of familiar gestures.[29] Umberto Eco, in an analysis of the stock situations in Rex Stout's Nero Wolfe novels, has suggested that the attraction of a book by Stout "lies in the fact that, plopped in an easy chair or in the seat of a train compartment, the reader continuously recovers, point by point, what he already knows, what he wants to know again: that is why he has purchased the book."[30] If this is so, then the formulaic quality of such popular entertainments is not just the shortcut of the hack (although it obviously solves numerous problems of composition at a stroke) but an essential aspect of the pleasure they afford.

In Kidō's stories, the motifs touched on already—the continual remarking of change and the rehearsal of defunct Edo period laws and customs—are only two among many. These other motifs can be roughly divided into two categories: those whose appearance in every story, in unvarying sequence, is all but guaranteed, and those that belong to a larger pool of optional but nonetheless frequently repeated devices that may be introduced freely at any point. To the first category belong the following conventions, which make up the master plot for every story in the series:

1. The story begins with the first-person narrator (Kidō) either visiting Hanshichi's house or meeting him somewhere by chance and then accompanying him home. They engage in conversation, often about the theater; some stimulus to Hanshichi's memory launches him into his narrative (*"Maa, okiki kudasai"* [I'll tell you all about it]). In all but a handful of instances, it is the story of a case that Hanshichi himself investigated during his service as a private agent or an assistant agent.[31]

2. The precise year and date (or, less often, only the year and month) of the case are given, and the third-person narrator takes over the story.

3. Some messenger, often one of Hanshichi's own assistants, arrives at his house in Kanda Mikawa-machi with news of a crime, a disappearance, or some suspicious incident. In especially sensitive cases, such as those involving the house of a samurai, the messenger arrives to tell Hanshichi he is wanted in Hatchō-bori. There he is given his assignment directly by a sergeant.

4. Hanshichi visits the scene of the incident and gleans his first clue, either in the form of physical evidence or the testimony of a witness.

5. Hanshichi gives assignments to one or more of his men, usually involving the gathering of information about the suspects or their families (*". . . o aratte koi"* [Go check out so-and-so] is the usual phrase of instruction). His men are unfailingly loyal and, with the exception of the always overeager Kumazō, expert at their work; their methods, however, remain obscure, since they accomplish their tasks off-stage, returning some hours or days later to report their findings to Hanshichi.

6. Hanshichi interrogates one or more suspects personally, using some combination of questions (whose degree of penetration takes both suspect and reader by surprise), verbal intimidation (*"Hakujō shiro!"* [Confess!], *"Shōjiki ni ie!"* [Tell it straight!]), and threatening jabs of his truncheon.

7. Just as the story arrives at its climax—which is either a confession or a capture (in the latter case, the criminal, if uncooperative, will be bound by a rope)—there is an interruption, and we are returned to the scene of Old Hanshichi's narration. Hanshichi asks Kidō whether he has solved the mystery.

8. Kidō offers an ill-formed and partial hypothesis, or simply admits he is baffled. Old Hanshichi then clears up the mystery, explaining both the circumstances surrounding the crime and the logic behind his own actions during the investigation.

9. Hanshichi tells us what punishment each criminal received and the fates of the other characters.

To the second category belong the following stock situations, characteristic gestures, and bits of business:

1. The decision, made in a mood of resignation, to take to the streets without any useful clue in hand at all, simply to make a beginning; this is invariably followed, first, by some unlooked

for *chance encounter or discovery* of great importance and, second, by Hanshichi's repetition of his favorite proverb, "Even a dog will come upon a stick, if only he will walk" *(Inu mo arukeba bō ni ataru).*

2. The early invocation of *the supernatural* as a possible explanation of some mysterious occurrence (such as the apparent killing of a woman by a fox in "In the Days of the Chrysanthemum Dolls"), usually combined with some allusion to the traditional genre of the *kaidan,* or the tale of the uncanny. This explanation will subsequently be debunked by Hanshichi and the mysterious occurrence revealed as a ruse of the criminal.

3. In cases involving murder or apparent suicide, Hanshichi's apologetic insistence upon *reinspection of the corpse,* during which he invariably discovers, thanks to an eye made sharp by long years of experience, some crucial detail (a broken fingernail, a scratch on the throat) overlooked by the coroner.

4. The scene of the *whispered plan* (as in the tangerine-rolling episode in "The Fire Bell Mystery"), in which Hanshichi gives to an assistant instructions that are kept from the reader; this is followed by the plan's execution, whose narration puzzles us since we do not know the premises from which Hanshichi is working.

5. Closely related to the whispered plan is the *omitted interview,* during which the reader suspects Hanshichi will learn important information but is kept in the dark about its precise nature because the narration cuts away to a later moment in time just as the interview is beginning.

6. Hanshichi's ready and skillful *assumption of a false identity* in order to question a suspect, or someone close to one, without putting that person on guard. (Hanshichi is not, however, a master of elaborate disguise. He generally uses only a simple prop or two and a convincing story.)

7. The *missing person,* who must be traced by Hanshichi's men because he or she holds the secret to the case.

8. The sudden appearance, just as the case seems to be nearing solution, of one of Hanshichi's men at the door, so breathless he can hardly gasp out the news of the *surprise murder* of the chief suspect.

9. Hanshichi's habit of *omairi,* or paying of respects, at every temple or shrine he happens to pass. This habit becomes

conspicuous enough to merit special justification. In "Kuma no
shigai" (The Corpse of the Bear), the twenty-ninth story, Hanshichi explains that "whether on official business or no, anyone
who's put the rope on so many people thinks about the world
to come.... Then too, places where lots of different people
gather are good for picking up information" (vol. 3, p. 25).

10. Hanshichi's stop, in mid-investigation, for a *meal of grilled eel* or,
     less often, buckwheat noodles; the subsequent *overheard conver-
     sation* in the restaurant.

11. The *secret investigation* that must be carried out with the great-
     est discretion because it involves the family of a high-ranking
     samurai.

12. The discovery of some *cryptic, fragmentary text*—such as an inter-
     cepted message—whose meaning, once deciphered, cracks the
     case.

13. The *semipoetic descriptions* of the weather and the landscape,
     given not only to lend atmosphere, but also as a device to stall
     the narrative during waiting of some kind (for a report from
     one of Hanshichi's men or for the appearance of a criminal for
     whom a trap has been laid).

Each story in Kidō's series presents the reader with a new puzzle, a new
set of suspects, and a new shock of surprise at the moment of the culprit's
exposure or confession. And yet these elements of novelty are always contained by the familiarity of the stock situations and motifs that unify the
series. Writing on the detective story, Umberto Eco has made the intriguing suggestion that although the genre might appear to "satisfy the taste
for the unforeseen or the sensational, [it] is, in fact, read for exactly the
opposite reason, as an invitation to that which is taken for granted, familiar,
expected. Not knowing who the guilty party is becomes an accessory element, almost a pretext."[32] In Kidō's stories, the role of the familiar and the
expected is so prominent as to give them a prescripted, ritual quality. Kidō
must surely have been aware of this aspect of his stories, since he plays with
the idea of their scriptedness in the story "Hiroshige to kawauso" (Hiroshige and the Otter).

Ironically, the first thing that one notices about "Hiroshige and the
Otter" is its difference from the usual run of the mill. Here is one story, at
least, that seems to violate the accustomed formula right away. Instead of
beginning with the familiar voice of Kidō the narrator describing a meeting with Hanshichi, it confronts us with lines of text that are introduced by
some voice—it is not immediately clear whose—as the script for a play:

To put it in the style of an old playbook, on the main stage is a single platform, at the front a temple gate painted red. Beyond the gate can be seen, in the distance, the precincts of [Asakusa] Kannon. There is a ginkgo tree positioned appropriately, with everything set to look like the Nakamise arcade. The curtain opens to the sound of the clackers at an Asakusa sideshow, and from stage left enters an old man, apparently just come from the Okada or another nearby eatery. From stage right enters a young man, and the two meet before the gate. They greet each other.

"Well, well...you're out for a look at the blossoms?"

"Not out for any particular reason at all...the weather is so nice I just thought I'd have a stroll."

"Oh? I've been to pay a visit to the temple in Hashiba....By the way, have you had your lunch?"

"I have."

"In that case, if you don't have anything particular to do, how about heading to Mukōjima together...?"

"That sounds fine. I'd be pleased to."

The...young man, thinking that he ought to have brought along his notebook, follows after the old one. The set rotates to the sound of the same clackers, revealing the scene of the riverbank at Mukōjima. In front, the Sumida River, the far bank visible in the distance, a row of cherry trees on it. A faint sound of waves, and the set comes to a stop....From stage right the same men enter, showing some surprise that the blossoms have already scattered. There are some lines here about how that is just as well because it means the crowd is much thinner, and the two stroll toward stage left. (Vol. 1, pp. 246–247)

But no sooner has this novel mode been introduced than the voice of Kidō breaks it off. His words of explanation reconnect the scene that we have just witnessed to the familiar formula:

> Having read this far, anyone will probably have figured out who the dramatis personae are. The old man is the usual Old Hanshichi, and the young man is me. Old Hanshichi, in response to my questions, began telling me what Asakusa used to be like...and eventually he took my bait.
>
> "Yes, in the old days there were all sorts of marvelous incidents....I'll tell you [about one] as we walk along."
>
> The events occurred on the seventh day of the first month of Ansei 5 [1858]. (Vol. 1, p. 247)

It turns out, then, that what at first strikes the reader as having been anomalous is in fact the same familiar story. It is the familiar story of Kidō meeting Hanshichi in order to listen to one of his adventures, and it is also the familiar story of the reader recovering the memory of what past experience has taught him, that the story will *always* begin with a meeting between Kidō and Hanshichi. The pattern of this scene—presentation of the seemingly unfamiliar, followed by its regrounding in the familiar—thus captures in miniature the fundamental narrative movement of all the Hanshichi stories: variation that is always finally contained by repetition.[33] By placing Kidō and Hanshichi on stage, assigning them lines, and portraying their world as one made up of so many sets, Kidō brings off in this story a dramatization, in the fullest sense, of all of the stories' ritualistic adherence to a predetermined script. This familiarity of the stock situations and motifs in the series ensures that the activity of the reader, who is continually invited to recover the memory of earlier episodes in the series, will parallel the series' more general mission of recovering the memory of earlier episodes in Japan's imagined historical past. Thanks to Hanshichi's own nostalgic memories of his younger days, the reader is transported to a gilt version of the old Japan. And thanks to the reader's own memories of the other stories in the series, their formal repetition gratifies the same desire to repeat the past that is embodied in each individual story's painstaking reconstruction of it. In this way the stories' rhetoric of repetition and their essentially conservative ideology become two sides of the same coin.

Conclusion: The Vagaries of Intercultural Transfer

As we have seen, Hanshichi's enactment of nationalistic and nostalgic remembrance depends on five interrelated aspects of Kidō's stories: their antiquarian attention to historical details, their shifting point of view, their hero's decidedly old-fashioned methods of detection, their latent anxiety concerning early Western incursions onto Japanese soil, and their use of the series form, in which each story ritualistically repeats the past by recycling familiar motifs from earlier stories in the series. For the reader who has learned the script to Hanshichi's stories, they hold no real surprises. No choice or accident ever sets off a wholly unexpected chain of events. There are localized moments of surprise (most surprising of all is the identity of the criminal), but these are always predicted by the larger requirements of the stories' formula. We know ahead of time that the criminal's identity will come as a surprise, and so it is no surprise when it does so.

The stories' ideological content is no less predictable than their stock situations and motifs. The stories consistently foster a fantasy of escape to an insular Japan of the past that can only be revisited in the realm of the imagination. It is no great leap from this nostalgia for Edo to the idea that the old Japan was preferable to the complications of the modern, Westernized one. In Kidō's stories, the benefits conferred by modernity are forever suspect; the electric lights are likely to fail at any moment.

What is surprising about the stories is that their nativistic and even xenophobic ideology should have made a home for itself in the narrative form of the detective story, given that both the form itself and its entry into Japan were by-products of the very modernity that the stories so doggedly resist. The ideological content was an odd match for the form. In those stories where happy coincidence or Hanshichi's sixth sense removes the need for logical deduction more or less completely, the form can seem close to losing its defining features—at least if one reads with the same expectations one brings to Conan Doyle. And the ambivalence in the scenes of violence against foreigners hints at the strain of uniting admiration for Conan Doyle's work with an impulse to maintain as staunchly as possible the purity of Japan's cultural identity. Despite these difficulties, the stories' basic Japanese nativism is never in serious danger of being compromised. Kidō's stories thus confirm that there can be many a slip betwixt original and copy, and that a form that begins as an emblem of Western rationality and modernity can, through the vagaries of intercultural transfer, end up as an emblem of ambivalent anti-Westernism, old-fashioned intuition, and traditionalism.

Anxieties
of Influence

Edogawa Ranpo's
Horrifying Hybrids

W hile Okamoto Kidō turned his back on Japan's modernization by staging an imaginary return to a culturally pure, more easily comprehensible past, Edogawa Ranpo (1894–1965)—who was the most prominent
detective story writer of the generation that followed Kidō—fixed his gaze
on his rapidly modernizing and Westernizing surroundings with fascinated
horror. Ranpo's corpus is peopled by characters who enact a dizzying variety
of bizarre impersonations, transformations, and monstrous hybridizations.
These characters include not only Inomata (in *The Pomegranate,* discussed
in Chapter 1), who undergoes plastic surgery in Shanghai at the hands of
foreign doctors, but also (to name only a few) a man who poses as a leather
armchair, a dwarf who alters his appearance by attaching and removing
prosthetic arms and legs, men and women driven to crime by sadomasochistic appetites run amok, and a pair of artificially conjoined Siamese twins.
Ranpo's handling of these characters and their activities frequently suggests
that behind his imaginings (and his readers' enthusiastic consumption of
them) there persistently lurked anxieties about Japanese Westernization
and the cultural hybridity it brought about.

These anxieties were part of a growing backlash in the 1920s and 1930s
against what some intellectuals and politicians saw as the pernicious effects
of Western influence (or *seiyō kabure,* the "Western infection") on Japan.
This view culminated in such documents as the modernist poet Hagiwara
Sakutarō's (1886–1942) now famous 1938 essay "Nihon e no kaiki" (Return
to Japan), a nostalgic lament for the loss of Japanese cultural identity,
and the reactionary manifesto "Kokutai no hongi" (Fundamentals of Our
National Polity), disseminated by the Japanese Ministry of Education in

1936.[1] The latter document captured the sentiments of the political right in particularly blunt form: "The various ideological and social evils of present-day Japan," it began, "are the result of lack of…judgment, and a failure to digest things thoroughly; and this is due to the fact that since the days of Meiji so many aspects of European and American culture, systems, and learning, have been imported, and that, too rapidly."[2]

Such anxiety about the mutation of Japanese cultural identity surfaces repeatedly in Ranpo. But this anxiety about Japanese cultural identity is also typically combined in Ranpo's works with a seemingly contradictory longing for the glamorous exoticism of Western culture as well as an admiration for Western literary models. And to complicate things still further, Ranpo's works also show signs of anxiety about the legitimacy of their own claim to membership in the genre of detective fiction, which Ranpo and critics contemporary to him were prone to viewing as fundamentally Western.

These anxieties translated, in Ranpo's work, into a persistent fascination with guilty impersonation, with the self-inflicted harm that half-successful impersonations could entail, and with the monstrosity of cultural hybrids. The inherent contradictions these works confront as they attempt to duplicate Western precedent without sacrificing Japanese national identity mirror the contradictions faced by Japan itself as it attempted to create a modern colonial empire that would earn it legitimacy in the eyes of the Western powers, while at the same time preserving its sense of national and cultural difference from the powers on which it felt compelled to model itself. This similarity does not seem to have been a matter of mere coincidence. Rather, it seems to have been a consequence of the way that, in both the literary and the geopolitical spheres, Japanese found themselves in a double bind that arose from their perception that Japan was arriving only belatedly in the modern world.

One symptom of this double bind is Ranpo's pen name (his given name was Hirai Tarō). As Ranpo explains in a brief essay on the subject, his pen name "is the result of playing on the sounds of [the name] of the American Edgar Allan Poe, the father of the detective novel, and then matching Japanese ideographs to them." The ideographs Ranpo strung together to represent the sounds of Poe's name confer upon these sounds their own meaning in Japanese, roughly translatable as "staggering drunkenly along the Edo River."[3] The name thus evokes not only an image that is wholly removed from the usual associations it has in English; it also evokes the long-standing tradition among Japanese literati of devising such clever, self-deprecating pen names.

Even though Ranpo's borrowing changes both the sound of the name and the associations it sparks, it still depends for its full effect on its allusion to his predecessor Poe. Ranpo, in other words, suffers from what the literary critic Harold Bloom called "belatedness," simply by virtue of having come to the genre of the detective story after Poe, whom he acknowledges as the genre's "father."[4] As Bloom understands the phenomenon of literary belatedness, it is potentially one of the most fruitful sources of creativity, as each subsequent "latecomer" (Bloom calls them "ephebes") in the tradition engages in the willful "misprision," or misreading, of his predecessors in order to clear a space from which to speak for himself. There is nothing inherently inferior in Bloom's belatedness; the strongest of the latecomers will in fact develop such powerful misreadings of their precursors that they cause us to reread the earlier tradition through the lens of their own achievement, rather than the reverse. As Miryam Sas has noted, influence, for Bloom, has very little to do with what he calls "source studies," which focus on "the history of ideas," "the patterning of images," or "verbal resemblances," and much more to do with a mutual relationship of antagonism between ephebes and the works of their literary fathers.[5] As Bloom famously declared, "An ephebe's best misinterpretations may well be of poems he has never read."[6]

The remarkable thing about Ranpo's work is how powerfully it invites the simple, unidirectional view of influence that Bloom's classic writings and other, more recent, work by theoreticians of international literary relations would urge us to discard.[7] Ranpo seems to have focused both in his works and in the construction of his literary persona precisely on such things as "the patterning of images" and "verbal resemblance," even to the point of deliberately renaming himself after Poe (although his literary borrowing is by no means limited to Poe's oeuvre). His works and his name are inevitably distinct from Poe's, simply by virtue of their radically different cultural context. Nor would one want to overlook in Ranpo's borrowing the possibility of parody or pastiche, or even self-parody. But Ranpo seldom exploits these possibilities, and to gloss over the patently derivative nature of much of Ranpo's work would be to ignore one of its most characteristic elements.

Admittedly, to describe Ranpo's work as "derivative" risks reinstating a dubious hierarchy of literary value in which the works that inspired Ranpo are implicitly valorized as "originals" and Ranpo's works themselves are demoted to the status of "copies." Such a binary opposition is rendered even more problematic than usual by the nature of the detective genre itself, which depends for its very identity on a strong family resemblance among its members. Such conventions as the locked room, the series of interviews with the suspects, the dramatic reappraisal of the evidence, the revelation of the intricate yet utterly compelling solution by the detective, and the guilt of the least likely suspect have been so widely circulated and recirculated as to make the question of originality largely moot. And perhaps not only detective stories but all texts are, as poststructuralist literary-critical theory has suggested, made up of fragments of other texts.[8]

But Ranpo's works come laden with so keen a sense of their indebtedness and their position on the periphery of the genre as to compel attention to this aspect of them, even if one would ultimately prefer to sidestep entirely the question of originality or the question of literary value. In their continual reworking of the interrelated themes of impersonation, self-destruction, and monstrous hybridity, Ranpo's stories persistently embody anxiety not only about the cultural transformations brought on by Westernization, but also about their own self-declared status as belated and only partially Japanized, Western-inspired literary artifacts.

Ranpo's Career

Born in 1894 in Mie prefecture, Ranpo (then Hirai Tarō) went as a teenager to Tokyo to be schooled at Waseda University, where he studied economics. It was there that he read Poe and Conan Doyle and G. K. Chesterton for the first time. He records that he was deeply impressed by the purity of their logic and by their eschewal of the sort of melodrama that afflicted Ruikō's translated works, which he had "read all of as a boy but...had lukewarm feelings" for.[9] By his graduation he was sufficiently enamored of the Western detective story to have ideas of going to America to become a professional detective story writer. Lack of funds kept him in Japan in a series of more than a dozen jobs, none of which held his interest, for the next eight years. He bounced back and forth between Osaka and Tokyo, living in the latter for long periods between 1919 and 1922, and then again from 1925 on. He worked for a time at a trading company, then as a typewriter salesman; he ran a used book shop and a noodle shop; he worked at Tokyo city hall and as a newspaper reporter in Osaka. During these years he also deepened his knowledge of the native Japanese literary tradition, reading Akutagawa Ryūnosuke, Satō Haruo, Uno Kōji, and above all Tanizaki Jun'ichirō. No Japanese writer is closer to Ranpo than Tanizaki, whose own works embody a famously deep ambivalence toward Westernization. Ranpo writes that he "read Tanizaki's stories omitting none."[10]

In 1923, when he was twenty-nine, the magazine *Shinseinen* (New Youth) published his first story involving detection, "Nisen dōka" (The Two-Sen Copper Coin). When "Nisen dōka" appeared, virtually all of the mysteries in *Shinseinen* were translations of foreign stories, and from the moment of the publication of this first story, Ranpo was compared to his Western counterparts.

Ranpo records that Morishita Uson (1890–1965), the founder of the three-year-old magazine, introduced him to readers as a "detective writer who could hold his own against the foreign authors."[11] Two years later, he was writing full time.

Ranpo's writing varied considerably from period to period. His early stories are, as a rule, told with economy. Many give the reader a chance to develop a theory based on the evidence presented ("Ichimai no kippu" [A Single Ticket]). Some, however, only show a detective at work discovering the identity of a criminal already known to the reader ("Shinri-shiken" [The Psychological Test]). And others are, strictly speaking, stories of the strange or the macabre rather than stories of detection, although crime can figure in these as well ("Kagami-jigoku" [The Hell of Mirrors], "Hakuchūmu" [Daydream], and "Imomushi" [Potato Bug]). Ranpo's most oft-used detective and the single character most strongly associated with him is the private eye Akechi Kogorō. In contrast to the consistently drawn Hanshichi of Okamoto Kidō, Akechi evolves during his career in a way that suggests increasing cosmopolitanism and cultural deracination. He begins as a bookish kimono-wearing man of uncertain occupation ("D-zaka no satsujin jiken" [The Case of the Murder at D. Hill, 1925]). In *Issun-bōshi* (The Dwarf, 1926–1927), he is a professional detective who wears traditional Chinese robes acquired in Shanghai. By the time of his appearance in *Kumo-otoko* (Spider Man, 1930), he is wearing white shoes and a white hat and has about him "the air of an Indian gentleman used to living in Europe."

After the mid-1920s, Ranpo's writing became more spasmodic. Once he had completed *The Dwarf*, which he agreed to write for the Tokyo *Asahi* newspaper on short notice when the serial writer they had under contract fell ill, Ranpo stopped writing for a year to travel because, as he later explained in his literary diary, he was overcome with feelings of "shame at my work, self-abhorrence, and misanthropy."[12] The word "self-abhorrence" *(jiko ken'o)*, in particular, seems to have been strongly associated in Ranpo's mind with this episode; he repeats it in an essay on his career that he wrote for the *Nihon keizai shinbun* (Japanese Economic News) nearly thirty years later, saying that he set off on his travels because he "felt an intense self-abhorrence *(hageshii jiko ken'o)* at the slovenliness of *The Dwarf*."[13] This was to be the first of several long vacations Ranpo took throughout his career for similar reasons. (*The Dwarf*, however, was at least popular enough to inspire a 1927 movie with a screenplay by Naoki Sanjūgo.)[14]

When he eventually returned to his writing desk, Ranpo produced *Injū* (Shadowy Beast, 1928), which was published in *Shinseinen* magazine. It is his most sustained work in the style of the English golden-age writers (that is, in the style in which the interpretation and reinterpretation of fairly presented evidence is made the overriding concern). Beginning with *Kotō no oni* (The Demon of the Desert Isle, 1929–1930), he turned out increasing numbers of the long, generally serialized pieces that the Japanese refer to as *tsūzoku-chōhen*, or "popular full-lengths." From this point on, Ranpo began to recycle ideas from his earlier works with increasing frequency, producing works that catered to an audience with a marked taste for the erotic and the grotesque and embodying an aesthetic sensibility that came to be known as *ero-guro*.

Many of the works from this period and later in Ranpo's career demonstrate the looseness with which the term *tantei shōsetsu*, or "detective story," came to be applied in Japan. Detection is often overshadowed in these works by sadism, dismemberment, and an indulgence in the bizarre for its own sake. Many either do not make use of the double-layered detective structure at all or else they hybridize it with other forms, a circumstance that led Ranpo to observe in a 1935 essay, "It is said that more than half of Japan's detective stories are not real detective stories. I myself concur with this theory."[15] In 1936 Ranpo began, rather improbably, to write children's books, the most famous of which was *Kaijin-nijūmensō* (The Twenty-Faced Wonder, 1936), about an Arsène Lupin–like thief with legendary powers of metamorphosis. During the war he wrote science fiction and spy stories, using the pen name "Komatsu Ryūnosuke" instead of his usual one, with its American overtones. After the war he was increasingly viewed as the elder statesman of Japanese detective writers; he founded and presided over a club of his fellows as well as writing numerous essays on foreign and Japanese detective fiction (collected in *Gen'eijō* [The Illusory Castle, 1951]). When he died in 1968, he had attained the status of undisputed father of the detective story in Japan, both validating the implicit claim made by his pen name that he was a Japanese Poe and at the same time posing more insistently the question of what the implications of such a designation might be.

Ambivalent Longing for the West

"The Human Chair" ("Ningen isu," 1925) offers an example of the preoccupation in Ranpo's writings with impersonation, hybridity, and ambivalent longing for the West. Although it does not draw direct inspiration from any Western source and it is a story of the weird rather than a story of detection, its deliberate creepiness is reminiscent of much of Poe's work. The story begins with a framing narrative in which we meet a beautiful, talented, and successful young writer of popular fiction named Yoshiko. She has received in the mail a particularly thick packet, which she at first assumes must be a manuscript from yet another amateur writer hoping to break into the literary world with her approval and support. When she opens it, however, it seems not to be a manuscript after all but a long letter. It begins stiffly. "Madam: Please be so kind as to forgive the breach of etiquette that I—a man with whom you are not acquainted in the least—commit by precipitously sending so ill-mannered a letter as this. What I have to say will no doubt surprise you greatly, Madam, but I am about to make before you a confession of sins, committed by me, of a most extraordinary sort."[16] It is the man's confession that makes up the main part of the story.

The writer of the letter explains that he "was born [with]...the ugliest looks imaginable." Women, naturally, shun him. In a cruel twist, he says, he also has "burning within [him] a lustfulness of unmatched power." By trade he is a furniture maker; his specialty is custom-made chairs. His clients are rich, and he often used to amuse himself by imagining the opulently appointed Western-style rooms in which his chairs would end up, entertaining fantasies of meeting the elegant women who must surely inhabit them. One day, he confides, having completed an order of large leather armchairs for a hotel, there came to him a plan for acting on his fantasies. He disassembled one of the chairs and rebuilt it to contain a cavity large enough to hide in, his knees beneath the seat, head and torso in the backrest. Providing himself with enough food and water to last several days and a rubber bag for his wastes, he climbed inside. The chair was delivered, secret payload and all, to a lounge in the hotel, where it was soon being used by unsuspecting guests:

> Judging by her voice [the chair maker writes of one guest], she was a tender young foreign girl. No one else was in the room, and she was singing softly to herself. I heard her just in front of the chair, and then suddenly her fleshy, lithe body was upon me. She laughed to herself at something, flapping her arms and legs and then squirming in the chair like a fish in a net.
>
> For about thirty minutes she was there in my lap, singing occasionally, wriggling the weight of her body as if she were keeping time with her song.
>
> This was, for me...absolutely earthshaking. I, to whom women were something sacred, even frightening—I, who refrained even from looking at their faces—was in the same room, in the same chair, with a foreign girl I had never seen, with just a single skin of leather between us, wedged in so closely that I could feel her body's warmth.[17]

He became, he says, addicted to his life inside the chair, preferring its dark confines to the outside world. But eventually the hotel's management changed and the chair was put up for auction. This brought new possibilities: "In those months I had come to feel affection for many members of the female sex, but because every one of them was a foreigner, no matter how fine and desirable their physiques, there was no way around feeling an odd dissatisfaction of spirit. When all is said and done, perhaps a Japanese person can't feel true love except for a fellow Japanese. . . . Maybe my chair would be bought by a Japanese person. And maybe it would be put in a Japanese household. This was my new desire."[18]

All happens as he had hoped. His chair is placed in the study of a Japanese woman. She spends long hours sitting in the chair to write. He can tell by her voice that she is vivacious and by the feel of her body that it is "satisfactorily proportioned." He falls in love. He does everything in his power to make the woman fall in love with him, in the guise of the chair. "When she settled her body on top of me," he explains, "I was careful to receive her with a featherlike gentleness of touch. When she would tire of sitting on me, I would move my lap by imperceptible degrees to adjust her position. And if she began to doze off, I would very lightly rock my knees to act as a cradle for her."[19]

The end of the man's letter reveals why he has singled out Yoshiko to hear his confession. As she herself has begun to fear halfway through the letter, and to fear strongly enough to leave the study where she began reading, the chair that the author of the letter has been inhabiting is her own. He now hopes she will agree to meet face-to-face. No sooner has she thrown down the letter in horror and indignation than another one arrives for her. It is from the same man. The story ends by quoting this second letter. "The letter that I sent under separate cover," he says, "was a little bit of fiction I wrote. I would be grateful for your opinion of it. . . . I thought I would call it 'The Human Chair.'"[20]

As usual, Ranpo produces a work rich with suggestive and varied imaginings. The work is dominated, however, by its focus on the psychopathology of the chair maker, whose embedded first-person narrative accounts for the bulk of the tale. Early on, this embedded narrative signals that the chair maker's view of the world is strongly colored by his sense of his own inferiority. At first this sense of inferiority is rather simply linked to the chair maker's congenital ugliness and his blue-collar status. Both these links are made clear, for example, in the wishful daydreams the chair maker relates to the reader: "This person I am, this poor, ugly person who is no more than a laborer, would in my world of fantasy become a handsome young nobleman sitting in the magnificent chair I had made. And next to me would be the beautiful lover who always appears in my dreams, smiling brightly as she listened to what I had to say."

Before long, however, the text complicates the chair maker's sense of inferiority by giving the erotic longings it inspires a racial twist. This racial element becomes legible in the explicit distinction drawn between the chair maker's feelings for foreign women and his feelings for Japanese women. When the chair maker describes his reaction to the first woman who sits on his chair while he is inside, her foreignness is mentioned as part of the series of conditions, breathlessly listed in an escalating sequence, that pushes the experience to the limits of imaginable ecstasy: "[I] was in the same room, in the same chair, with a foreign girl I had never seen, with just a single skin of leather between us, wedged in so closely that I could feel her body's warmth." And as the story unfolds, it becomes clear that it is the foreign women at the hotel who arouse him the most, even if he cannot bring himself to fall in love with one of them. Indeed, their arousing effect is perhaps the main impediment to feeling the "true love" that he develops for Yoshiko. When Yoshiko sits on the chair, he is restrained and solicitous, receiving her "with a featherlike gentleness of touch." With the foreign women in the hotel, in contrast, he is moved to give his sexual desire the freest possible rein. "Inside the chair I could pretend to hug her close to me," he says about one of these foreign women. "Through the leather I could kiss the tender flesh of her neck. And in addition to these things I was free to do anything else I pleased."[21]

This racial component in the chair maker's narrative sets up a dynamic of intermingled desires and anxieties that carry the weight not merely of interpersonal relations but of intercultural ones. The chair maker exhibits a yearning for the allure of the West, or at least his imaginary version of it, that is figured as his all but uncontrollable sexual desire for white women. But this yearning is undercut by a feeling of unworthiness to engage the West on equal terms, figured as the necessity to adopt the servile posture of a chair in order to close the distance between himself and the women he desires. In this intermingling of desire and anxiety directed toward an imagined "West," Ranpo's story reflects the same psychology seen in Tanizaki Jun'ichirō's novel *Chijin no ai* (A Fool's Love, published in 1924, the year before "The Human Chair"). In what is perhaps that novel's most memorable scene, the main character, a Japanese man named Jōji, takes a lesson in ballroom dancing from a Russian countess named Madame Shlemskaya. "When Madame Shlemskaya presented her white hand," Jōji records, "my heart skipped a beat and I hesitated, uncertain whether it was all right to take it." Jōji's trepidation is not lessened by the ensuing dance with the countess, who stands a full head taller than he does. When the two dance, the material of the countess' blouse functions no less powerfully as a token of transgressive bodily contact than the thin layer of leather in Ranpo's story: "Drawn to her breast with only her soft, thin blouse between us," he tells us, "I felt as though I were doing something absolutely forbidden. Maybe my breath's bad, I fretted. She's offended by my greasy hands."[22]

The inequality between the chair maker and the foreigners who sit on him is further underscored when he has a momentary fantasy of inverting the relationship. When "the ambassador from a certain powerful country in Europe" sits down, the human chair at first feels an excited pride. But soon his imaginings turn murderous. "I wondered," he says, "what would happen if, from behind the leather, I were to make a violent stab at his heart with a sharp knife."[23] This fantasy is, however, entirely impotent. The chair maker has no knife, and in the end he gives not the slightest sign to the ambassador that he is inside the chair.

Combined with this volatile mix of desire and anxiety, one can also discern a further latent desire of the chair maker to assume a Western identity (even, absurdly, if that means doing so as a piece of furniture) and a concomitant fear of the possibly monstrous result of such an imposture. The story takes pains to mark the leather armchair into which its maker metamorphoses as a specifically Western object (a point that should go more or less without saying, since such chairs have no place among traditional Japanese furnishings). When the chair maker has his fantasies of transformation into a young nobleman, he imagines that the chairs he makes must be delivered to what are clearly Western-style rooms "with famous oil paintings on the walls and magnificent jeweled chandeliers suspended from the ceiling." The chair in which he conceals himself is ordered by a Western-style hotel and one managed, at that, by foreigners. At the hotel, the room in which the chair is placed is foreign enough in its conception to challenge the narrator's descriptive powers for a moment. "It was not a private room," he says, "but rather the sort of room where you wait to meet people, read the newspaper, or smoke, and where lots of people come and go; a room of the sort that could be called [and here he uses the English word] a lounge."[24] The new company that takes over the hotel is Japanese, and the reason the chair is sold is that the place is to be run as a Japanese-style inn *(ryokan)*. When the chair is then bought at auction by Yoshiko's wealthy husband, it is "placed in a spacious study in the Western-style wing *(yōkan)*" of their mansion.[25]

No less conspicuous than this overdetermination of the chair as a Western object is the story's marking of the man-chair hybrid as a perversion and a monstrosity. The confessional letter's first-person point of view puts the reader himself inside the chair, and Ranpo's descriptions of what one feels in that position are numerous and specific enough to suggest the story is meant to provide an erotic thrill to the heterosexual male reader it presumably addresses. But at the same time the story ensures that the reader's identification with the armchair maker cannot be complete. This identification is severely tempered by (if nothing else) the presence in the framing narrative of Yoshiko, who, we feel, is reading the letter at the same time we are. And from her point of view, the human chair is so disgusting as to make her want to run and hide. Halfway through the letter, we are told, "she unconsciously rose up and fled from the study, where the creepy armchair stood, to the sitting room in the Japanese wing."[26]

Perhaps most telling of all, it is not only the hybrid combination of man and chair that the story renders monstrous. Before the story's end, the man's addiction to life as a chair has made him a deformed, monstrous figure in his own right. "Because I was keeping my arms bent and my legs folded in this extremely cramped space almost all day long, my whole body would become numb, so that I couldn't stand up straight anymore," he explains. "Eventually I was making my trips to the bathroom or the kitchen by scooting on my bottom like a cripple."[27] The man's attempt to transform himself into the chair ultimately proves futile and self-destructive, and his confession does nothing to win the sympathy of Yoshiko—let alone that of the more distant and more erotically alluring foreign women he has left behind at the hotel.

"The Human Chair," then, begins as a story about attempting to remake personal identity but ends by developing a conflicted subtext about the temptations and dangers of attempting to remake cultural identity. Given this imagining of cultural impersonation as a sort of helplessly self-imposed deformity, what is one to make of the story's final twist? Certainly this ending underscores the sheer power of fabulation to evoke a palpable terror, and in this sense it is a literary triumph. But at the same time the story's conclusion stages a conspicuous dismissal and deflation of its own narrative labor. By altering its own label from confession to mere fiction, the story inscribes on itself the same sense of inferiority that it portrays in the chair maker. If one accepts the idea that the story itself is as deliberately Poe-like in its overtly creepy sensibilities as the chair is Western in its exterior presentation, then the story and the chair become roughly functional equivalents. The chair maker hopes to have the chair carry him into a world of "Western" erotic possibility to which he would be denied access were his true identity apparent. Likewise, Ranpo (rather like the writer who submits his manuscript for Yoshiko's approval) writes with the hope that his story will win him acceptance in the club of Western writers—a membership that he would not enjoy if he did not use borrowed forms or borrowed tropes. At the same time it is a membership that he seems to claim with deep ambivalence, both because of the worry that he is not worthy to claim it and because of the sacrifice of cultural identity that such a claim would entail.

Horror in the Modern Cityscape

Several of Ranpo's works contemplate yet another variety of cultural hybridity—that of the Westernized and modernized Japanese urban landscape. These works envision this hybridity with a mixture of fascination and horror that is of a piece with that in "The Human Chair."

Like "The Human Chair," Ranpo's story "The Red Room" ("Akai heya," 1925) has, at least in its opening passage, a gothic atmosphere obviously reminiscent of Poe, though the main armature of the story is derived from a Japanese source, Tanizaki Jun'ichirō's story "On the Way" ("Tojō," 1920).[28] "The Red Room" is about a secret society of Japanese men that gathers regularly to frighten one another with horror stories. The room of the story's title is the site of their meetings. Its décor is stagy, and Ranpo's description of it is probably indebted to the description Poe provides of the seven colored rooms in his "Masque of the Red Death" (1842).[29] The windowless walls are draped from floor to ceiling in heavy pleats of silk the color of "blood flowing freshly from its vein." Red velvet covers the deep armchairs that the men occupy and the table they encircle. On the table three "Romantic" (Ranpo inserts the English word) candles flicker in a silver candelabrum, casting long shadows that have the appearance, as they move over the wall hangings, of giant insects. A newly inducted member of the society, a man introduced only as "T.," starts speaking.

As T.'s tale begins, "The Red Room" shifts from the creepiness of the secret society's chamber to the modern Tokyo cityscape, which turns out, in its way, to be far scarier. T. announces to the assembly that although he believes himself in full possession of his senses, he has been desperate for some time to fight off an oppressive and chronic ennui. After trying every sort of thrill seeking he could imagine (he mentions "playing at crime and detection, séances and other experiments in spiritualism, the enactment and the filming of 'obscene pictures,' other sexual games, prisons, lunatic asylums, the study of autopsy"), he finally hit upon something that held his interest: murder. He claims to have committed nearly one hundred murders, none of which has been detected. His method, he explains, is to cause fatal accidents in such a way that he will seem to have had no responsibility for them. It turns out that the hazards of the modern city fit his designs perfectly:

> Here is one I pulled off successfully with an old woman from the country who was about to cross some trolley tracks. Imagine that just as she places one foot on the tracks—and of course it's not just trolleys that she has to worry about, but also cars, bicycles, carriages, and rickshaws streaming in both directions, so there is no doubt her mind is in a

whirl—at the moment she puts one foot on the tracks, imagine an express trolley appears, coming like the wind. At that moment, if the old woman doesn't notice the trolley and simply continues across the tracks, she will be unharmed. But if someone were to yell loudly, "Look out!" she would suddenly become flustered and hesitate, unsure whether to keep going across or to return the way she came. And if the trolley were too close to be able to make an emergency stop, the simple words "Look out!" would be enough to injure the old woman or perhaps even to cost her life. As I said, I once killed a woman from the country with complete success in just this way.[30]

This scene of murder literalizes the onslaught of modernity as a trolley. The haplessness of the victim—a generation behind the times and obviously far more used to the leisurely pace of life in the countryside than to the hurly-burly of machine-age urban culture—underlines a basic anxiety in the passage about the dehumanizing effects of a modern, originally Western, technology.

Seen through the madly acute vision of T., the metropolis and its environs become a minefield of such deadly hazards. In another murder, surely the most bizarre of Ranpo's entire corpus, the scene of the killing is a modern suburban development (a *bunka-mura*, or "culture village") of Western-style buildings *(seiyō-kan)*. As Jordan Sand has documented, the first such major housing development in the Tokyo area was built in Ochiai near Mejiro station in 1922, and a second went on the market in 1923.[31] By the time Ranpo published "The Red Room," additional "culture villages," "garden cities," and "college parks" were proliferating like mushrooms, as a sign of the increasing commodification of Western life and culture in the Japanese marketplace. As Sand explains, these housing developments, and indeed any architecture designated by the catchword *bunka*, or "culture," "connoted a cosmopolitan modernity that was the common currency of educated urbanites."[32] This cosmopolitanism clearly involved a hybridization, in the minds of Japanese real estate developers and their clientele, of Western and Japanese urban life. Sand reports that the advertisements for one such Mejiro development depicted an American visitor exclaiming, "Why, it's a miniature Los Angeles!"[33]

Strolling through such a development, T. notices a sparrow alight on a wire running from a lightning rod atop the most imposing of the "concrete Western buildings." When the sparrow almost immediately topples dead from the wire, he realizes that the lightning rod must have somehow picked up an electrical charge from the atmosphere. T. sees approaching a group of children pretending—rather ominously—to be soldiers, and soon he has singled out his next victim:

A small boy of six or seven lagged behind the rest of the group. I watched him, wondering what he was going to do. Standing on a little knoll in front of the wire from the lightning rod, he pulled his pants down and began to urinate. When I saw that, I came up with another ingenious trick. I had learned in school that water is a conductor of electricity. It would be an easy matter to urinate onto the uninsulated portion of the wire from the knoll where the child stood....I called to the child, "Hey, sonny, try peeing on that wire there. Can you reach it?" He said, "That's easy! Watch me!" No sooner had he said this than he turned around and aimed for the exposed wire. The moment he hit it—how frightening it was—the child jumped upward as if dancing for a moment and then collapsed in a heap....It was the first time in my life I had seen a person die of electrocution.[34]

The marvels of electricity had begun in the early 1920s to loom ever larger in the Japanese popular imagination, as refrigerators, toasters, radios, and electric lights became increasingly commonplace in middle-class urban homes and especially in the new "culture houses."[35] Ranpo here capitalizes on ignorance and vague unease about the technical details of electricity's workings (T. himself scratches his head over just how the ground wire could have become so powerfully charged). Building on the association between electricity and the culture village dwellings, this episode represents the 1920s fad for Western-style construction as a deadly blight upon the landscape, something from which one would recoil in horror, a notion that is almost absurdly literalized in the effect of the shock on the boy's body and the likely reaction of the reader to it. Given the fuzzy science, the menace here seems to have been projected onto the landscape as much as discovered in it and to be at least as much a cultural one as an electrical one.

After having T. relate the details of a number of other similar deaths he has caused, Ranpo ends "The Red Room" with the same sort of disavowal of his own story that he makes in "The Human Chair." T. stages what is at first a convincing charade involving a pistol, a confederate, and his own bloody death by gunshot, but then, laughing maniacally, reveals the truth to his listeners: the "bullet" in the pistol was fashioned of material cut from a cow's bladder and then filled with red ink. What is more, he now confesses, the entire tale he has told is also a lie, all contrived solely to entertain the other members of the society. The story concludes on a note of grim disappointment: "The scarlet silk hangings, the scarlet carpeting, the matching table cloth and the armchairs, and yes, even that imposing candelabrum—how shabby they all appeared now! In 'the red room,' even if one searched its every nook and cranny, there was not a trace of dream or fantasy to be found."

"The Red Room" reiterates all the characteristic contradictions of Ranpo's works. On the one hand it strives to re-create and pay homage to the gothic sensibilities of Poe's writings. Yet on the other hand it seems to embody both a horror of the hybridity that such intercultural imitation may yield and—given the story's final deflation of itself—a lack of conviction concerning its own worth as an imitation in the first place. It is as if, rather than mustering the material and the gravitas to sustain a fantasy in the manner of Poe, Ranpo found it easier in the end to declare the whole thing (not just T.'s story but his own as well) a charade.

In the serialized novel *The Dwarf* (*Issun bōshi,* 1926–1927), which ran simultaneously in the Tokyo and Osaka *Asahi* newspapers, Ranpo again sets his macabre fantasies in a Westernized Tokyo cityscape. This time he focuses most memorably on the multistory department store. Such stores made their first appearance in the Ginza shopping district in the wake of the Great Earthquake of 1923. In the previous two decades, the large Japanese retail houses had gradually evolved from storefronts where customers were brought goods to inspect from an interior storage area to the open plan epitomized by the Wanamaker Department Store in Philadelphia. When Ranpo began *The Dwarf* in 1926, Japanese department stores had only recently incorporated Wanamaker-style sales floors designed to be walked through while wearing one's shoes, as opposed to removing them at the entry. The glass case displaying goods with tags indicating predetermined, fixed prices and the display mannequin were also notable novelties.[36]

Part of the inspiration for *The Dwarf* was probably supplied by Fortuné du Boisgobey's *La main coupée* (The Severed Hand, 1880), which Kuroiwa Ruikō translated into Japanese as *Katate bijin* (The One-Handed Beauty) in 1889. The plots of Ranpo's work and Ruikō's translation are quite dissimilar, but both works do make a point of having severed limbs turn up in unlikely places. In any case, *The Dwarf* stands out for its persistent use of the emblems of Western cultural influence to create cartoonish scenes of horror.

The novel is one of Ranpo's longest, and some of its implausible turns of plot suggest that it was only sketchily outlined before the early episodes were committed to print. The main interest in the novel centers on the attempt of the detective (Akechi Kōgoro) to explain the suspicious doings of the dwarf for whom the novel is named. The dwarf turns out to have put together a blackmail scheme hinging on his knowledge of a murder committed by a young, comfortably upper-middle-class woman named Yamano Michiko. Yamano's victim was her own illegitimate half sister Komatsu (who also happens to serve as the family's maid). Michiko's father, desperate to keep the crime a secret, hires the dwarf, who has useful underworld connections, to dispose of Komatsu's body. The dwarf, however, defiantly dismembers the body and begins leaving parts of it around the city in places likely to attract attention, with the idea that Michiko's father will be forced to pay him to stop, lest his daughter's crime come to light. The dwarf is made more horrible by the vague suggestion that he himself is a sort of stumplike result of dismemberment. Comparisons are drawn between his body and that of the victim. And to disguise his small stature, he occasionally wears a set of four prosthetic limbs, which are prone to detaching in the hands of pursuers chasing him at close range.

Early in the novel the dwarf appears at night on the third floor of "a famous Ginza department store." Ranpo's third-person narrative voice seizes on the potential of this novel, large, dark space to inspire dread: "The display cases in the sales area were all swathed in white cloth; their varied white forms—large and small, high and low—stood in rows like countless coffins.... There were, here and there, thick cylindrical pillars that somehow made an impression as of living giant men."[37] But it is on three life-size display mannequins that the narrator's attention comes to rest. These mannequins, "the spookiest things [in the store]," are so real-looking as to seem alive: "While [the night watchmen were] on duty, they would pause to stand in front of the dolls, staring steadily at their faces, feeling that [the dolls] were about to break suddenly into a smile."[38] On this particular night, the watchmen discover standing among the mannequins the dwarf himself, as he momentarily poses, doll-like, in the beam of their flashlights before they realize he is alive and chase him away.

It is not until the store opens for business the next morning that we discover what the dwarf has been up to. One of the mannequins catches the eye of a schoolchild because its arm looks uncannily real to him. His grandmother assures him that it cannot possibly be a real arm. Another woman suggests that if it will put him at ease, he should slip under the rail and check the doll for himself. He does this, to quite the opposite effect: "The boy pulled off its right forearm and waved it high in the direction of the shoppers. When they saw it, there was pandemonium. The root of the forearm, which had until then been hidden by the sleeve of the kimono, had been violently cut off from the elbow, and a reddish black membrane of blood adhered lumpily to the wound."[39]

With this scene Ranpo transforms the department store into a sort of charnel house. The impulse to do so must have sprung partly from nothing more complicated than the inherent uncanniness of mannequins and their posable, detachable limbs. But the text also appeals to a sense of weirdness and horror that goes beyond this, to touch the sheer alien quality of the mannequins as novel, imported objects. (Tellingly, the mannequins draw a small crowd in Ranpo's scene even before the substitution of the arm is noticed.) It is typical of Ranpo's works that he locates the uncanny most readily in the accoutrements of Westernized Japanese culture. Even when these things are somehow disturbing in their own right, Ranpo seems to depend on their foreignness to make them even more so. And in this instance, the attachment of the Japanese human arm to the Western display mannequin creates a horrible hybrid that only renders more plain the hybridization of cultures represented by the presence in the Tokyo cityscape of the department store itself.

The imagery of detached limbs is, along with the attempt to identify the owner of the arm (it does eventually prove to have been Komatsu's), one of the few things unifying a rather wayward narrative. This image series, initiated in the department store scene and continued through the descriptions of the dwarf and his prostheses, culminates in the climactic discovery of Komatsu's delimbed body. She is discovered, near the novel's end, in a doll-making shop, encased in a giant plaster Kewpie doll.

Jordan Sand reports that the chubby blue-eyed celluloid Kewpie doll was originally designed in the United States but was being manufactured by the late 1920s in numerous countries worldwide. In Japan, he adds, the manufacture of celluloid toys (presumably including Kewpie dolls) had by 1928 become a newly booming business, and the country supplied over 70 percent of the world's consumption.[40] The dolls were thus both a reminder of racial difference and a sign of the spread into Japan of modern capitalism, mass production, and mass consumer culture. Ranpo was hardly a coherent critic of any of these latter things (and indeed his own livelihood as a writer depended on them). But the ambivalence that his works display toward them hints at the deep sense of cultural dislocation that Japan's confrontation with modernity caused. In this case, by constructing a trail for his detective Akechi to follow that ends with the revelation of Komatsu's delimbed body inside the Kewpie doll—both supplying a horrible completion to her maimed body and obscuring her identity—Ranpo gives a nightmarishly gruesome aspect to the very hybridization of Japanese and Western culture that he participated in as a detective writer.

Guilty Impersonation
in Shadowy Beast

Ranpo's 1929 novel Shadowy Beast, like "The Human Chair" and "The Red Room," also revolves around an act of guilty criminal impersonation. The novel, however, is perhaps unique in Ranpo's output thanks to the specificity with which it associates this guilty impersonation with the figure of the detective writer and with Ranpo's own writings. The note of irresolution on which the narrative closes represents a departure from the tidily unambiguous confessions (often followed by suicides) that end so many of his stories. But the irresolution keeps alive in the text a lingering hope that is ultimately identical to that expressed in *The Pomegranate* and many of his other works—the hope that the guilty impersonation at the heart of the case might turn out not to have been an impersonation at all. At the same time the novel also contains its quota of thematic material having to do with Western cultural influences, which in this case are portrayed primarily as influences on Japanese sexuality. The representation in the novel of these influences as a form of sadomasochistic perversion indicates a continuing, powerful ambivalence in Ranpo's works toward their imagined West, which comes off in this novel—as so often in Ranpo—looking both enticing and pernicious.

The narrator of the *Shadowy Beast* is a middle-aged writer of detective fiction, Samugawa by name. He presents the story to us as a set of detailed notes, based on his own experience, that he plans someday to turn into a novel. In fact, it is Ranpo's single most elaborately and cohesively plotted full-length work and one of the few that allows the reader a sense of genuinely matching wits with the detective.

Samugawa is pulled into the life of Shizuko, the alluring young wife of a rich businessman, when she confides that she is receiving threatening letters from a jealous jilted lover. She explains that this lover, who is named Hirata, has been stalking her ever since she and her family left the provincial town where the two grew up. In the meantime he has earned his living by writing notoriously morbid detective stories under the pseudonym "Ōe Shundei." The name is well known to Samugawa, who prides himself on the genteel intellectualism of his own writing and regards Shundei as his archrival.

Now that Shundei has located Shizuko, he is apparently planning revenge for her heartlessness. His letters threaten to murder first her husband Oyamada and then Shizuko herself. As proof of his lurking presence, he records in his letters the most minute and intimate details of Shizuko's life for several nights running (what book she read, how she drank her wine, what time her husband got home, and whether or not they had sex). Shizuko expresses her worry that Shundei has taken a page out of one of his stories and is spying on her from above the ceiling. When he examines the attic, Samugawa does in fact find telltale disturbances in the dust as well as a loose button. Shundei seems to be lurking, just as he claimed. Any doubts Samugawa still has about this disappear when Shizuko reports glimpsing the face of a man on the ledge outside her second-story bedroom window. Two days later, Oyamada turns up dead, his apparently knifed body afloat in the Sumida River beneath the ferry docks near Azuma Bridge. The police begin a manhunt for Shundei.

Meanwhile, Samugawa has gotten to know the taxi driver that customarily answers calls from Shizuko's house. He notices that the driver wears a pair of gloves with a missing button and that the remaining buttons match the one he found above Shizuko's ceiling. When the driver says he was given the gloves by Mr. Oyamada, Samugawa begins to form a theory. He has already deduced that Oyamada had sadistic tendencies; nothing else could explain the way Shizuko blushed when he asked her about a riding crop he found in the couple's bedroom or the lash marks he has noticed at the nape of Shizuko's neck. When Oyamada was found dead, he was wearing a toupee to cover his baldness, though Shizuko claims she never knew him to wear one. Samugawa realizes that if the sadistic Oyamada had known about Shizuko's past, he might have taken a perverted pleasure in impersonating Shundei. He could have sent the threatening letters to her. He could have spied on her from the attic. He could have shown himself from the window ledge, wearing the toupee as a disguise. And, what is more, Samugawa realizes, Oyamada could also have slipped and fallen from that ledge, impaling himself on the glass shards in the high wall below and creating wounds that had seemed to be inflicted by a knife. His body could then have slipped into the river and been carried by the current to the ferry terminal below the bridge.

The apparent knifing by Shundei thus seems to have been nothing but an accident that Oyamada richly deserved. With the case apparently solved, the search for Shundei is dropped. Samugawa now begins a love affair with Shizuko. But one day, to his surprise, he learns from the taxi driver that Oyamada had given him the gloves with the missing button as long ago as the previous year, at the end of November. This is a surprise because he remembers Shizuko mentioning that the attic where he discovered the button was cleaned with absolute thoroughness at the end of December. He now realizes that the button could not have simply fallen off Oyamada's glove while Oyamada was in the attic. Something else must have happened to it between the time it came off the glove and Samugawa's own discovery of it in March. He suspects the button was deliberately planted for him to find, and he suspects Shizuko herself of planting it.

In the climactic scene of the novel, Samugawa confronts Shizuko with a new theory of the case: that she herself is Shundei, that she wrote both the books published under his name and the threatening letters she pretended to receive, and that she murdered her sadistic husband by pushing him from the window ledge during some sex game involving the toupee. As Samugawa outlines this theory of impersonation for Shizuko, she tries to distract him from his reasoning by whispering in his ear, snuggling up to him, and finally stripping herself naked:

> Before I could finish speaking, Shizuko brought out the foreign-made riding crop from the corner of the room. No sooner had she made me grasp it than she took off her kimono without warning and got on all fours on the bed. From beneath her smooth-skinned arm, she turned her face toward me. "What does it matter? What does it matter?" she said, repeating herself like she had gone mad. "Come on, whip me! Whip me!" she yelled, undulating her upper body like a wave.[41]

But the farther Shizuko carries this attempt to seduce him, the more confident Samugawa becomes that she is doing so because his reasoning is correct. Carried away by his anger at her deception, he lashes at her repeatedly with the riding crop she has placed in his hand. Shizuko responds to Samugawa's accusations by collapsing in tears, and Samugawa walks out on her, unable to continue a liaison with the woman he has revealed as a murderer.

But it is not long before Samugawa is stricken with remorse. He reads in the paper the next morning that Shizuko's dead body has turned up in the river in the same place her husband's did and with the same wounds. He assumes that Shizuko has committed suicide and done so by jumping from the same window that he accused her of pushing her husband from. He at first interprets her suicide as an admission of guilt. But then he finds himself plagued by doubts:

> I had not heard even a single word of confession directly from Shizuko. Even though various pieces of evidence had come together, their interpretation was, every bit of it, my own imagining. It could not be a scientific and immovable certainty like two plus two equals four. In putting together the plausible-seeming series of inferences that I made from the testimony of the taxi driver and the cleaning crew, hadn't I been able to interpret various pieces of evidence in ways virtually opposite [from the way I had first interpreted them]? How could I say with certainty that the same thing could not happen again, leading to still other conclusions?[42]

He decides that Shizuko's suicide is not in itself a confession of guilt. She may well have killed herself in despair at being doubted by her only confidant. He reconsiders the possibility that Shundei actually does exist and that he has murdered both Shizuko and her husband after all. He makes inquiries in the town where Shizuko told him Hirata Ichirō, a.k.a. Shundei, was from.

He half hopes he will be told that there is no such person there, but in fact there is a Hirata Ichirō in the town register, and no one knows where he has gone. But then again, Samugawa thinks, this proves nothing. Shizuko could easily have used the name of an old acquaintance in crafting her story. The narrative ends on this note of irresolution: "Now six months have already passed since Shizuko's tragic death. Hirata Ichirō still has not materialized. My awful irrepressible doubts only deepen with each passing day."[43]

The mystery in *Shadowy Beast* is structured to make the reader repeatedly confront the question of Shundei's identity. This question, in turn, is explicitly connected to a question of authorship—the question of who wrote the threatening letters and who wrote the morbid detective stories published under Shundei's name. Each possible explanation of Oyamada's death offers a different scenario. We are first led to think that Shundei is the pen name of Shizuko's jilted lover, that he is the author of both the letters and the stories, and that he is responsible for Oyamada's death. Then we are led to think that the threatening letters were written by Oyamada impersonating Shundei and that his death was an accident. Next we are led to think that there is no such person as Shundei at all and that Shizuko herself has impersonated him and his wife (who often acted as "Shundei's" intermediary in his dealings with publishers), writing both the stories and the letters. In this scenario Shizuko has murdered Oyamada. Finally, in the novel's closing pages, we are led to reconsider the possibility that the very first scenario is the correct one after all.

The novel's working through of these possibilities is further complicated by its overt self-referentiality. In a maneuver reminiscent of the references to Eric Bentley's novel *Trent's Last Case* in *The Pomegranate*, Ranpo incorporates into *Shadowy Beast* numerous allusions to other detective stories, with the difference that in this case they are allusions to other stories written by Ranpo himself. Every story that Shundei is supposed to have written has a title that recalls the title of one of Ranpo's own previously published works. When, for example, Shizuko expresses fear that Shundei has taken a page from one of his own works and is spying from above the ceiling, the work in question is specified as "Yaneura no yūgi" (Attic Entertainments). This title is an allusion to Ranpo's own "Yaneura no sanposha" (The Attic Walker, 1925), in which a crazed cross-dresser spies from above the ceiling on the fellow boarders in his boardinghouse.[44] Five other stories by Shundei are mentioned in the novel by name; their titles all similarly allude to stories by Ranpo. "Ichimai no kitte" (A Single Stamp), mentioned in connection with the forging of handwritten notes, recalls the name and the plot of Ranpo's "Ichimai no kippu," or "A Single Ticket" (1923). "B-zaka no satsujin jiken" (The Case of the Murder at B. Hill), mentioned as having "suggested that the wounds on Shizuko's back were those of a masochist," is an allusion to Ranpo's "D-zaka no satsujin jiken" ("The Case of the Murder at D. Hill," 1925), which also hinges on the revelation of a sadomasochistic relationship. The title of Shundei's *Panorama-guni* (Panorama Land) alludes to Ranpo's *Panorama-tō kidan* (The Strange Tale of Panorama Island, 1926), a novella about a man inspired by Poe's story "The Domain of Arnheim" to build an artificial island utopia. Shundei is also credited with a story called "Hitori futayaku," or "One Person, Two Roles," which has allegedly given Shizuko the idea of impersonating Shundei; this title duplicates that of a 1925 story by Ranpo about a man who leads a double life. Last, the novel refers to a story by Shundei called "Issen dōka," or "The One-Sen Copper Coin," as a source of insight into the techniques of disguise Shizuko used to impersonate Shundei's wife. This title recalls Ranpo's "Nisen dōka," or "The Two-Sen Copper Coin," published in 1923.

These repeated allusions as well as the ironically self-deprecating descriptions of Shundei as "notoriously morbid" and "sick" make Shundei into more than the perpetually elusive object of the novel's investigations: they set him up as a surrogate within the text for Ranpo's own authorial identity. The central mystery of the novel, then—whether Shundei has an independent existence of his own or is merely a phantasm created through impersonation—can be read as posing the same question about Ranpo's own identity as a writer. It perhaps poses this question in a spirit of playfulness, and indeed the deliberate ontological confusion created by the text tends to confirm this possibility. Even as Shundei is set up as a stand-in for Ranpo, it is Ranpo's own extratextual works that are implicitly granted the position of priority here, as the works replicated by Shundei rather than as the replications.[45] (And Samugawa's name bears a notable resemblance to Edogawa's own so that—given Samugawa's profession as a detective writer—he too potentially becomes yet another stand-in.) But playfully intended or not, this concern with imitative impersonation is persistent enough in the text and in Ranpo's oeuvre to be taken seriously as a defining feature of both.

In *Shadowy Beast* the basic question, posed this time through Shizuko's possible impersonation of Shundei, remains essentially the same as in so many of his other works, namely, whether Ranpo can claim an independent authorship of his own or whether his work is merely derivative of things previously published. The question itself, as is typical in Ranpo, becomes framed in starkly binary terms. The structure of logical possibilities offered by the narrative does not seem to allow recognition of an essential derivativeness in all writings in the detective genre (whether Japanese or not) that does not simultaneously cause a crisis of identity for the individual authors who work in that genre. Either Shundei exists in his own right, and he is the author of the writings attributed to him, or he has no existence of his own and is nothing more than an artifact of the writings penned by Shizuko. By the end of the novel, the intermediate possibility—that Shundei both exists and has also been impersonated (by Oyamada)—is no longer alive, thanks to the irreconcilable discrepancy concerning the button found in the attic.

The irresolution of the novel's end probably reflected, at least in part, a modernist's sense of the basic flimsiness of outmoded epistemological certitudes. But it also seems significant that the novel's irresolution should hinge on precisely the question of whether there is a Shundei who exists in his own right or whether his works are the result of Shizuko's impersonation. The detective himself, believing he has revealed Shizuko as a guilty impersonator, falls back at the novel's end on the lingering hope that she might have been telling the truth after all and that there really is a Shundei. This would not only absolve Shizuko of having murdered her husband and deceived Samugawa. In the symbolic language that the novel seems to construct in order to carry out its displaced meditation on authorship and impersonation, this would also confer upon Ranpo's writing a more than merely phantasmal or parasitic status. But this possibility is not allowed to come to fruition since the novel's own stubborn lack of resolution casts it into doubt.[46]

In the course of arriving at this ending, *Shadowy Beast* develops a striking association between the body of Shizuko and what Roland Barthes has called the striptease of classic narrative—that is, a story's gradual, progressive revelation of its truths.[47] When Shizuko is first introduced, Samugawa notes her elegant femininity, but his interest in her is aroused most fiercely by the reddish lashes on the back of her neck, just visible above her kimono collar, which are described as "probably extending all the way down her back." This description poses the enigma of these marks' origin, setting in motion what turns out to be one of the novel's central story lines. It also offers the ostensibly titillating prospect of further narration—narration that might confirm how far down her back the marks extend, revealing more of Shizuko's body in the process. Indeed, as the story unfolds, Shizuko's body is subjected to a narrative gaze that becomes, by gradual degrees, increasingly far-reaching. When, for example, Samugawa goes above Shizuko's ceiling in order to test the theory that Shundei has been spying on Shizuko from that position, the description of his view directs upon Shizuko a penetrative visual attention that both underlines the power of her body to arouse raw sexual desire and hints at still further revelations to come:

> The wondrousness of the scene made by the world below, seen from
> the opening in the ceiling planks, surpassed anything I had imagined.

Especially when I looked at Shizuko…I felt surprise at how different a person could look depending on the angle of view.…In Shizuko's shiny hairdo, in the hollow between the hair at the front and her chignon, there had accumulated a layer of dust, very thin to be sure, but dirty beyond compare next to the other, clean parts of her hair. Beyond her chignon—since I was looking from directly above at the valley formed by the collar of her kimono at her back—I could see all the way to the hollow between her shoulder blades. Those cruel welts continued painfully over the surface of her pale white skin even down into the darkness beyond where I could see. Observed from above, Shizuko seemed to have lost some of her elegance, but in its place I felt the force of her marvelous eroticism attack me with an even greater intensity.[48]

When, in the climactic final scene, Shizuko strips off her clothes at the same time that Samugawa announces his solution to the mystery, the novel forges an unmistakable link between Shizuko's body, which is presented as a gratifier of the scopophilic urge to see, and the form of the detective narrative, as a gratifier of the epistemophilic urge to know. The final complete unveiling of Shizuko's body, of the signifying marks on her back, and of those marks' origin in Shizuko's now openly enacted masochistic desire becomes for Samugawa in this scene the ultimate verification of the solution to the mystery that he has announced, which is no less revelatory in its naming of Shizuko as the murderer of her sadistic husband. His further marking of Shizuko with the punishing lashes of the riding crop reinforces that identity, inscribing it directly on her body.

The marking of the storytelling body in this scene is all the more significant because of the text's association of these marks with distinctly Western cultural influences. As we have seen, the novel grants the erotic desires of its protagonists a central place both in the crimes it portrays and in the solution, or attempted solution, of them. It is therefore striking that the novel should trace its characters' sadomasochistic impulses back to a West that is imagined as a perverting influence on Japanese sexuality. This West's influence is most powerfully concentrated in the riding crop, which in the course of the novel comes to take on an almost talismanic significance. The crop, on the half dozen occasions it is mentioned, is only once referred to as simply "the riding crop." Otherwise it is always "the foreign-made riding crop" *(gaikoku-sei jōba muchi)*. Both the riding crop and its associated sadism have, it turns out, been brought back by Mr. Oyamada from Europe. "About four years previously," the narrator tells us, "Mr. Oyamada Rokurō had traveled to Europe on business, spending two years mainly in London but also in two or three other cities. His vice had no doubt budded and blossomed in one of those cities."[49]

The transformation that Oyamada's sexual appetites undergo in Europe is sufficiently radical to bring about changes in the couple's Japanese house. They now require greater privacy from the prying gaze of the neighbors, and the property becomes an eyesore: "Making an ill match for the villa-like appearance [of the house] were the horribly vulgar, apparently newly built, concrete wall surrounding the compound (complete with shards of glass embedded along the top to ward off intruders) and the two-story Western addition that towered above the main house. Both were completely out of harmony with the old Japanese architecture and stank of the uncouth taste of the rich."[50]

Shizuko herself is similarly transformed in the course of the novel. She is aligned with the East at the book's opening. Samugawa first sees her in the Ueno Imperial Museum. He is standing before a glass showcase, studying an ancient image of a bodhisattva. Shizuko appears behind him, her reflection in the glass doubling and matching the contours of the wooden statue. But by the book's end she has been transformed into the shadowy beast of the novel's title, a woman of flesh and blood and appetites, a being who could not be farther removed from the bodhisattva. She assents to Samugawa's plan to rent the upstairs of a small warehouse and convert it to a special apartment for secret assignations. They furnish this apartment with Western items of Shizuko's choosing: "On the second floor of the warehouse we installed carpeting, a bed *(beddo)*, a sofa, and the like, besides lining up rows of several giant mirrors, all to decorate as effectively as possible the setting for our entertainments. Shizuko bought, in spite of my protests, preposterously expensive matching furniture."[51] And when Shizuko, kneeling on the bed, begs to be whipped with the foreign riding crop, we are directed to understand that her own erotic desires have been reshaped by Oyamada's: "long [exposure] to Oyamada's sadism had finally infected her too with the perversion, until she was tormented by irrepressible masochistic passions."[52]

Even the narrator is in danger of contagion by this foreign predilection. When Shizuko first asks him to use the riding crop on her, he feels, to his surprise, a "peculiar thrill" *(fukashigina yuetsu)* at the sight of the welts he raises. He confesses, "If my trysts with her had continued in that manner for half a year, I surely would have fallen victim to the same disease *(yamai)* Mr. Oyamada had."[53]

The novel thus enacts, through its manipulation of Shizuko's body, the situation of its own, conflicted position in the field of Western cultural influences. The narrative centers itself on the revelation and contemplation of a body that, thanks to the marks inscribed on it, not only instigates the story given voice by the narrator, but also inspires, in the climactic scene, further inscription and accompanying narration. This pattern continues even after Shizuko's death, when her corpse surfaces at the ferry terminal bearing wounds that Samugawa traces back to the glass shards in Oyamada's wall. The fundamental condition for the narrative's existence—its sine qua non—is the marking of the narrated body at its center with what the novel persistently figures as foreign cultural influences, whether in the form of the foreign-made riding crop or the glass shards spiking out of the unneighborly and tasteless wall surrounding Oyamada's house. The novel thus embodies—in every sense of the word—its own subjection to the Western influence of the detective form from which it derives its basic narrative impetus. The novel, moreover, shows unmistakable signs of ambivalence about these signs of influence that it bears. This ambivalence is legible in the novel's representation of that influence—of the story-instigating marks on Shizuko's body—as the manifestations of a perverted, sadomasochistic relationship. Having been brought back from Europe by Mr. Oyamada, this sadomasochism threatens to spread from one character to the next like an infection, altering the spaces they inhabit and ultimately rendering lethal their most intimate encounters with one another. These signs of ambivalence are also legible, as we have seen, in the novel's meditation, through its handling of the elusive character of Shundei, on its own potentially phantasmal and derivative status. Taken together, these signs of deep ambivalence toward Western cultural influence—and more specifically toward that influence's enablement of the narrative and its underwriting of Ranpo's own identity as an author—reaffirm and amplify the ambivalence present in "The Human Chair," "The Red Room," and *The Dwarf.*

Hybridizing the Locked Room Mystery with the Japanese Cultural Milieu

The conficts inherent in Ranpo's struggle to establish his credentials in the genre of detective fiction are perhaps most apparent of all in his locked-room mysteries, which also show the persistence of his fascination with the marked, storytelling body that is so central to *Shadowy Beast.* Since its origin in Poe's "Murders in the Rue Morgue," the locked-room mystery (in which a corpse is found in a room that apparently affords no ingress or egress) has had an iconic status in the Western tradition of detective fiction. Under the logic of Ranpo's self-positioning in the shadow of his Western models, it became a virtual requirement that he should write locked-room mysteries of his own. But this forced him into what he saw as a difficult position, given the scarcity of securely locking rooms in traditional Japanese architecture. Ranpo seems to have devoted considerable effort to solving this problem, and the effort involved him in some of his most conspicuously Westward-looking experimentation. His devotion to solving this self-imposed problem suggests how thoroughly caught he was in the idea that his worth as a writer would hinge upon how he fared in comparison to his Western progenitors, even though he was working in a genre whose rules they had written only to please themselves.

Ranpo in fact contrived two different Japanese locked-room mysteries, in two different works, "The Case of the Murder at D. Hill" and *The Demon of the Desert Isle*. Both works conspicuously hybridize what they construe as an originally Western genre with a distinctively Japanese cultural milieu in which traditional architecture plays a crucial role. *The Demon of the Desert Isle*, in particular, devotes a great deal of its narrative energy to the theme of hybridization (both bodily and cultural) and to fending off its potentially monstrous consequences.

The setting that Ranpo chooses for "The Case of the Murder at D. Hill" is Dango-zaka, the steep hill in the Sendagi district of Tokyo famous since about the 1860s for the chrysanthemum doll festival held there. (The locale is the same as that of Okamoto Kidō's "In the Days of the Chrysanthemum Dolls," the story in which the angry mob stones the group of foreigners.) More specifically, he uses as the scene of the crime in the story a *nagaya*, a type of long, narrow building that had been in use since the late Edo period. Fronting the street with its long dimension, a *nagaya* houses under one roof a number of rented shops and dwellings, each with a separate entrance.

As Ranpo conceives his setting, the close living conditions of the *nagaya* and its surrounding neighborhood result in a constant, if unintentional, mutual surveillance by its inhabitants. The narrator, for example, reports overhearing the waitress at the coffee shop across from the *nagaya* gossiping about one of its residents—the wife of the bookshop owner—after having seen her at the local bath. "The bookseller's wife is such a beauty," the waitress remarks to her coworker, "but when she takes her clothes off she has cuts all over her body—they've got to be marks from being hit and scratched. It's odd, since she's not on especially bad terms with her husband." The urgency of decoding these marks is heightened when the narrator and the amateur detective Akechi Kogorō (who makes his debut in this story) discover the strangled corpse of this same bookseller's wife behind the *nagaya*'s bookshop.

They call the police, who begin their inquiry by questioning the owners of the shops in and around the *nagaya*. They prove to know one another's habits well. When asked about the whereabouts of the victim's husband, the owner of the neighboring clock shop says, "He goes out every evening and sets up a street stall [to sell books]. He always comes home sometime after midnight."[54] This clock shop owner and the *tabi* maker on the bookshop's opposite side both testify on further questioning that they have heard no unusual sounds. This might seem at first to indicate a breakdown in the regime of neighborly surveillance that Ranpo is establishing for the story. In fact, in a nod to the Sherlock Holmes story "Silver Blaze" (in which Holmes deduces that a crime was an inside job because no one heard a dog on the premises bark in the night, though it would have had the culprit been a stranger), the absence of sounds proves to be an important clue in its own right. As we learn when Akechi explains his solution at the story's end, the victim did not fight or scream because she and the killer were illicit lovers, her death an accident of sadomasochistic sex gone too far. "Almost," Akechi observes, "a murder by consent."[55] Although the sadomasochism in this mystery is crucial to its solution, and although it is linked, in passing, to Western culture (the woman's lover is said to have "drunk from the stream of the Marquis de Sade"), the connection is not made as insistently as the one in *Shadowy Beast*. Instead "The Case of the Murder at D. Hill" makes its most conspicuous gestures toward Western precedent in its handling of the neighbors' mutual surveillance, which becomes in the story a means of effectively sealing off the entrances and exits to the *nagaya*.

Further testimony reveals that no one was seen entering or leaving the bookshop around the time of the murder. The front entrance to the shop was watched by the narrator, who was at a table by the front window of the café just across the street. At the back of the *nagaya* is a fence with gates opening into an alley. But this alley has only one exit, and that too turns out to have been watched, by a man selling ice cream nearby. "After it got dark," he says, "not so much as a cat went by me. . . . All of my customers ate their ice cream where I could see them and then left right away in the direction they had come from."[56]

The only other means of entrance to the *nagaya* are the upstairs windows. But their use is also ruled out by the presence of still other watchers who were taking the air out on the clothes-drying platforms. Questioning of the sweet-shop owner reveals that he was up on the rooftop playing his bamboo flute and that he was "positioned so as not to miss anything going on at the second-floor window of the bookshop."[57] The testimony of these watchers thus allows an important deduction. "If the statements of the ice-cream man [and the others] are to be believed," Akechi says, "the criminal is either still hiding somewhere inside the *nagaya* . . . or he is one of the tenants. Those are the only alternatives."[58] With the search thus narrowed, Akechi is eventually able to identify as the culprit the owner of the noodle shop in the same *nagaya* where the victim lived. Taking advantage of his own wife's absence, he went out his back gate into the alley. From there, he used the bookshop's alley gate and back door to get back inside the *nagaya* for his tryst. After accidentally killing his neighbor's wife, he returned the way he had come. Since he never left the alley, the ice-cream man on the corner at its open end never saw him.

"The Case of the Murder at D. Hill," then, is a story based on the locked-room mysteries of Poe and Conan Doyle with the curious twist that there is not actually a locked room anywhere in it. It is the casual watchfulness of the people in and around the *nagaya* that takes the place of the fastened windows in Poe's "Murders in the Rue Morgue" and the stone chamber in Conan Doyle's "Speckled Band." Although sealing off the building requires a large cast of watchers, they are plausible enough given the realities of life in an urban *nagaya*.

The story, however, shows signs of concern that doing away with the locked room might invalidate its membership in the Western tradition of locked-room mysteries. Apparently as a precaution against this, the narrator, after reporting the testimony of the rooftop flute player (whose presence seals off the last possible way into the building), interrupts the story to mention Poe and Conan Doyle by name. "Dear readers," he says, "you are probably reminded by this story of Poe's 'Murders in the Rue Morgue' or Doyle's 'Speckled Band.' You may be thinking that the criminal in this case is not a human but a poisonous snake from India or an orangutan. As a matter of fact that occurred to me too. But it is unthinkable that such animals would be found in Tokyo around D. Hill."[59] This suggestion that the reader is "probably reminded" by the story of Poe and Conan Doyle leaves little doubt about the text's bid to position itself in the tradition of these literary fathers. Indeed, Ranpo puts yet a further interjection into the mouth of his narrator, to the same effect: "It is often said," the narrator observes, "that with Japanese architecture, the sort of intricate crimes that there are in foreign detective stories do not occur, but I don't think that's true at all, because there are in fact cases just like this one."[60] The story grafts the locked-room mystery onto its Japanese cultural milieu with admirable ingenuity, but these comparisons, by so conspicuously identifying Western precedents as the measuring standards for the genre, implicitly underline what the story in effect constructs as its own secondary and derivative status.

Ranpo revisited the problem of conjoining the locked-room mystery and the Japanese milieu in *The Demon of the Desert Isle*. *The Demon of the Desert Isle*, however, devotes considerably more energy than "The Case of the Murder at D. Hill" to exploring the problems of hybridization suggested by this conjoinment. Initially it presents hybridization as a problem of narrative genre, by foregrounding the difficulty of identifying the genre to which the novel itself belongs. The problem later resurfaces when the novel unveils the solution to its locked-room puzzle. And by the novel's end, the problem of hybridization has been reconfigured in bodily terms through the novel's handling of a pair of Siamese twins and an abortive homosexual union between two of its characters. At each of these junctures the novel shows distinct signs of uneasiness with its own narrative and cultural hybridity.

The Demon of the Desert Isle—which certainly numbers among the most deliberately, bizarrely outré of Ranpo's works—shows signs of discomfort with its own hybrid quality as a narrative from its earliest pages. In these pages, the narrator, an ordinary accountant named Minoura, explains that his motive for writing the book is to explain why he, not yet thirty, has a head of white hair and why his wife has a huge irregular scar on her hip of "exactly the sort that would be left behind if another leg had been growing there but had been cut off."[61] In the course of identifying these bodily markings as the instigators of his story, the narrator shows himself to be at something of a loss about how to categorize the story itself. In the space of only two short paragraphs, he refers to his account with five different labels, including *koi monogatari* (love story), *tantei shōsetsu* (detective story), *kaiki shōsetsu* (thriller), *kaii-dan* (story of the grotesque), and *keiken-dan* (story of personal experience). His description of the account further emphasizes the ramshackle quality of its structure and its resulting generic ambiguity:

> Although this tale resembles what are called detective stories or thrillers, the thing that makes it extraordinarily peculiar is that before the main story line gets under way, the main character (or rather the secondary main character), my girlfriend Kizaki Hatsuyo, is killed, as is one other person, Miyamagi Kōkichi, an amateur detective whom I admire and whom I asked to solve Hatsuyo's strange murder. Moreover, the grotesque tale that I have to tell merely takes these two strange deaths as its point of departure, and the main story is a story of my personal experience, which has to do with a large-scale evil and a heretofore unimagined scheme that is much, much more deserving of your astonishment and your shivers.[62]

The story is in fact all of the things suggested by these different generic labels, a congeries of different discourses melded together into a hybrid whole.[63] The narrator begins by describing his love affair with and engagement to Hatsuyo; he then describes Hatsuyo's murder (it is here that the locked-room mystery figures) and the detective work that leads to its solution. But the identification of the murderer, who turns out to be a ten-year-old child contortionist, and his means of ingress and egress still leaves the motive for the murder unclear, and the child is himself murdered before he can be made to explain.

At this point the narrative begins to metamorphose into something like a combination of an adventure tale and a piece of science fiction. The narrator's attempt to determine the motive behind his girlfriend's murder leads him to the desert isle of the novel's title, which is presided over by Takegorō, a hunchbacked, Dr. Moreau–like man with a diabolical scheme to "rid Japan of every last one of its healthy people and overrun it with freaks."[64] Takegorō is manufacturing these freaks on his island by altering the bodies of abducted children. His methods include confining the children in tight-fitting boxes to stunt their growth and surgically grafting onto them foreign body parts, including animal fur. The narrator and his companion Moroto eventually deduce that a treasure belonging to Hatsuyo's family is buried on the island and that Takegorō masterminded her murder in order to get a treasure map she possessed. Hoping to beat the hunchback to the discovery of the treasure, the narrator descends together with his companion into a system of catacombs beneath the island. There the two become lost, wandering for days in constant fear of being drowned in an underground cave by the incoming tide. Eventually finding the treasure and an exit from the catacombs, the two are able to thwart Takegorō and to free the freakish children that he has so far manufactured. Included among these children are an adolescent pair of opposite-sex Siamese twins who have been surgically attached at the hip. One of these twins proves to have been Hatsuyo's sister and heir to the buried treasure. At the novel's close, the narrator arranges for her to undergo further surgery to free her from her twin before marrying her and her newfound fortune. Taken as a whole the text thus "augments," as Jim Reichert has noted, "a...murder mystery with a plethora of seemingly incompatible generic formulas, topics, and images."[65]

The murder mystery itself is noteworthy for its own hybridizing of the locked-room convention with the novel's Japanese setting. In staging Hatsuyo's murder, Ranpo, as he had in "The Case of the Murder at D. Hill," foregrounds the effort required to fashion a locked-room mystery out of what he considered the less-than-promising materials afforded by traditional Japanese architecture. The episode begins when Hatsuyo is found dead, stabbed in the heart with a knife while she slept in her own house. Her house is a traditional, one-story, four-room place with sliding wooden rain shutters and latticework doors. The narrator provides an inventory of the possible entrances and exits, and rules them out one by one:

> The house had three places normally used as entrances. The first was the lattice door at the front, the second was the double paper doors at the kitchen entrance, and the third was the veranda outside Hatsuyo's

room. Otherwise it was just walls and sturdily latticed windows. The night before, all of these entrances had been carefully latched. The doors leading onto the veranda were [of the type] fitted with pegs so they could not be pried from their grooves [from the outside].[66]

The narrator also rules out the kitchen skylight (tied shut with a string from the inside), the space under the veranda (fitted with a wire grate to keep out cats and dogs that shows no signs of tampering), and even the toilet shaft (too tight a fit). Having convinced the reader that the victim's room was completely sealed off, Ranpo pauses to remark, through the mouth of his narrator, on the success with which he has managed this. The interjection is once again conspicuous for its mention of Western models:

> In Poe's "Murders in the Rue Morgue" and [Gaston] Leroux's *Mystère de la chambre jaune,* and the like, I have read of similar cases. All of them are cases of murder in rooms sealed from the inside. But I believed that sort of thing could not happen without architecture of the foreign type, that it could not happen with the delicate boards and paper of the Japanese style. I now realized, however, that this was not entirely true. Even if the boards are delicate, evidence will remain if they are broken or removed. So from the point of view of the detective, there is not the slightest difference between a narrow wooden slat and a concrete wall one foot thick.[67]

This is a thoroughly convincing conclusion. That it should find its way into the text in such explicit and triumphant terms, however, demonstrates how seriously Ranpo took the problem of inserting himself into the foreign tradition of detective writers.

Later, when Miura's companion Moroto solves the mystery of Hatsuyo's death, one cannot help feeling again that Ranpo is making self-conscious international comparisons. Before announcing the solution, Moroto observes that it has been hidden in plain sight all along. "Among Edgar Poe's stories there is one called 'The Purloined Letter'—have you read it?" he asks the narrator. "…In Hatsuyo's case, too, once I state [the solution], you'll ask how you could have overlooked something so simple."[68] With this statement, the narrative both admits the possibility that the solution will be something of a letdown and also latches onto Poe's precedent as a validation of the solution's simplicity. Moroto explains that the killer gained entry into Hatsuyo's house from the attached shop next door. Descending through the waste hatch in the floor of the kitchen, he then crawled to the under-floor space beneath Hatsuyo's own kitchen, where he came up through the waste hatch there. "[When two dwellings] share a single roof, it is customary in Japanese architecture for the two to share one attic and one under-floor crawl space," Moroto notes.[69] The solution thus foregrounds the narrative's own hybridizing of the locked-room mystery with its Japanese setting, in effect turning the peculiar features of Japanese architecture—the very thing that posed such a problem in the first place—into the key to the mystery.

Unfortunately the solution is marred by the clunky subterfuge that has been used to carry it off: we have been previously told that Hatsuyo's house and the shop next door both stand out in their neighborhood of two-story buildings, since they are only one story high, but we have not been told that they actually share a single roof.[70] Indeed, the narrative itself shows some discomfort with this subterfuge in Moroto's next remark: "It is odd, isn't it?" he says. "We Japanese are very heedless—so conscientious about shutting up at the front and back of the house but then leaving the attic and the way beneath the floorboards wide open."[71] Ranpo seems to use this remark of Moroto's to pass off his own calculated neglect to mention the structural connection between the neighboring buildings as an oversight in the Japanese conception of home security rather than a gap in the narrative itself. Because the text resorts to the language of Japanese national identity ("we Japanese are very heedless") at the very moment this subterfuge is being papered over, it subtly associates its own clunkiness of execution and the Japanese identity of its author.

The discomfort apparent here with this only partially successful cultural hybridization looms larger when it is read alongside the examples of bodily hybridization that Ranpo concocts in this novel, hybridizations that he persistently represents as monstrosities. There are two main examples of monstrous hybridization in the narrative, both of which also become, through their connection to the enigma of the bodily markers that launch the tale (the narrator's white hair and the scar on his wife's hip) additional figures for the narrative's own uneasy hybridizing of genres and cultures.

The first of these instances of hybridization is that of the artificially conglomerated "Siamese twins," Shū-chan (the beautiful young woman who becomes the narrator's wife) and Kit-chan (a perpetually unkempt, foul-mouthed boy given to frequent masturbation). The body of these twins itself tells the story of their origin because, as Moroto (who is trained as a doctor) observes, it is impossible for naturally born Siamese twins to be of the opposite sex, since they must grow from the union of a single egg and sperm. The pair are thus the very embodiment of monstrous hybridization, of the unnatural stitching together of opposites at odds with one another.

The striking thing about Ranpo's narrative is how very far it goes to undo and correct this embodiment of hybridization at its center. The narrative's overcompensation in this area suggests that it is unable to countenance any sort of deviation from the "normal," an intolerance that places the narrative itself in crisis, given its own rampant literary hybridizing. Not only does Moroto, the doctor, perform surgery to separate Shū-chan and Kit-chan, leaving the huge, enigmatic scar on Shū-chan's hip. The text performs still further normalizations on the body of Shū-chan: "I can't tell you," Minoura says, "how overjoyed I was when she appeared before me with her incision healed, her hair properly done, her face made up, wearing a beautiful crepe kimono and speaking to me in the Tokyo dialect."[72] That the narrative should carry its rehabilitation of Shū-chan so far as to have her learn the Tokyo dialect seemingly overnight (she has lived her whole life on the hunchback's island) threatens to render absurd the text's policing of the boundary between the "normal" and the "abnormal," as Reichert notes. But to read this overcompensation as nothing more than a gesture at the absurd would be reductive. It seems more fruitful, while acknowledging the basic absurdity of Shū-chan's transformation, to read it as a significant component of the text's fundamental unease with hybridization, which it goes to considerable lengths first to equate with monstrosity and then to vanquish with such ostensibly iconic signs of Japanese cultural identity as the kimono and the Tokyo dialect, firmly established by the time of the novel's publication as *hyōjungo,* or "standard language." This impulse to vanquish and normalize deviance and monstrosity is equally clear in the use to which Shū-chan's fortune is to be put. With their newfound wealth, the couple endow a special house for the physically deformed as well as a clinic devoted to plastic and reconstructive surgery, "with the goal of sparing no effort to exhaust the surgical possibilities for remaking the deformed into normal human beings."[73]

The second main example of monstrous hybridization in the novel provides the solution to the enigma of the narrator's prematurely white hair. The narrator mentions at the beginning of the tale that he knows of cases in which people subjected to episodes of great fright—such as going over Niagara Falls in a barrel or being buried alive—have had their hair turn white more or less instantaneously. His own hair, we learn, turned white sometime during the days he and Moroto spent in the catacombs beneath the desert isle, in constant fear of being trapped there and drowned. His explanation for the dramatic loss of pigment in his hair, however, hints that it was not fear of death alone that turned his hair white: "I had been threatened repeatedly by the horror of death," he says, "and with horrors still greater."[74]

What were these "horrors still greater" than that of death? Apart from the danger of entrapment in a cave below the high tide level, there is only one other thing that the narrator has faced underground: the unwelcome homosexual advances of his companion Moroto.

Exhausted, hopelessly lost in the catacombs, and in despair of ever emerging alive, the two men have ample time to lie in the dark and talk. There Moroto pleads with the narrator to accept his long-standing love, pointing out that they are now completely free of the morals, customs, and shame of the world above. Minoura, however, feels an "indescribable revulsion" at Moroto's plea. Moroto's subsequent advances are terrifyingly bestial and predatory: "When I noticed what was happening," the narrator says, "the snake was already quite close to me. . . . I slipped and fell on the rocks. The snake came crawling slimily over my body. I asked myself whether this could be Moroto. It was no longer human; it was, rather, a disgusting animal. . . . A fiery cheek came to rest on my own, which was perspiring with horror. [I was aware of] a rough panting like that of a dog, an odd body odor, and a hot slimy membrane seeking out my lips, crawling all over my face like a leech."[75] Moroto's advance is ultimately interrupted, but this scene gestures at a same-sex conglomeration of bodies that the text presents as a thing no less horrifying than the opposite-sex union of Shū-chan with her artificial Siamese twin. Minoura's description of the fear he feels as Moroto preys on him—"a fear still more awful and more indescribable than the fear of death"—leaves no question that the narrator's subjection to these advances is meant to be the height of spine-tingling deviance and horror, and that they are the very things, previously alluded to as still more horrible than death, that have caused the narrator's hair to turn white.[76]

This potential hybridization of the two male bodies—one homosexual and one heterosexual—is no less energetically forestalled and corrected by the narrative at its end than the surgical grafting together of Shū-chan and Kit-chan. Not only does the narrative inaugurate Shū-chan as Minoura's sexual partner by the device of their marriage. Moroto is also summarily killed off by an unnamed disease. "This was the one regrettable thing," Minoura says, protesting too much, "in the midst of every other thing going as one would have hoped."[77]

The novel, then, foregrounds its own eccentric hybridization of multiple narrative discourses (most notably the murder mystery, the adventure tale, and science fiction) through its linking of the very bodily marks that generate the narrative to two conspicuously "unnatural" conglomerations: that of the Siamese twins, on the one hand, and that of the two main male characters, on the other. Fundamental to this hybridization of narrative discourses is a no less important cultural hybridization: that of the locked-room mystery into a Japanese setting, for it is the attempt to solve the mystery of Hatsuyo's death that provides the pretext for the adventure tale and its concomitant science-fiction-like elements.

At the same time, the novel carries out, at the thematic level, a grand meditation on the monstrosity of hybridization in general, which it takes almost absurd pains to render "normal." This overcompensatory bid for normalization can be read as a sign of the deep discomfort in the novel with its own mutation of the detective story, which it has accomplished by grafting it to other narrative discourses in its new Japanese context.

Essays in Self-Criticism *(Shinseinen)*

The Demon of the Desert Isle only obliquely expresses its discomfort with the results of the detective story's transplant to Japan, but more direct indications of that discomfort are to be found in the pages of the magazine *Shinseinen* (New Youth), which was published, beginning in 1920, by Hakubunkan.

Under the editorship of Morishita Uson, *Shinseinen* played a crucial role in Ranpo's development as a writer and in the more general development of Japanese detective fiction between World Wars I and II.[78] Within a few years of its launch, the magazine found a secure niche as a general-interest monthly targeted at young urbanites. It offered a wide variety of reading matter, ranging from essays on current events and coverage of sports, fashion, travel, and movies, to humorous sketches, cartoons, and light fiction. Almost from its beginning the magazine included detective fiction as a regular feature, and eventually the genre became central to the magazine's identity. There were times during the late 1920s and 1930s when, depending on who was overseeing the magazine's art, the cover of nearly every issue featured a splashy illustration of a bloody knife or a sprawling corpse or a pistol-wielding man wearing a monocle, or some variation on these motifs.

At first the detective fiction in the magazine consisted exclusively of translated works. The authors represented included Poe, Conan Doyle, Maurice Leblanc (creator of Arsène Lupin), Gaston Leroux, L. J. Beeston, G. K. Chesterton, Herman Landon, Wilkie Collins, Freeman Wills Crofts, and a host of lesser-knowns. But after 1923, when Ranpo published "The Two-Sen Copper Coin," about breaking an elaborate braille-based code in order to solve a robbery, the magazine made gradually increasing use of detective stories written by Japanese authors. By 1925 the magazine was running contests calling for submissions from readers, publishing essays by newly established authors on their own favorite detective writers, running articles explaining how to order detective fiction by mail from abroad, putting out thick supplementary issues devoted solely to detective fiction, and printing critical essays that sized up the detective stories recently published in the magazine. The list of Japanese writers who went on to notable careers after publishing detective stories in *Shinseinen* includes not only Edogawa Ranpo but Yokomizo Seishi, Yumeno Kyūsaku, Kōga Saburō, Unno Jūza, Hisao Jūran, Kigi Takatarō, and Oguri Mushitarō. These writers' appearances did not, however, crowd out the translations of foreign detective stories, which continued to command the bulk of the pages committed to the genre throughout the magazine's life span. Soon after World War II *Shinseinen* ceded its prominence to a newly launched competitor, *Hōseki* (Gem), but during its heyday between the wars, *Shinseinen* was the undisputed publication of record for detective fiction in Japan. "The history of this magazine is the history of the Japanese detective story," Ranpo wrote of *Shinseinen*. "If one were to compile an index for it, it would be a *Britannica* of the detective story."[79]

Despite the rapid growth in the output of Japanese detective stories in *Shinseinen* during the 1920s and early 1930s, and despite the commercial success the magazine enjoyed, the critical essays published there are full of hand-wringing over Japan's failure to produce a "master" detective writer or "good" stories. These essays show that the anxiety in Ranpo's detective stories was not limited to him alone and that it shaped a significantly broader narrative of Japanese achievement and failure in the genre as well.

Kozakai Fuboku (1890–1929), an early commentator on Japanese crime literature, set the tone for much of this criticism in 1922, in an installment from a history of crime literature he was then publishing as a serial in *Shinseinen:*

> This is the age of translation in the Japanese detective novel. Even supposedly original works are generally adaptations. Why does no master writer of detective stories appear in Japan? Japanese are known as an uncreative people. That is probably one reason. And another is probably the shallowness of our so-called scientific research. But beyond that, it is also probably because the state of Japanese people's life and society is too impoverished in content to make for a good detective novel. Detective novels need extreme—even sick—social conditions as a background.[80]

Kozakai's comments here anticipate all of the main lines of thought that would be pursued by critics of detective writing in *Shinseinen* during the next decade. He first poses the question (itself already assuming a Japanese lack) of why there is "no master writer" of detective stories in Japan. He then offers three answers: one is that the problem lies in the Japanese

mind, which he deems uncreative; the second is that Japan is not scientifically advanced enough; and the third is that the fault lies in the conditions
of Japanese social life. "Too impoverished in content" is a rather vague turn
of phrase, but taken together with the subsequent mention of insufficiently
"extreme" social conditions, it suggests a collective life in which economic
stratification is too attenuated and in which deviance and crime are too
rare or mild to offer suitable material for detective stories.

Kozakai's basic question ("why does no master writer of detective stories appear in Japan?") would be posed again and again in the pages of
Shinseinen. However one parses it, the question points to a Japanese sense
of self-dissatisfaction born of international comparison. If one rejects the
value judgment the question implies (because one believes that writers
such as Kuroiwa Ruikō, Okamoto Kidō, and Edogawa Ranpo are in fact
masters in their own right), then the question's very premise demonstrates
a self-defeating insistence on using the wrong standards of judgment, with
the result that the worth of Japanese achievement is overlooked or denied.
If instead one accepts the question's premise that Japan had no master
detective writers, one is still left wondering why it should matter so much
whether Japan has any master detective writers or not. The critical essays in
Shinseinen suggest that the supposed lack of good Japanese detective writers
mattered because it was a symptom of other, more obviously serious lacks in
national character and national achievement. In a sign of just how powerfully the discourse of inadequacy gripped the critics penning these essays,
even when Japan's lack of good detective writers pointed them to a positive
characteristic of Japanese life (such as a lack of crime), their analyses could
still threaten to twist those characteristics into faults.

After Kozakai's early essay, speculation about a mismatch between the
Japanese mind and the genre of detective fiction surfaced almost as often
in *Shinseinen* as the question of why there were no good Japanese detective
writers. This speculation usually somehow combined Kozakai's assertion
about lack of creativity with his assertion about Japan's lack of scientific
progress. Hirabayashi Hatsunosuke, the most penetrating and prolific critic
of Japanese detective fiction during this period, was typical in this regard,
although he seems to have been somewhat more optimistic than his contemporaries that good writers would emerge in due course. "The reason the
detective novel has hardly developed in Japan," he wrote in 1924, "is...that
the Japanese mind—especially the mind of the novelist—is antiscientific
(hikagakuteki) and lacking in the kind of knowledge required by outstanding
detective novels. Even so, in the near future I think two or three detective
novelists will emerge in Japan. Readers are already demanding it."[81]

In April 1925, three months after Ranpo published "The Case of the Murder at D. Hill," Katō Takeo (1888–1956) published an essay titled "The Works of Edogawa Ranpo," in which he continued the line taken earlier by Hirabayashi. "Why don't good detective novels appear in Japan?" he asked, taking up the usual refrain. "...The real reason is that the Japanese mind is not given to close reasoning *(nihonjin no atama ga ōzappa dakara de aru)*. [The Japanese] are not logical, and they are not scientific. They suffer from a poverty in their powers of plotting."[82] Katō went on to develop the notion of a fundamental gap between the sensibilities of Japanese literature and the detective novel. "The tendency in Japanese literature," he wrote, "is more toward contemplation than ratiocination and more toward feeling than contemplation. One must say that Japanese literature is at the furthest possible remove from the detective novel. The detective novel is—it goes without saying—a literature of logic and of science."

In the same April 1925 issue of *Shinseinen*, Hirabayashi made another appearance, and again he connected the dearth of detective writers to the belatedness of Japan's national and scientific progress:

> Japan is fifty or one hundred years behind the West, as one can tell from the development of the modern novel; when one contemplates this fact, it seems natural that there should be almost no works worthy of being called detective novels in Japan and almost no writers of them. That is for no other reason than that Japan's scientific culture is not sufficiently advanced to give rise to detective novels. The reason the detective novel hasn't developed in Japan is...that Japanese civilization is scientifically infantile and primitive. That is the root cause of all the reasons people give for the lack of the detective novel's development in Japan.[83]

With this observation, Hirabayashi compounds Katō's notion of a gap between the Japanese and Western mental characters with the notion of a gap in time. This subtly recasts Katō's language of difference (contemplation versus ratiocination) into a language of Spencerian hierarchy familiar from the discourse of Meiji period intellectuals such as Fukuzawa Yukichi, in which Japan is figured as the child (Japan is "infantile") to the West's adult and as the "primitive" counterpart to the West's more enlightened civilization.

While some critics following Kozakai Fuboku developed his early suggestion that Japan's mental temperament and its lack of scientific progress lay behind the shortage of Japanese detective writers, other critics picked up on Kozakai's notion that Japanese social conditions were responsible. In an assertion that sheds some light on Ranpo's interest in locked-room mysteries, Kume Masao blamed Japanese living conditions and Japanese architecture. "At the moment," he wrote in a pessimistic 1924 essay, "Japanese buildings are…made of paper and bamboo, which leak secrets, so maybe some special form of detective novel will come into being [to accommodate that fact], but at this point one can't help thinking that it doesn't look possible."[84]

In an essay published in the same issue of *Shinseinen*, the writer Nagata Mikihiko (1887–1964) declared that he had "given up on the idea of the Japanese detective novel long ago."[85] Pondering the reason for his own lack of success in writing detective fiction, he also placed much of the blame on Japanese living conditions, and—in concurrence with Kume Masao— specifically on Japanese domestic architecture:

> Isn't the reason probably that this life of the Japanese just isn't suited to detective novels? The life of a family is concentrated in a single-unit house and separated from other lives by nothing more than hedges, rain shutters, and paper doors; its depth could hardly be less. In most houses, if you crawled beneath the floor and listened, you could get to the bottom of any secret. In the worst cases, even voices speaking on the phone can be heard leaking out to the street in front—that's the kind of life we lead.

Nagata's essay contributed to a growing acceptance in *Shinseinen* criticism of the proposition that the work of foreign writers was uniformly superior to Japanese efforts. "For anyone who wants to read detective novels," he wrote later in the same piece, "there's really nothing for it but to go poking around in Maruzen [i.e., in search of foreign works]."

These critics' persistent focus on Japanese architecture seems like something of a red herring, given Okamoto Kidō's ability to find perfectly suitable places for his crimes even in the old city of Edo. But if this focus on architecture lacks explanatory power in its own right, it nonetheless underscores the basic sense of futility that Japanese detective writers felt as they confronted the vast gap that separated Japan and the West on their mental maps.

The writer Satō Haruo (1892–1964), who in 1918 had published the novella *Shimon*, or *Fingerprint* (about a man who fears he has committed murder while under the spell of an opium dream), also weighed in on the question. Perhaps perceiving the merely peripheral role of architecture in the creative process, he diplomatically suggested that "the fact that at present no good detective novels appear in Japan is owing partly to the form of our buildings—but the form of the buildings as they symbolize our entire lives." In a remark reminiscent of Kume Masao's observation that Japanese domestic architecture ensured one could "get to the bottom of any secret," he added: "It seems possible to say that the Japanese lead lives without depth, even when it comes to criminality."[86] Satō Haruo's well-known romanticism and decadence come out in this remark, which echoes Kozakai Fuboku's earlier suggestion that Japanese life is "too impoverished in content" for crime fiction. Like Kozakai, having defined a characteristic communalism and transparency in Japanese social life, Satō Haruo then interprets these things as elements in an oppressive and limiting regime of normalcy, and he does so in order to explain a lack that is apparent only in comparison to the Western literary tradition.

The discourse of Japanese inadequacy persisted in *Shinseinen* criticism through the end of the decade. Even after Ranpo published *Shadowy Beast* in 1928, Hirabayashi found fault with it: "*Shadowy Beast* is suspenseful," he wrote, "...but it is not an extraordinary masterpiece. It is not up to [L.J.] Beeston...or even his own earlier standard" (Hirabayashi had praised "The Case of the Murder at D. Hill" for its logic in an earlier essay). "*Shadowy Beast* is muddy," he continued. "It's too effortful, like a woman with too much makeup on. He overdoes it in re-rehearsing the possibility that Shizuko might have been the criminal after she has committed suicide. Ranpo is wrestling with no one but himself. The ending doesn't resolve. That is a comfortable way out for the writer, but it's not satisfying to the reader."[87]

In 1929, seven years after having broached the topic, Kozakai Fuboku still did not believe any good Japanese detective writer had materialized. "Japan has just emerged from the era of translation," he wrote that year in another magazine, "and whether we'll reach a golden age or not depends on whether a good writer appears.... Many people are responding to writing contests, but good submissions are very rare." Following the pattern that was typical of nearly all the analysis on the topic in this period, Kozakai's essay runs inexorably toward an explanation of this lack that is rooted in the Japanese national character: "From time to time it occurs to me to wonder whether the Japanese are weak when it comes to the ability to write detective novels. I think this all the more when I realize that there is nothing all that good even among the experimental attempts of highbrow writers to do a detective novel."[88]

Conclusion: The Burden of the Would-Be Imitator

Reading these critical essays in *Shinseinen* together with Edogawa Ranpo's works reveals a complex of intermingled desires and fears surrounding Japanese literary and cultural borrowing. These writings show a powerful aspiration to follow Western precedents, both because of their inherent attractions and because of the cultural cachet they had as products of Western, scientific modernity. But these writings also contain an equally powerful, unresolved anxiety about the likelihood of falling short of the mark set by those precedents. Ranpo's stories suggest that this anxiety was in turn connected to other, related anxieties: fear of discovery as a literary or cultural impersonator, worry about being proven unworthy or inferior as an imitator, angst that the connection between one's imitation and its model would go unrecognized, and horror at the monstrously hybrid results of cultural imitation that was only half complete.

The writings of Ranpo and those of the critics contemporary to him suggest the difficulty their authors faced when it came to seeing themselves as something other than second-rate copies of their Western counterparts. They also hint at the profound weight of that self-perception. Here is one instance, then, in which the notions of cultural imperialism and colonialism seem an apt fit for the data. Homi Bhabha has proposed that the hallmark of the colonial relation is its dependence on "fracturing the subjectivity of its subordinates through encouraging the non-Western subject to identify with metropolitan cultural forms and values."[89] The evidence suggests that many detective writers in the 1920s and 1930s were under the sway of just such a split subjectivity and that they were nearly powerless to free themselves from it. On the one hand a writer such as Ranpo embraced the Western detective novel as the example of the form most worthy of emulation, even to the point of staking his literary identity on the act. Yet on the other hand he never seems to have been able to carry off the emulation with complete satisfaction. This seems to have been at least partly the result of having internalized a self-generated discourse of inferiority that, while certainly not a necessary result of the Japanese encounter with the Western detective novel, ultimately became for Ranpo and his contemporaries almost inextricably bound together with it.

Coda

Cultural Borrowing
Reconsidered

A mong all of Ranpo's stories of failed imposture, it is in "The Masked Dancers" ("Fukumen no buyōsha," 1926) that he forges the most obvious link between imposture and Japanese Westernization. "The Masked Dancers" begins as another story about a secret society of wealthy men. Compared to the society in "The Red Room," which is devoted strictly to telling horror stories, this society is more wide-ranging in its search for offbeat entertainment. "Do you read novels?" the narrator's friend Inoue asks him. "It's the kind of strange society that turns up a lot in foreign novels, like *The Suicide Club*—that one is a little *too* strange—but it's a sort of fraternity looking for powerful thrills of that sort."[1] Intrigued, the narrator attends a meeting of the society. The thrill scheduled on this occasion is a masquerade ball. The president of the society has arranged for a woman to be present for each man, with the couples to be formed by a dealing of numbered cards. When this is done, the narrator has a moment to study his masked partner, who looks somehow familiar, before the lights are put out and the dancing begins. The narrator finds that the mysterious woman is thrillingly forward. Later, after having drunk and danced himself into a stupor, he wakes up in a strange room to find a note from the woman telling him what a cad he has been. The note is apparently from his friend Inoue's wife, Haruko.

The element of detection in the story is provided by the narrator's attempt to reconstruct the events of the night before and puzzle out the true identity of the woman. At first he is stunned that the president of the club should have arranged for the members of the club to swap wives unwittingly. Then he thinks that he must have been set up to think that he spent the evening with Inoue's wife and that the woman had merely borne a close resemblance to her. He pays a visit to the president's house to tell him, in a congratulatory way, how hard he fell for this trick. There he finds gathered some members of the club who are joking about the masquerade ball. From their conversation the narrator realizes that there was no trick and that there was supposed to have been one. Everyone but he and Inoue had actually danced with his own wife, although none of the men knew it at the time. The wives were in on the joke from the start, and the cards had been fixed so as to pair married couples. But he and Inoue, he realizes, both mistook their numbers (one was 11 and the other 17), with the result that they inadvertently spent the evening dallying with each other's wives, who were also deceived until the masks came off. When his deductions lead him to see that the woman he spent the evening with was indeed Inoue's wife, Haruko, the narrator is revealed to himself as the unwitting culprit in a horrifying transgression. He is devastated. There is not the slightest hint of erotic thrill in his realization. "I had no strength left to think," he says. "Only one thing impinged itself on my mind like a hot iron—the sickening feeling, not likely to go away so long as I lived, that I had toward my wife, toward Inoue, and toward his wife, Haruko."[2]

This story asks that we accept some unlikely things (the coincidence of both men mistaking their numbers and the inability of either wife to recognize she had the wrong man) for the sake of staging not one but two failures of impersonation. The first of these failures is obvious to the narrator before the masked ball has gotten fully under way. The ball has none of the splendor that he is sure would define the affair if it were being held in the West of his imaginings:

> When I [describe the ball] in this way, my readers may call to mind a Western-style masquerade ball, but it was not that by any means. The room was a Western one, and the people were generally wearing Western costumes, but that room was a Western room in the mansion of a Japanese man, and, as the people were Japanese people costumed in the Western style, their whole carriage was extremely Japanese; it was nothing like a Western masquerade ball. Their costumes were very skillful as far as concealing their identities was concerned, but everyone was wearing things too subdued or too unrefined to be appropriate to the name of "masquerade ball." In addition the women were strangely shy, and the languid air with which they walked about had nothing whatsoever to do with the perkiness of Western women.[3]

These costumes may allow the masquers to cast off their identities temporarily, but they do not transform them into Westerners or even into convincing imitations. The narrator notes with chagrin that when the lights are doused and the music starts, so few of the members actually know how to dance that the couples are reduced merely to walking around the room holding hands.

The second failure (the result of the mix-up with the numbers) is only obvious after the fact. It is not a failure to impersonate Westerners sufficiently but a failure to stop short of impersonating them fully, a failure to carry out properly the intended, merely pretend, impersonation. The result is that the narrator is left recoiling in disgust from himself because he has become more "Western" than he is capable of being.

The story, through Ranpo's typical layering and relayering of identities, imagines the role of the would-be cultural imitator as a thoroughly ambivalent one, in which he is torn between his desire to imitate and his realization that he is not capable of an imitation that will be the equal of the original. And it leaves little doubt that the focus of its characters' ambivalent longing is indeed Western culture, or at least their own loosely conceived, imaginary version of it.

Taken as a whole, Ranpo's corpus of detective writings embodies the same ambivalence that is so clearly limned in this story. These writings' frequent borrowing (not only of the form of the detective narrative itself but of things such as Bentley's trick of the killer who impersonates his victim or the device of the locked room) indicates the strength of Ranpo's desire to replicate for his Japanese audience the pleasures of foreign works. But their repeated, often self-referential, enactments of failed impersonations and their persistent horror at the resulting hybrids give them an unmistakable aura of pained self-consciousness about that very borrowing.

This ambivalence was consonant with Japan's national frustration at its seeming inability to make headway in the quest for membership in the club of Western powers, despite its dutiful replication of Western legal systems and Western patterns of colonial rule. In this instance, then, the national impulse to emulation, together with its accompanying contradictions and disappointments, translated more or less predictably into particular texts and into particular writers' and critics' perception of their relationship to their Western models.

But the most important aim of this book is to show that there were other responses possible to the problem of writing in the shadow of the West and that the sort of ambivalent longing evident in Ranpo—while undeniably an important aspect of Japanese response to Western contact—must not be allowed to stand for the whole. The examples canvassed in this book show that there is more than one type of "imitation" and that the term itself is too blunt to tease them apart.

The agenda of political reform and muckraking that Kuroiwa Ruikō carried out through his translation of detective novels—whether promoting the abolition of the death penalty or exposing the corruption of the mid-Meiji establishment—was inspired by Western ideals of liberalism and investigative journalism. But the translations themselves were so quirkily reworked to fit his particular local needs, and they took on such new meanings in the process, that they threatened the conventional understanding of the relationship between original and copy. Unlike Ranpo's generation, he had no compelling desire to insert himself into a Western tradition of detective writing, and his own political and commercial agenda almost completely overrode any consideration of fidelity to the thing he had borrowed. As a result, the hybrids that he created bespoke self-possession and élan rather than the horror and the impulse toward self-destruction that are so characteristic of Ranpo's works. Where for Ranpo cultural borrowing seems to have simply underscored Japanese inferiority to the West, for Ruikō cultural borrowing, both in his politics and in his translations, was an unambiguous good, a means to the end of national improvement.

Okamoto Kidō's borrowing presents yet another response to the problem of writing in a borrowed genre. While Ruikō's translations led him and his readers to look forward and outward, and to think of themselves as citizens of the world, Kidō's stories of Hanshichi, the Sherlock Holmes of Edo, turned his readers backward and inward to the insular world of Japan's premodern past. Rather than using the form of the detective novel to celebrate the values of Western modernity and rationality embodied in the original Holmes, he unapologetically subverted the form into a nostalgic, nativistic, ritualistic celebration of Japanese traditionalism. Like Ruikō (but unlike Ranpo) Kidō showed an almost complete lack of compunction when it came to appropriating and modifying the borrowed form to suit his own local purposes.

The one thing that all these writers had in common was their perception of a wide gap in cultural achievement between Japan and the West. Ruikō would have had no doubt that the Meiji legal system was a vast improvement over the Tokugawa one, with its aura of infallibility surrounding the magistrates and shogunal commissioners. But the oligarchic character of mid-Meiji governance was still an obvious affront to his democratic sensibilities, sensibilities that had been formed during a Freedom and People's Rights Movement that rested heavily on Western notions of natural human rights. These values came conspicuously to the fore in his frequent criticism of Japanese institutions, which grew from the implicit premise that

Japan could be bettered by emulation of the West. Kidō's stories, too, are informed by a recognition of the profound differences between Western modernity and Japanese traditionalism, although he stands on the opposite side of the fence from Ruikō. The threat that his stories perceive in the loss of the past is premised entirely on this sense of difference and on the fear that Japan will be the worse if this difference is not preserved. Ranpo and his contemporaries, who so often found themselves stuck in a pattern of decrying their own failure to live up to the standards of Western detective writing, were the most keenly fixated of all upon this cultural gap. They were also the most assiduous in their maintenance of its width, even as they expressed a longing to cross it. This deep-seated belief in the gap between East and West, and the concomitant anxiety over Japan's partially success-ful attempt at bridging it underlay most of the Japanese detective fiction produced before World War II.

Although none of these writers' awareness of the gap was a happy one, their very anxiety about it led them to produce a body of writings that are uniquely representative of their time and place, one that could never be mistaken for the product of another culture. And on this basis, ironically enough, they stake a claim to an unmistakable identity of their own, in spite of their inhabitation of a borrowed form.

Notes

Chapter 1: Introduction

1. Sukehiro Hirakawa, "Japan's Turn to the West," in *The Cambridge History of Japan*, vol. 5: *The Nineteenth Century*, ed. Marius P. Jansen (Cambridge: Cambridge University Press, 1989), p. 433. Quoted in Conrad Totman, *A History of Japan* (Malden, Mass.: Blackwell, 2000), p. 301.

2. Jim Reichert, "Tsubouchi Shōyō's *Tōsei shosei katagi* and the Institutionalization of Exclusive Heterosexuality," *Harvard Journal of Asiatic Studies*, vol. 63, no. 1 (June 2003), p. 72. The reviewer was Takada Sanae, and the review is reprinted in *Nihon kindai bungaku taikei*, vol. 57 (Kadokawa shoten, 1988), p. 60.

3. When Keene describes the much more favorable reaction to Futabatei's novel *Ukigumo*, he again reveals contemporary critics' (and his own) tendency to measure Japanese works against a Western standard: "Critic after critic," Keene notes, "expressed the thrill of discovery that a work written by a Japanese and faithfully describing contemporary Japanese society could possess the depth and intensity of a European novel." *Dawn to the West: Japanese Literature of the Modern Era* (New York: Henry Holt, 1984), pp. 107 and 112.

4. See, for example, James A. Fujii, *Complicit Fictions: The Subject in the Modern Japanese Prose Narrative* (Berkeley: University of California Press, 1993); Dennis C. Washburn, *The Dilemma of the Modern in Japanese Fiction* (New Haven: Yale University Press, 1995); and Seiji M. Lippit, *Topographies of Japanese Modernism* (New York: Columbia University Press, 2002).

5. Tzvetan Todorov, who provides perhaps the most quoted characterization of the whodunit, observes that it "contains not one but two stories: the story of the crime and the story of the investigation. In their purest form, these two stories have no point in common.... The first story, that of the crime, ends before the second begins.... The characters of the second story, the story of the investigation, do not act, they learn.... The hundred and fifty pages which separate the discovery of the crime from the revelation of the killer are devoted to a slow apprenticeship: we examine clue after clue, lead after lead. The whodunit

thus tends toward a purely geometric architecture." Tzvetan Todorov, *The Poetics of Prose,* trans. Richard Howard (Ithaca, N.Y.: Cornell University Press, 1977), pp. 44–45.

6. Hirabayashi Hatsunosuke, "Nihon no kindaiteki tantei shōsetsu," *Shinseinen,* vol. 6, no. 5 (April 1925), pp. 156–157.

7. Ibid., p. 158.

8. Miryam Sas, *Fault Lines: Cultural Memory and Japanese Surrealism* (Stanford: Stanford University Press, 1999), p. 36.

9. Lydia Liu, *Translingual Practice: Literature, National Culture, and Translated Modernity—China 1900–1937* (Stanford: Stanford University Press, 1995), p. 27.

10. Arthur Conan Doyle, "The Red-Headed League," in John Hodgson, ed., *Sherlock Holmes: The Major Stories with Contemporary Critical Essays* (Boston: Bedford, 1994), p. 56.

11. Conan Doyle, "The Speckled Band," in Hodgson, *Sherlock Holmes,* p. 171.

12. Shu-Mei Shih, *The Lure of the Modern: Writing Modernism in Semi-Colonial China, 1917–1937* (Berkeley: University of California Press, 2001), p. 374.

13. Jordan Sand has made a similar point in his study of Japanese domestic architecture between 1880 and 1930: "It is…appealing…to point to the creative ways in which particular forms were appropriated as Japan progressively joined global trends of fashion and of thought. Yet the appropriations were never made freely. The choice of things Western, which seems at times to transcend all other evaluative criteria, replicated relations of power, since the modes of interpretation available for Japanese to conceive their social and material world were determined by the forces of their political world." *House and Home in Modern Japan: Architecture, Domestic Space, and Bourgeois Culture, 1880–1930* (Cambridge, Mass.: Harvard University Asia Center, 2003), p. 365.

14. The story was first published in the September 1934 issue of the magazine *Chūō kōron.*

15. Edogawa Ranpo, *Zakuro,* in *Edogawa Ranpo zenshū* (Tokyo: Kōdansha, 1978–1979), vol. 12, p. 38. Unless otherwise noted, all translations are my own.

16. Ibid., p. 40.

17. The presence of a nearby waterfall makes Inomata's plunge to his death more than a little reminiscent of Doctor Moriarty's death at Reichenbach Falls in Conan Doyle's story "The Final Problem."

18. Howard Haycraft, for example, says of *Trent's Last Case* that it "stands truly first among modern examples of the genre." *Murder for Pleasure: The Life and Times of the Detective Story* (New York: D. Appleton-Century, 1941), p. 119.

19. Edogawa, *Edogawa Ranpo zenshū,* vol. 12, p. 11.

20. Edogawa Ranpo, *Tantei shōsetsu yonjūnen* (Tokyo: Chūsekisha, 1994), p. 214.

21. Ibid.

22. Ibid.

23. Ibid.

24. Ibid., pp. 215–216.

25. Ibid., p. 217.

26. Ibid., p. 216.

27. Ibid., p. 219.

28. Edogawa, *Edogawa Ranpo zenshū*, vol. 12, pp. 41–42.

29. Ibid., p. 10.

30. My interest in this question and my approach to it have been inspired by Jeffrey Kinkley's *Chinese Justice, The Fiction: Law and Literature in Modern China* (Stanford: Stanford University Press, 2000). See especially chapter 3, titled "Shadows."

31. The major works in Japanese on Japanese crime literature are Nakajima Kawatarō, *Nihon suiri shōsetsu shi* (A History of the Japanese Mystery Novel) (Tokyo: Tōkyō sōgensha, 1993–1996); Itō Hideo, *Taishō no tantei shōsetsu* (The Taishō Detective Novel) (Tokyo: San'ichi shobō, 1990), *Shōwa no tantei shōsetsu* (The Shōwa Detective Novel) (Tokyo: San'ichi shobō, 1993), and *Kindai no tantei shōsetsu* (The Modern Detective Novel, covering the Meiji, Taishō, and Shōwa periods) (Tokyo: San'ichi shobō, 1994); Gonda Manji, *Nihon tantei sakka ron* (On Japanese Detective Writers) (Tokyo: Gen'eijō, 1975) and *Gendai suiri shōsetsu ron* (On the Modern Mystery Novel) (Tokyo: Daisan bunmeisha, 1985); and Kasai Kiyoshi, *Tantei shōsetsu ron* (On the Detective Novel) (Tokyo: Tōkyō sōgensha, 1998).

Nakajima and Itō are the most comprehensive, but both sacrifice depth of analysis to attain their broad coverage. Of the two, Nakajima is the more penetrating, although he still devotes more energy to behind-the-scenes publication history, plot summary, and biography than he does to critical reading. And since much of his book is made up of articles that were originally written for different magazines over a period of several years, the whole suffers somewhat from a lack of continuity. Even so, both Itō and Nakajima are indispensable for getting one's bearings and as reference works. Gonda Manji's *Nihon tantei sakka ron* is refreshing in its focus on fewer writers (eighteen) and on textual analysis, though some of the latter perhaps overemphasizes biography. Its greatest drawback is that it begins with Kozakai Fuboku (who was active in the 1920s), thus omitting entirely consideration of the Meiji and most of the Taishō period. Kasai's book is perhaps the most theoretical of the lot, but it is focused on the even later post–World War II era, as is Gonda's second book.

In the field of *torimono-chō*, or crime stories set in the Edo period, see Nawata Kazuo's book *Torimono-chō no keifu* (A Genealogy of the *Torimono-chō*) (Tokyo: Shinchōsha, 1995), which includes four chapters on Okamoto Kidō's Hanshichi stories.

There are a small number of book-length works in Japanese on individual crime writers, including two of the writers treated here—Kuroiwa Ruikō and Edogawa Ranpo. On Ruikō, see the following: Itō Hideo, *Kuroiwa Ruikō: tantei shōsetsu no ganso* (Kuroiwa Ruikō: Father of the Detective Story) (Tokyo: San'ichi shobō, 1988); Iida Momo, *Kuroiwa Ruikō* (Tokyo: Riburopōto, 1992);

and Takahashi Yasuo, *Monogatari yorozu chōhō* (The Story of *Yorozu chōhō*) (Tokyo: Nihon keizai shinbunsha, 1989). Only the first of these is primarily concerned with Ruikō's activities as a detective-story writer and translator. It contains a bibliography of writings on Ruikō and on Meiji period crime literature. On Ranpo, see Matsuyama Iwao, *Ranpo to Tōkyō* (Ranpo and Tokyo) (Tokyo: PARCO, 1984); and Matsumura Yoshio, *Ranpo ojisan* (Uncle Ranpo) (Tokyo: Shōbunsha, 1992). A good collection of essays on Ranpo (including contributions by Matsumoto Seichō and Yokomizo Seishi) and a bibliography of Ranpo criticism are contained in Nakajima Kawatarō, ed., *Edogawa Ranpo: hyōron to kenkyū* (Edogawa Ranpo: Criticism and Research) (Tokyo: Kōdansha, 1980). A further bibliography of Ranpo criticism, conceived as a supplement to that in Nakajima, can be found in *Kokubungaku kaishaku to kanshō*, vol. 59, no. 12 (December 1994), pp. 159–166. This entire issue of the journal is devoted to Ranpo.

Notable scholarship on Japanese detective fiction in Western languages includes Sari Kawana's *Sleuthing Japan: Detective Fiction and Modern Culture* (Minneapolis: University of Minnesota Press, forthcoming); Amanda C. Seaman's *Bodies of Evidence: Women, Society, and Detective Fiction in 1990s Japan* (Honolulu: University of Hawai'i Press, 2003), which focuses primarily on women writers of the 1990s; and a substantial portion of Cécile Sakai's *Histoire de la littérature populaire japonaise: Faits et perspectives (1900–1980)* (Paris: l'Harmattan, 1987). Marred by inaccuracies but useful for its brief profiles of major writers and its bibliography is Kazuo Yoshida, "Japanese Mystery Literature," in the *Handbook of Japanese Popular Culture*, ed. Richard Gid Powers and Hidetoshi Kato (New York: Greenwood Press, 1989).

32. Edogawa Ranpo, "Nihon tantei shōsetsu no keifu," *Chūo kōron*, November 1951, rpt. *Edogawa Ranpo zenshū*, vol. 19, pp. 217–227; see p. 223.

Chapter 2: Affirmations of Authority

1. Quoted in Itō Hideo, *Kuroiwa Ruikō: sono shōsetsu no subete* (Tokyo: Tōgensha, 1979), pp. 199–200.

2. Not only trial proceedings but the details of laws themselves and of the exact range of penalties possible for their violation were generally kept secret from the public. See Daniel Botsman, *Punishment and Power in the Making of Modern Japan* (Princeton: Princeton University Press, 2005), pp. 33–35.

3. Ihara Saikaku, *Tales of Japanese Justice*, trans. Thomas M. Kondo and Alfred Marks (Honolulu: University of Hawai'i Press, 1980), p. xv. Discussion of *T'ang ying pi shih* is based on Kondo and Marks' discussion on the same page.

4. The exception, number 6 of the *T'ang ying pi shih* ("Ping Chi Tests a Child"), is similar to Saikaku's story "The Cloud-Clearing Shadow" (part I, 2). *Tales of Japanese Justice*, p. xv.

5. Ihara, *Tales of Japanese Justice*, p. xii.

6. Botsman, *Punishment and Power*, p. 35.

7. Ibid., p. 36.

8. Ibid., p. 38.

9. Botsman's *Punishment and Power*, contains a discussion of the varieties of capital punishment in Tokugawa Japan and the crimes to which they were matched. See pp. 28–33.

10. "They Did Not Know What Was Inside the Drum," in Ihara, *Tales of Japanese Justice*, pp. 8–11.

11. "The Short Bow of the Ten Night Nenbutsu," in ibid., pp. 23–25.

12. Nishino Tatsukichi, ed., *Ōoka seidan*, Genbon-gendai yaku 67 (Tokyo: Kyōikusha, 1989), p. 239.

13. Tsukamoto Tetsumi, ed., *Ōoka seidan* (Yūhōdō, 1928), p. 488. Subsequent references to this story appear in the main text.

14. For mention of this and still other titles, see Nakajima Kawatarō, *Nihon suiri shōsetsu shi*, vol. 1, pp. 18–19.

15. Kodama Kōta et al., eds., *Meiji jidai*, Zusetsu nihon bunka shi taikei, vol. 11 (Tokyo: Shōgakukan, 1967), p. 185.

16. The term *gesaku* encompasses a variety of subgenres of popular fiction that began appearing after about 1750, including *sharebon* ("clever books," primarily about the pleasure quarters), *kokkeibon* (humorous books), *kibyōshi* ("yellow books," heavily illustrated popular romances, often a medium for adult satire), *gōkan* ("bound [or union] volumes," collecting several yellow-book fascicles as a set and therefore permitting greater length and complexity than their unbound predecessors), *yomihon* ("reading books," books without pictures, including popular historical romances), and *ninjōbon* ("books about human feeling," set, like the *sharebon* from which they were derived, in the pleasure quarters but offering a generally more sympathetic treatment of their characters). In its early period *gesaku* is associated with such names as Hiraga Gennai (1728–1779), Ōta Nanpo (1749–1823), and Santō Kyōden (1761–1816), and after 1800 with Takizawa (Kyokutei) Bakin (1767–1848), Jippensha Ikku (1765–1831), Shikitei Sanba (1776–1822), Tamenaga Shunsui (1790–1843), and Ryūtei Tanehiko (1783–1842). Edo *gesaku* is typified by flippancy, elaborate puns, in-jokes, and literary allusions, a concern for accurate rendering of the spoken idiom, and a penchant for whimsical digression.

17. John Pierre Mertz has suggested that such publications played a part in the "construction of a literary idea of national community, a space within which people could imagine the future of their society." *Novel Japan: Spaces of Nationhood in Early Meiji Narrative, 1870–88* (Ann Arbor: University of Michigan Center for Japanese Studies, 2003), p. 117.

18. Okitsu Kaname quotes the following lines from yet another competitor, the *Ukiyo shinbun*: "About the story of Oden, for which we ran no more than an advertisement in yesterday's paper: on the same day the *E-iri*, the *Kana-yomi*, and the *Tōkyō* all showed forth their writing brushes at their most winning, and since they are all going to [cover the story] with full-length accounts *(naga-monogatari)*, we are leaving the detailed reporting to them." *Meiji shinbun koto hajime: bunmei kaika no jānarizumu* (Tokyo: Taishūkan shoten, 1997), p. 102.

19. *Kana-yomi shinbun,* February 4, 1879. The truncated newspaper run is quoted in full in Okitsu Kaname, ed., *Meiji kaika-ki bungakushū* 2 (Tokyo: Chikuma shobō, 1967), p. 426.

20. *Yūbin hōchi shinbun,* February 1, 1879. Reprinted in Katō Shūichi et al., eds., *Buntai,* Nihon kindai shisō taikei 16 (Tokyo: Iwanami, 1989), pp. 303–304.

21. The account in the *Tōkyō nichi nichi shinbun* was printed September 12, 1876. It has been reprinted in Ishida Bunshirō, ed., *Shinbun kiroku shūsei: Meiji Taishō Shōwa dai jiken shi* (Tokyo: Kinseisha, 1966), pp. 65–68; see p. 65.

22. On this point Kisen's version, as Wada Shigejirō points out, probably reflects the influence of Oden's own deposition, in which she claimed to have samurai blood (Wada Shigejirō, *Kindai bungaku sōseiki no kenkyū: riarizumu no seisei* [Tokyo: Ōfūsha, 1973], p. 250). Kisen's version, titled *Sono na mo Takahashi dokufu no Oden: Tōkyō kibun,* began appearing on February 13 and concluded twenty-four installments later, on April 22, 1879.

23. Hirata Yumi's "The Story of the Woman, the Woman in the Story: Takahashi Oden and the Discourse of the Poison Woman" contains a comprehensive reconstruction of the probable events leading to Kichizō's death, drawing on contemporary newspaper accounts and testimony independent from Oden's own. Her analysis in the same article of the tale's place in a larger system of traditional "women's narratives" is also indispensable. See *Gender and Japanese History: The Self and Expression / Work and Life,* vol. 2, ed. Wakita Haruko et al. (Osaka: Osaka University Press, 1999), pp. 221–252. For a cogent, thought-provoking treatment of Oden as a female deviant, see Christine Marran, "'Poison Woman' Takahashi Oden and the Spectacle of Female Deviance in Early Meiji," *U.S.-Japan Women's Journal,* English supplement no. 9 (1995): 93–110. Marran's book *Poison Woman: Figuring Female Transgression in Modern Japanese Culture* (Minneapolis: University of Minnesota Press, forthcoming) is likely to be a definitive treatment.

24. Kanagaki Robun, *Takahashi Oden yasha monogatari,* in Okitsu Kaname, ed., *Meiji kaika-ki bungakushū* 2 (Tokyo: Chikuma shobō, 1967), pp. 3–61; quoted on pp. 3–4. Subsequent page references appear in the main text.

25. For examples, see ibid., pp. 9, 10, 15, 24, 36, and 47.

26. There is, however, an error concerning Oden's age that seems to have escaped Robun's notice. On p. 11 (in Okitsu, ed., *Meiji kaika-ki bungakushū* 2) we are told that "Oden reached her twenty-eighth spring *(nijū hachi no haru o mukae),* and around the time that the cherries deep in the mountains reached full blossom, her desire for the male sex became apparent *(otoko koishiki fuzei mo araware);* she began coquettishly making herself up and hanging about the shrines and temples." The phrase "twenty-eighth spring" *(nijūhachi no haru)* in this passage must be an error for "eighteenth spring" *(jūhachi no haru).* The error is repeated on p. 42, where we are told in a flashback to the time before she married Naminosuke that Oden was "twenty-eight and at the height of her beauty" *(nijū hachi no hana no kao).* Quite apart from the unlikelihood of any

dokufu reaching age twenty-eight before having her sexual awakening, accepting Oden's age as twenty-eight on p. 11 would throw off entirely the chronology of the subplot of her father's imprisonment and return. Even more important, if one were to accept Oden's age as twenty-eight when she meets Seikichi (and marries Naminosuke), then her adventures would last just one very full year, since the introduction *(itoguchi)* gives Oden's age as twenty-nine when she is sentenced to death, and her execution occurs on that same day. But the span of Oden's adventures, from the time of her leaving home to her capture, must actually be five or six years, from about 1871 to 1876. (Oden's own deposition in fact gives Meiji 4 [1871] as the year of her running away from home. A report printed in the *Nichi nichi shinbun* on September 12, 1876, gives the year of her running away as Meiji 2 [1869].) Such an oversight on Robun's part might seem to suggest that dates and chronology do not really matter to him and his readers so much after all. But even if one takes that view, it is still significant that he provides enough information about chronology for us to turn up such inconsistencies in the first place. As Ian Watt says of similar inconsistencies in Defoe, "The mere fact that such objections arise is surely a tribute to the way the characters are felt by the reader to be rooted in the temporal dimension. We obviously could not think of making such objections to Sidney's *Arcadia* or *The Pilgrim's Progress;* there is not enough evidence of the reality of time for any sense of discrepancies to be possible" (*The Rise of the Novel* [Berkeley: University of California Press, 1957], p. 24).

27. Robun's revisions introduce some inconsequential lexical variations and, in the court verdict, recast the *katakana* script of the *Yūbin hōchi* version as *hiragana*. Both documents have been reprinted in Katō Shuichi et al., *Buntai,* pp. 303–307.

28. The deposition has been reprinted in ibid., pp. 303–307. The excerpt from the deposition that Robun incorporates into the twenty-fourth installment, long as it is, is cut short well before the end. It does not include the section quoted here, in which Oden gives her own account of the events on the night of Gotō Kichizō's death.

29. Ibid., pp. 306–307.

30. In this regard, *Takahashi Oden yasha monogatari* is an important transitional text not only in the history of Japanese crime literature but in the history of Japanese literary realism in general. See Mark Silver, "The Lies and Connivances of an Evil Woman: Early Meiji Realism and *The Tale of Takahashi Oden the She-Devil,*" *Harvard Journal of Asiatic Studies,* vol. 63, no. 1 (June 2003), pp. 5–67.

31. Roland Barthes, *The Rustle of Language,* trans. Richard Howard (New York: Hill and Wang, 1986), p. 146. Quoted in Marston Anderson, *The Limits of Realism: Chinese Fiction in the Revolutionary Period* (Berkeley: University of California Press, 1990), p. 17.

32. The autopsy was reported in the *Tōkyō nichi nichi shinbun* on February 5, 1879. See Edamatsu Shigeyuki et al., eds., *Meiji nyūsu jiten* (Tokyo: Mainichi komyunikēshonzu, 1983–1986), vol. 2, p. 409.

33. This happens, for example, after Oden and Naminosuke have become separated in their escape from the henchmen of Genji Katsunuma, whom the two have cheated out of the money he put up as Oden's guarantor at a brothel called the Sakuraya (p. 35). It happens again when Oden returns to her home village after Naminosuke's death and is reunited with her adoptive father after an absence of a year or more (p. 46). On both occasions she edits her narrative in the retelling, omitting important details. In otherwise full accounts of her doings, she does not tell Naminosuke that she has slept with Genji, and she keeps from her adoptive father her strangling of Naminosuke. Neither man suspects the truth, so that the reader clearly sees Oden using these accounts of herself to shape these men's notions of who she is.

A no less striking example of Oden's use of creative autobiography occurs when the police arrest her for questioning because she is traveling with a fugitive named Terugorō. "Being a silver-tongued, crafty femme fatale," Robun tells us, "she wielded her words adroitly" (p. 45). Oden gives an account of herself in which she conceals her murder of Naminosuke but owns up to having run away from home. Her story is calculated to square with what she knows her adoptive father and brother-in-law will say about her when they are questioned. By thus "mixing the true and the false" (makoto soragoto uchimazete), she transforms herself into a victim who had no one to turn to, when her husband died of leprosy, but the shady Terugorō, of whose crimes she claims to know nothing. The police let her go.

34. Even after the ban on vendettas took effect in 1873, according to Kenzo Takayanagi, "a subsequent enactment permitted a child or grandchild to kill the murderer of his parents or grandparents on the spot." See Takayanagi, "A Century of Innovation," in Law in Japan: The Legal Order of a Changing Society, ed. Arthur Taylor von Mehren (Cambridge, Mass.: Harvard University Press, 1963), p. 20.

35. Strictly speaking, the pun is a partly visual one, since the characters for "a brief life story" are normally read shōden, not oden, but o is a reading of the first character in other contexts.

36. For a brief discussion of the practice and an illustration of sample tattoos, see Edo machi-bugyō, Rekishi gunzō raiburarii 3 (Tokyo: Gakken, 1995), p. 185.

37. Toyoda Takeshi, Myōji no rekishi (Tokyo: Chūōkōronsha, 1971), p. 150.

38. Ibid., pp. 150–151.

39. Richard Torrance's book The Fiction of Tokuda Shūsei and the Emergence of Japan's New Middle Class (Seattle: University of Washington Press, 1994) offers a vivid account, built from Tokuda Shūsei's memoirs and autobiographical writings, of the economic consequences of the abolition of the status system. See especially the excerpts from Shūsei's novel Hikari o ōte on pp. 10 and 12.

40. On the acute financial disorder of the 1870s, see William W. Lockwood, The Economic Development of Japan (Princeton: Princeton University Press, 1968), pp. 13–14.

41. Earl Kinmonth, The Self-Made Man in Meiji Japanese Thought (Berkeley: University of California Press, 1981), p. 11.

42. Oden is not the only swindler in her world. She herself falls victim in one episode to an elaborate fraud, engineered by a Tatematsu, involving the purchase of mulberry seedlings in large quantities. And she is shocked to discover, after going to the trouble of killing Kichizō, that her victim has tricked her about how much money he has with him. She finds in his bellyband not the agreed upon two hundred yen, but only a fraction of that amount in a deceptively thick bundle of what prove to be mere ten-*sen* notes.

43. The first domestic Japanese newspaper, the *Chūgai shinbun* (Domestic and Foreign News), was begun in 1868 by Yanagawa Shunsan (1832–1870); in addition to domestically produced items, it also carried translations from foreign newspapers. See Okitsu Kaname, *Meiji shinbun koto hajime,* pp. 2–5.

44. Okitsu Kaname, ed., *Meiji kaika-ki bungakushū 2,* p. 3.

Chapter 3: Borrowing the Detective Novel

1. Shōyō published the translation under the pen name Harunoya Oboro (literally, "Misty Spring Night") in the *Yomiuri shinbun.* Nakajima Kawatarō, *Nihon suiri shōsetsu shi,* vol. 1, p. 36.

2. The translation appeared under the pen name Takenoya Shujin in the *Yomiuri shinbun.* Ibid.

3. These counts are based on Itō Hideo's catalog of Japanese crime literature. See his *Kindai no tantei shōsetsu,* pp. 323–396.

4. As is mentioned below, the tabloid newspaper that Ruikō founded, *Yorozu chōhō,* was the most widely circulating newspaper in Tokyo by 1902 (120,000 copies daily). See Yamamoto Taketoshi, *Kindai nihon no shinbun doku-sha-sō* (Tokyo: Hōsei daigaku shuppan, 1981), p. 96. It was in this tabloid, in serialized form, that most of Ruikō's translations of Western crime literature first appeared.

5. The result appeared as "Futaba-gusa" (Violets), published by Kunshidō in 1888. See Kuroiwa Ruikō kai, ed., *Kuroiwa Ruikō* (Tokyo: Nihon tosho sentā, 1992), pp. 16–17.

6. Kuroiwa Ruikō, trans., *Makkura* (Tokyo: Kin'ōdō, 1889), pp. 4–5.

7. Ibid. The interpolation quoted appears on p. 53.

8. Kuroiwa Ruikō, trans., *Kettō no hate* (Tokyo: Sanyūsha, 1891), unnumbered page. The foreword was signed by one Kasazono Kazuhito, who seems to have had no special claim to fame.

9. The information given here is taken from the chronology in Kimura Ki, ed., *Kuroiwa Ruikō shū,* Meiji bungaku zenshū 47 (Tokyo: Chikuma shobō, 1971), pp. 398–407 (prepared by Takamatsu Toshio), and Tsurumi Shunsuke's vividly imagined portrait "Kuroiwa Ruikō" in *Taishū geijutsuka no shōzō,* ed. Katō Hidetoshi, Nijisseiki o ugokashita hitobito 8 (Tokyo: Kōdansha, 1963). A chronology also appears in Itō Hideo, *Kuroiwa Ruikō: Tantei shōsetsu no ganso,* pp. 379–383, but it seems to have been derived exclusively from Takamatsu's. The ages Takamatsu gives in his table are, by Western conventions, one year too

great (Ruikō is listed as one year old in 1862, the year of his birth, according to the Japanese convention) and have been changed.

10. This school went through many changes over the years and is itself something of a study in the flux of early Meiji. It had been opened in 1869 as the School of the West (Yōgakkō) and was eventually to become Osaka's number three high school. In between, it was renamed Kaimei gakkō (School of Enlightenment) in 1873, Ōsaka gaikokugo gakkō (Osaka School of Foreign Language) in 1874, and Ōsaka eigo gakkō (Osaka School of English) later that same year. In 1879 its name was changed yet again, this time to Ōsaka senmon gakkō (Osaka Professional School).

11. "Kaitakushi kanri no shobun o ronzu." The piece is reprinted in Kimura, *Kuroiwa Ruikō shū*, pp. 349–351.

12. Tsurumi, "Kuroiwa Ruikō," p. 219.

13. Ibid., pp. 228, 230.

14. For a list of the titles Ruikō ran and the dates they appeared, see Itō, *Tantei shōsetsu no ganso*, pp. 421–435.

15. Itō Hideo, *Kuroiwa Ruikō kenkyū* (Tokyo: Gen'eijō, 1978), p. 159; and *Tantei shōsetsu no ganso*, pp. 381–382. Circulation figures for *Yorozu chōhō* and all the other major Meiji period newspapers are available in Yamamoto, *Kindai nihon no shinbun dokusha-sō*, p. 96.

16. Tsurumi, "Kuroiwa Ruikō," p. 240.

17. Quoted in Yamamoto, *Kindai nihon no shinbun dokusha-sō*, p. 96.

18. Takahashi, *Monogatari yorozu chōhō*, p. 436.

19. Haycraft, *Murder for Pleasure:* for Du Boisgobey, see p. 104; for Gaboriau, see p. 36.

20. Both libraries were published in New York, the Seaside by George Munro and the Lovell by the John W. Lovell Company.

21. "International Copyright Relations of the United States," Circular 38a (Washington, D.C.: U.S. Copyright Office, 2003).

22. Ruikō Shōshi [Kuroiwa Ruikō], trans., *Hōtei no bijin* (Tokyo: Kunshidō, 1887), p. 3.

23. For a study in English of the general phenomenon of Meiji period literary adaptation and its theoretical implications, see J. Scott Miller, *Adaptations of Western Literature in Japan* (New York: Palgrave, 2001). In Japanese, the standard work on the subject is Yanagida Izumi, *Meiji shoki honyaku bungaku no kenkyū*, vol. 5 of his *Meiji bungaku kenkyū* (Tokyo: Shunjūsha, 1961).

24. Ruikō, who did not know French, made his translation from still another translation of this work, from French into English, that appeared as *The Widow Lerouge*, no trans., Seaside Library (New York: George Munro, 1874).

25. This information is from Itō Hideo's chronology of Japanese crime literature. See his *Kindai no tantei shōsetsu*, pp. 323–396. *Hito ka oni ka* has been reprinted in Kuroiwa Ruikō, *Ruikō zenshū* (Tokyo: Takara shuppan, 1979), vol. 2, pp. 168–418. The *Konnichi shinbun*, where *Hito ka oni ka* first ran, seems to have had a much more modest circulation than *Yorozu chōho*—Yamamoto

Taketoshi does not list it in his table of circulation figures (see n. 15 above). The novel was, however, reprinted in book form very soon after and no doubt found its way into reading rooms and lending libraries.

26. Itō Hideo lists the novel as being based "perhaps on either *Lady Audley's Secret* or *Hostages to Fortune*," both by the English writer Mary Elizabeth Maxwell, a.k.a. Miss Braddon (*Tantei shōsetsu no ganso*, p. 428). In fact *Hito no un*'s resemblance to them is only slight. For mention by Ruikō of having omitted parts of the original, see his note at the conclusion of the last installment, *Yorozu chōhō*, no. 568 (October 24, 1894), p. 3.

27. As Lydia Liu has observed in a discussion of Walter Benjamin's theory of translation, "The original and translation complement each other to produce meanings larger than mere copies or reproduction." *Translingual Practice*, p. 15.

28. John Owen Haley, *Authority without Power: Law and the Japanese Paradox* (New York: Oxford University Press, 1991), p. 69.

29. Ibid.

30. The entire code of 1871 has been translated into English by Paul Heng-Chao Ch'en in his *Formation of the Early Meiji Legal Order* (Oxford: Oxford University Press, 1981).

31. For a wonderfully full and vivid description of civil court procedures under the Tokugawa, see Dan Fenno Henderson, *Conciliation and Japanese Law, Tokugawa and Modern*, vol. 1 (Seattle: University of Washington Press, 1965), pp. 127–181. The phrase "Confucian stratification" is Henderson's and appears on p. 145. On the crawling expected of litigants, see John Henry Wigmore, ed., *Law and Justice in Tokugawa Japan: Materials for the History of Japanese Law and Justice under the Tokugawa Shogunate 1603–1867*, part 1 (Tokyo: Kokusai bunka shinkokai, 1969), p. 40.

32. *Kuroiwa Ruikō, Hito ka oni ka*, in *Ruikō zenshū*, vol. 2, pp. 168–418; quote on p. 169. The word *gigoku* in modern colloquial Japanese usually means "scandal." But the *Kōjien* (the most authoritative Japanese dictionary) also gives the following definition: "a court case *(saiban jiken)* in which because of complex circumstances the truth is unclear." It is with this definition in mind that I have translated *gigoku shōsetsu* as "mystery narrative." Also apropos of the issue of genre formation and genre naming: on the title page, Ruikō gives to *Hito ka oni ka* the subtitle *saiban shōsetsu*, or "trial narrative."

33. Ibid., p. 173. Subsequent references appear in the main text.

34. The translation first appeared as a serial in the *E-iri jiyū shinbun*, from September 9 to November 28, 1888 (Itō, *Kuroiwa Ruikō: tantei shōsetsu no ganso*, p. 422).

35. Ruikō Shōshi, trans., *Yūzai muzai* (Tokyo: Inoguchi Matsunosuke, 1889), unnumbered page.

36. Hirakawa, "Japan's Turn to the West," p. 473.

37. The one glaring difference was the Japanese decision not to adopt the jury system.

38. The reader is also rather oddly reminded of the process of name trans-lation when the minor character of the servant Densuke appears. He is so minor that he has been left out of the initial table of equivalences, and Ruikō inserts in parentheses after the first appearance of his name the words *genmyō Denisu,* or "original name 'Denis'" (p. 313).

39. The illustration appears in *Ruikō zenshū,* vol. 2, pp. 344–345.

40. This discussion is on pp. 86–87 of the Seaside Library edition of Gabo-riau's *Widow Lerouge.*

41. Gaboriau, *Widow Lerouge,* pp. 235–236.

42. *Ruikō zenshū,* vol. 2, p. 410.

43. Gaboriau, *Widow Lerouge,* p. 238.

44. See, for example, Tsuda Mamichi, "Shikei wa kei ni arazu," *Meiroku-sha zasshi,* no. 8 (1875). For a bibliography of writings in Japanese on capital punishment from 1867 on, see Mihara Kenzō, *Shikei haishi no kenkyū* (Tokyo: Seibundō, 1990), pp. 553–590.

45. Ch'en, *Formation,* pp. 40–41.

46. The tallies of executions are from Toshiyuki Nishikawa, "Capital Pun-ishment in Japan," *Asian Thought and Society: An International Review,* vol. 10, no. 29 (July 1985), pp. 84–85.

47. "Hakkan no ji," *Yorozu chōhō,* no. 1 (November 1, 1892), p. 1. Reprinted in Kimura, *Kuroiwa Ruikō shū,* p. 355.

48. The word *chikushō* in the column's title may well have been intended as a pun since it not only means "to keep a woman," but it is also, when written with different characters, a common expletive. One can imagine the word coming to the lips of the men that Ruikō targeted when they saw their names in his paper.

49. For excerpts from the column, see Itō, *Tantei shōsetsu no ganso,* pp. 171–172.

50. For a report of a betting pool made up of foreigners resident in Yoko-hama, see *Yorozu chōhō,* no. 280 (October 27, 1893), p. 2.

51. The summary given here of the Sōma Affair is indebted to Itō Hideo's explanation of it in *Tantei shōsetsu no ganso,* pp. 140–145. The hypothesis regard-ing Tomotane's schizophrenia has been put forward in Miyamoto Tadao, "Sōma jiken," *Heibonsha daihyakka jiten,* vol. 8 (Tokyo: Heibonsha, 1984), p. 974.

52. "Yo ga shinbun ni kokorozashita dōki," quoted in Kuroiwa Ruikō kai, *Kuroiwa Ruikō,* pp. 16–17.

53. *Yorozu chōhō,* no. 229 (August 8, 1893), p. 1.

54. *Yorozu chōhō,* no. 219 (July 27, 1893), p. 2.

55. For an example, see *Yorozu chōhō,* no. 229 (August 8, 1893), p. 1.

56. For a likely example of a letter to the editor submitted by Ruikō him-self, see *Yorozu chōhō,* no. 230 (August 9, 1893), p. 1, the letter signed Shōma Mabito ("true man who sheds light on evil").

57. "Dokusatsu hikokunin kotogotoku menso to naru," *Yorozu chōhō,* no. 278 (October 25, 1893), p. 2. The verdict exonerating the Shiga faction is reported (and reprinted verbatim) in *Yorozu chōhō,* no. 278 (October 25, 1893), p. 2.

58. "Hōshiki no saiban to shakai no saiban," *Yorozu chōhō*, no. 279 (October 26, 1893), p. 1, and no. 280 (October 27, 1893), p. 1. Ruikō also ran a brief announcement of the editorial under the same title in the issue preceding these two. See *Yorozu chōhō*, no. 278 (October 25, 1893), p. 2.

59. *Yorozu chōhō*, no. 279 (October 26, 1893), p. 1.

60. Ibid.

61. *Yorozu chōhō*, no. 529 (September 8, 1894), p. 3.

62. *Yorozu chōhō*, no. 532 (September 12, 1894), p. 3.

63. Kuroiwa, *Makkura*, p. 23.

64. Kuroiwa, *Kettō no hate*, p. 11.

65. Ibid., p. 12.

66. For a fuller discussion of this and other related provisions in the French Napoleonic Code, see H. D. Lewis, "The Legal Status of Women in Nineteenth-Century France," *Journal of European Studies*, vol. 10, part 3, no. 39 (September 1980), pp. 178–188.

67. Kuroiwa, *Kettō no hate*, pp. 236–237.

68. Mehren, *Law in Japan*, p. 20.

69. Carl Steenstrup, *A History of Law in Japan until 1868* (Leiden: E. J. Brill, 1991), p. 129.

70. "Kettō-zai," in Shinmura Izuru, ed., *Kōjien*, 5th ed. (Tokyo: Iwanami, 1998), p. 842.

71. Kuroiwa, *Kettō no hate*, p. 11.

72. Ibid.

73. Ibid.

74. Other notable French-inspired reforms of the period included the opening of courts to the press (1872), prohibition of torture in civil cases (1872), abolition of class distinctions at court trials (1872), abolition of confession by the accused as a requisite for imposing punishment (1876), and the total ban of physical torture (1879). See Mehren, *Law in Japan*, pp. 19–20.

75. The section in question appears on pp. 234–235 of F. Du Boisgobey, *Consequences of a Duel*, trans. A. D. Hall, Seaside Library (New York: George Munro, 1885).

76. Kuroiwa, *Kettō no hate*, p. 246.

77. The conjecture about the age of the phrase appears in the entry for *gemen* in Shinmura, *Kōjien*.

78. The link established in Ruikō's Japanese version between Moriyama's evil deeds and her violent death is not, however, completely without ground in the English version, where Coulanges (Kobayashi's equivalent) "point[s] out the manifest intervention of Providence in the punishment of the guilty couple" (Du Boisgobey, *Consequences of a Duel*, p. 234).

79. Kuroiwa, *Kettō no hate*, p. 246.

80. Such a double-page illustration appears between p. 239 and p. 240 in *Kettō no hate* (Tokyo: Sanyūsha, 1891).

81. Ibid., p. 246. The proverb in question, rendered into Japanese, is *Dokusho hyappen, i onozukara tsūzu.* There is a variant form, with the same meaning: *Dokusho hyappen, gi onozukara arawaru.*

82. Kuroiwa Ruikō, *Hito ka oni ka,* in *Ruikō zenshū,* vol. 2, pp. 253–254.

Chapter 4: Arresting Change

1. The discussion of Japan's wartime economic development is based on William W. Lockwood, *The Economic Development of Japan,* pp. 38–40.

2. Okamoto Kidō, "*Hanshichi torimono-chō* no omoide" (Memories of *Hanshichi torimono-chō*), *Bungei kurabu,* August 1927. Quoted in Okamoto Kyōichi, "Kaisetsu," in Okamoto Kidō, *Hanshichi torimono-chō* (Tokyo: Kōbunsha,1986), vol. 6, p. 342.

3. Okamoto Kidō, *Hanshichi torimono-chō,* vol. 1, p. 33. All subsequent citations of *Hanshichi torimono-chō* appear in the main text and refer to this six-volume edition (Kōbunsha, 1986). Imai Kingo, ed., *Hanshichi torimono-chō,* 6 vols. (Tokyo: Chikuma shobō, 1998), is less widely available but includes helpful maps, commentary, and illustrations. Fifteen of Kidō's stories appear in English translation in Ian MacDonald, trans., *The Curious Casebook of Inspector Hanshichi: Detective Stories of Old Edo* (Honolulu: University of Hawai'i Press, 2007).

4. This gloss appeared when the story was first printed in the January 1917 issue of the Hakubunkan company's magazine *Bungei kurabu;* it was not, however, repeated in later editions. (Nawata, *Torimono-chō no keifu,* p. 20.)

5. Quoted in Nawata, *Torimono-chō no keifu,* p. 20.

6. The six stories are "Kanpei no shi" (The Death of Kanpei), "Obake shishō" (The Ghost Teacher), "Yūya no nikai" (The Second Floor of the Bathhouse), "Haru no yukidoke" (The Spring Thaw), "Mikawa manzai" (The Traveling Performer from Mikawa), and "Fugu daiko" (The Blowfish-Skin Drum). All but the last starred Onoe Kikugorō VI in the role of Hanshichi. (Musashino Jirō, "Kaisetsu," in Okamoto, *Hanshichi torimono-chō,* vol. 5, p. 370.)

7. Ishimaru Hisa, "Bungei kurabu," in *Shinchō nihon bungaku jiten* (Tokyo: Shinchōsha, 1988), p. 1097.

8. Okamoto Kyōichi, "Kaisetsu," p. 344.

9. Edward Seidensticker, *Tokyo Rising: The City since the Great Earthquake* (New York: Knopf, 1990), p. 130.

10. It was Shirokiya that built the first four-story department store, in Nihonbashi. See Seidensticker, *Low City, High City* (New York: Knopf, 1983), pp. 110–114.

11. Seidensticker, *Tokyo Rising,* p. 27.

12. See "The Face of the City," in Jinnai Hidenobu, ed., *Process: Architecture,* no. 72 (April 1, 1987), p. 54.

13. *Tokai no shinpi* (The Mystery of the City, 1926), quoted in Suzuki Sadami, "Modan toshi no gensō," *Taiyō,* supplement 88 (Winter 1994), p. 16.

14. It was also with this collection that the stories first appeared under the name *Hanshichi torimono-chō* (Hanshichi's Arrest Records). In 1921 Ryūbunkan had published a smaller collection of stories as *Hanshichi kiki-gaki-chō* (Hanshichi in His Own Words). See Nakajima Kawatarō, *Nihon suiri shōsetsu shi,* vol. 1, p. 188.

15. Okamoto Kyōichi, "Kaisetsu," p. 344.

16. Ibid., p. 342.

17. *Yasha* (*yaksa* in Sanskrit) are Buddhist guardian deities with origins in the Hindu tradition.

18. The description of the administrative hierarchy in Edo is based on *Edo machi-bugyō,* pp. 50–51 and 114–117.

19. Between 1702 and 1719, there were at times three commissioners in office, a "central" post having been added to the northern and southern ones. For a list of the names and dates of service for all the commissioners between 1604 and 1868, see *Edo machi-bugyō,* pp. 202–203.

20. The figures given for the numbers of inspectors and sergeants are taken from *Edo machi-bugyō,* p. 115.

21. The very first story, "Ofumi no tamashii" (The Spirit of Ofumi), is the lone exception. The first-person narrator hears this story not from Hanshichi but from "K no ojisan," the uncle of his friend "K." Hanshichi is the hero all the same.

22. As Nawata Kazuo points out, this gives a possible double meaning to the suffix *-chō* in Kidō's title. It can be understood as referring not only to the transcriptions of interrogations kept in the commissioner's register, but also to the notes kept by the "author" during his visits to the old Hanshichi's house (*Torimono-chō no keifu,* p. 30).

23. A certain number of the stories begin immediately with this third-person narrator's voice, but they do not violate the typical pattern so much as take it for granted. As a rule, the first-person narrator's voice emerges at the end of these stories, where we are returned to the scene of their telling in Old Hanshichi's house. See, for examples, "Benten musume" (Benten's Daughter), "Mukōjima no ryō" (The Mukōjima Villa), and "Ijin no kubi" (The Foreigner's Head). The atypical opening of "Hiroshige to kawauso" (Hiroshige and the Otter) is discussed below.

24. For an example, see "Shin-kachikachiyama" (Mt. Kachikachi Revisited), in Okamoto, *Hanshichi torimono-chō,* vol. 5, p. 6.

25. Hodgson, *Sherlock Holmes,* pp. 170–171.

26. In Meiji 30 (1897), as the story's narrator records, electric lighting was only beginning to come into use in private homes. In Meiji 40 (1907), kerosene and gas lamps were still dominant. It was not until the last years of Meiji, with the introduction of hydroelectric power plants and tungsten filaments, that electric lighting came into widespread use. See Sone Hiroshi, "Toshi no meian," in *Nihon bungaku o yomu,* vol. 6 (Tokyo: Yūseidō, 1993), p. 5.

27. See Stephen Vlastos, ed., *Mirror of Modernity: Invented Traditions of Modern Japan* (Berkeley: University of California Press, 1998).

28. "Ninin nyōbō" (Two Wives), in Okamoto, *Hanshichi torimono-chō*, vol. 6, p. 199.

29. The quotation is taken from an interview of Conan Doyle in *Tit-Bits* magazine (December 15, 1900) and appears in Richard Lancelyn Green's introduction to his edition of *The Adventures of Sherlock Holmes* (Oxford: Oxford University Press, 1994), p. xiv.

30. Umberto Eco, "The Myth of Superman," in *The Role of the Reader: Explorations in the Semiotics of Texts* (Bloomington: Indiana University Press, 1979), p. 119. My debts to this essay and to Eco's "Narrative Structures in Fleming," contained in the same volume, will be apparent to all who have read them.

31. The exceptions are "Kojorō-gitsune" (Kojorō the Vixen), "Hakuchō kai" (The Mystery of the White Butterfly), "Yasha jindō" (*Yaksa* Shrine), "Tabi eshi" (The Itinerant Artist), "Yaritsuki" (The Spear Stabbings), and "Tsunokuniya" (Tsunokuni Tavern). These are all adventures either of Hanshichi's adoptive father (also a private agent) or of other agents before Hanshichi's time. In the former case, Hanshichi has heard the story directly. In the latter case, the premise is that Hanshichi refers to the old arrest record as he tells the story to Kidō.

32. Eco, "The Myth of Superman," in *The Role of the Reader,* p. 120.

33. Theodor Adorno, in his oft-quoted essay "On Popular Music" (1941) has called this ploy "pseudo-individualization," and he contends that it is a distinguishing characteristic of all popular works (as opposed to what he considers the serious works of high culture—Beethoven's symphonies, for example). See Antony Easthope and Kate McGowan, *A Critical and Cultural Theory Reader* (Toronto: University of Toronto Press, 1992), pp. 217–218. But Kidō's stories are an unusual case, even in the realm of popular culture more broadly considered, given the hand-in-glove fit between their use of repetition as a formal device and their ideology of nostalgic longing to retell and repeat the past.

Chapter 5: Anxieties of Influence

1. Hagiwara Sakutarō's essay is contained in Muramatsu Takeshi, ed., *Shōwa hihyō taikei 2* (Tokyo: Banchō shobō, 1968). A translation of "Kokutai no hongi" appears in Ryusaku Tsunoda et al., comps., *Sources of Japanese Tradition* (New York: Columbia University Press, 1958), 785–795.

2. Tsunoda et al., *Sources of Japanese Tradition,* p. 786.

3. Ranpo has downplayed the drunkenness. "There are some people who guess that [the name] must be based on memories of walking along the banks of the Edo River in a drunken stupor, but although I did live next to the river in Ushigome during my student years, at the time I had no taste for liquor, and I never staggered around drunk. [I chose the characters for] 'Ranpo' simply for their sound, but it may be that I was half conscious of the idea of a step that was somehow abnormal *(dokoka seijō narazaru ashi-nami)* when I named myself."

Edogawa Ranpo, "Watakushi no pennēmu" (My Pen Name), in *Edogawa Ranpo, Shinbungei-tokuhon* (Tokyo: Kawade shobō shinsha, 1992), p. 212.

4. Bloom's classic works on literary influence are *The Anxiety of Influence* (New York: Oxford University Press, 1973) and *A Map of Misreading* (New York: Oxford University Press, 1975).

5. Bloom, *A Map of Misreading*, p. 19. Quoted in Sas, *Fault Lines*, p. 39.

6. Quoted in ibid.

7. See, for example, Lydia Liu's *Translingual Practice* and Cornelia Moore and Raymond Moody, eds., *Comparative Literature East and West: Traditions and Trends* (Honolulu: University of Hawai'i, East-West Center, 1989).

8. Much of the seminal work in this area is contained in Julia Kristeva's *Desire in Language* (New York: Columbia University Press, 1980) and *The Revolution in Poetic Language* (New York: Columbia University Press, 1984).

9. The biographical information given here is drawn from Ranpo's "Watashi no rirekisho" (My Resumé) and the chronology accompanying it in Nakajima Kawatarō, ed., *Edogawa Ranpo wandārando* (Tokyo: Chūsekisha, 1989), pp. 122–131. "Watakushi no rirekisho" originally appeared in the *Nihon keizai shinbun,* in six installments, between May 3 and May 10, 1956.

10. The single most significant point of intersection between Ranpo and Tanizaki is Tanizaki's story "Tomoda to Matsunaga no hanashi" (The Story of Tomoda and Matsunaga, 1926), a mystery about a man with two identities. He lives for years at a time as Tomoda, a man of Falstaffian appetites who loves all things Western (including foreign prostitutes). As Tomoda, he gains so much weight eating and carousing that his features are altered beyond recognition. His pleasure sprees, however, are inevitably interrupted by attacks of nervous longing for things Japanese. He then resumes his identity as Matsunaga, a timid, sickly, waif of a man who spends all his time at home with his Japanese wife.

11. "Watakushi no rirekisho," reprinted in Nakajima, *Edogawa Ranpo wandārando*, p. 129.

12. Edogawa Ranpo, *Tantei shōsetsu yonjūnen*, p. 97. Ranpo details the circumstances of his accepting the assignment on p. 82 of the same volume.

13. "Watakushi no rirekisho," in Nakajima, *Edogawa Ranpo wandārando*, p. 129.

14. This version of *Issun bōshi* is the only prewar film based on a work by Ranpo. Remakes appeared in 1948 and 1955, and since World War II over two dozen Ranpo films have come out. For a survey, see Katsura Chiho, "Ranpo shōsetsu no eigaka ni tsuite," *Kokubungaku kaishaku to kanshō*, vol. 59, no. 12 (December 1994), pp. 70–75.

15. Edogawa, "Nihon tantei shōsetsu no tayōsei ni tsuite" (The Multifariousness of the Japanese Detective Story), in *Edogawa Ranpo zenshū*, vol. 16, p. 140.

16. Edogawa, "Ningen isu," in *Edogawa Ranpo zenshū*, vol. 2, p. 9.

17. Edogawa, *Edogawa Ranpo zenshū*, vol. 2, p. 16. Confirmation that Ranpo has in mind a European foreigner comes from an English translation of this story that Ranpo himself checked line by line. The Japanese for the first

sentence quoted is *Koe ni yotte sōzō sureba sore wa mada ura-wakai ikoku no otome degozaimashita. Ikoku no otome* means "a girl from a foreign country." James B. Harris' closely supervised translation, however, reads, "Judging solely by her voice, she was European" (Harris, trans., *Japanese Tales of Mystery and Imagination,* by Edogawa Rampo [Ranpo] [Tokyo: Charles E. Tuttle, 1956], p. 13). According to Harris' preface, when this translation was made, he spoke but did not read or write Japanese, and Ranpo read but did not speak or write English. "Hence, for each line translated," he says, "the two collaborators…were forced to overcome manifold difficulties in getting every line just right, the author reading each line in Japanese several times and painstakingly explaining the correct meaning and nuance, and the translator sweating over his typewriter having to experiment with sentence after sentence until the author was fully satisfied with what had been set down in English" (p. xi). The resulting translation is relatively free, and in some places entire paragraphs have been excised. It is nonetheless a useful gloss on Ranpo's work in Japanese.

18. Edogawa, *Edogawa Ranpo zenshū,* vol. 2, pp. 18–19.

19. Ibid., p. 20.

20. Ibid., p. 21.

21. Ibid., p. 16.

22. Tanizaki Jun'ichirō, *Naomi (Chijin no Ai),* trans. Anthony Hood Chambers, (New York: Vintage, 2001), pp. 67–68.

23. Edogawa, *Edogawa Ranpo zenshū,* vol. 2, pp. 17–18.

24. Ibid., pp. 13–14.

25. Ibid., p. 19.

26. Ibid., p. 21.

27. Ibid., p. 17.

28. Tanizaki's story, first published in the magazine *Kaizō* in January 1920, is about a man who plots to kill his wife by placing her in situations where she is vulnerable to lethal dangers and then relying on probability to take care of the rest. Ranpo's borrowing from this story is mentioned in Nakajima, *Nihon suiri shōsetsu shi,* vol. 1, p. 163.

29. Here is Poe's description of the seven rooms of the castle in which Prince Prospero has sequestered himself and his revelers: "To the right and left, in the middle of each wall, a tall and narrow Gothic window looked out upon a closed corridor which pursued the windings of the suite. These windows were of stained glass whose color varied in accordance with the prevailing hue of the decorations of the chamber into which it opened. That at the eastern extremity was hung, for example, in blue—and vividly blue were its windows. The second chamber was purple in its ornaments and tapestries, and here the panes were purple. The third was green throughout, and so were the casements. The fourth was furnished and lighted with orange—the fifth with white—the sixth with violet. The seventh apartment was closely shrouded in black velvet tapestries that hung all over the ceiling and down the walls, falling in heavy folds upon a carpet of the same material and hue. But in this chamber only, the color

of the windows failed to correspond with the decorations. The panes here were scarlet—a deep blood color" ("The Masque of the Red Death," p. 486 in Edgar Allan Poe, *Poetry and Tales* [New York: Library of America, 1984]).

30. Edogawa, *Edogawa Ranpo zenshū*, vol. 1, p. 166.

31. Jordan Sand, *House and Home in Modern Japan*, p. 234.

32. Ibid., p. 233.

33. Ibid., p. 245.

34. Edogawa, *Edogawa Ranpo zenshū*, vol. 1, p. 169. This passage is omitted in James B. Harris' translation into English in the volume *Japanese Tales of Mystery and Imagination*. The omission was presumably made at Ranpo's own direction, since Harris' preface to the translation describes an unusually close collaboration between translator and author.

35. Sand, *House and Home*, p. 205.

36. The early evolution of the Japanese department store and the influence of Wanamaker's are described in Hatsuda Tōru, *Hyakkaten no tanjō* (Tokyo: Sanseidō, 1993), pp. 60–72.

37. Edogawa, *Edogawa Ranpo zenshū*, vol. 3, pp. 121–122.

38. Ibid., p. 122.

39. Ibid., p. 125.

40. The statistic is taken from Sand, *House and Home*, p. 219. As an indication of the iconic status that the Kewpie doll attained in Japan, Sand includes on the same page an early-twentieth-century photographic studio portrait of a Japanese infant who has been posed alongside a round-eyed, open-armed Kewpie doll twice the infant's size.

41. Edogawa, *Edogawa Ranpo zenshū*, vol. 3, p. 256.

42. Ibid., p. 261.

43. Ibid., p. 263.

44. The title of "The Attic Walker" ("Yaneura no sanposha") is itself reminiscent of Uno Kōji's story "The Bachelor of Laws in the Attic" ("Yaneura no hōgakushi," 1918).

45. Sari Kawana has noted Ranpo's use of Shundei as a "literary double," remarking that by "giving Ōe a similar biography to his own, Ranpo plays with the notion of authorial presence and uses it as a device of trickery." "The Price of Pulp: Women, Detective Fiction, and the Profession of Writing in Inter-War Japan," *Japan Forum*, vol. 16, no. 2 (2004), p. 226.

46. More than one Japanese critic suggested that Ranpo had ruined an otherwise perfectly good novel with this ending. Ranpo quotes in *Tantei shōsetsu yonjūnen* criticism of the novel's ending by both Kōga Saburō and Hirabayashi Hatsunosuke. Kōga declared the novel's doubt-sowing coda "unnecessary," and Hirabayashi felt that it showed a regrettable desire to "conquer the reader," that is, to make the logical possibilities in the work so intricate as to ensure that no reader could figure them all out (p. 127).

47. The analysis here is inspired by Peter Brooks' *Body Work: Objects of Desire in Modern Narrative* (Cambridge, Mass.: Harvard Univesity Press, 1993), especially

pp. 18–21. For Barthes on narrative as striptease, see his *Pleasure of the Text*, trans. Richard Miller (New York: Hill and Wang, 1975).

48. Edogawa, *Edogawa Ranpo zenshū*, vol. 3, p. 41.

49. Ibid., p. 240.

50. Ibid., p. 218.

51. Ibid., p. 252.

52. Ibid., p. 247.

53. Ibid.

54. Ibid., vol. 1, p. 99.

55. Ibid., p. 113.

56. Ibid., p. 101.

57. Ibid., p. 102.

58. Ibid., p. 101.

59. Ibid., p. 103.

60. Ibid., p. 104.

61. Ibid., vol. 4, p. 10.

62. Ibid., pp. 10–11.

63. Jim Reichert has perceptively called the novel "a veritable Frankenstein's monster" and a "freakish" text. The discourses he identifies in the novel include those of criminology, sexology, and eugenics. See "Deviance and Social Darwinism in Edogawa Ranpo's Erotic-Grotesque Thriller *Kotō no Oni*," *Journal of Japanese Studies*, vol. 27, no. 1 (Winter 2001), pp. 113–141.

64. Edogawa, *Edogawa Ranpo zenshū*, vol. 4, p. 159.

65. Reichert, "Deviance," p. 120.

66. Edogawa, *Edogawa Ranpo zenshū*, vol. 4, p. 28.

67. Ibid., p. 29.

68. Ibid., p. 61.

69. Ibid., p. 60.

70. For the mention of the two buildings' conspicuous height, see ibid., p. 25.

71. Ibid., p. 60.

72. Ibid., pp. 172–173.

73. Ibid., p. 173.

74. Ibid., p. 170.

75. Ibid., p. 162.

76. For the phrase quoted, see ibid., p. 162.

77. Ibid., p. 173.

78. Yamashita Takeshi, *Shinseinen o meguru sakka-tachi* (Tokyo: Chikuma, 1996), provides a history of the magazine and profiles of the major writers associated with it. Nakajima Kawatarō, *Nihon suiri shōsetsu shi*, vol. 1, also includes a useful, briefer, history of the magazine in a chapter titled "The Birth of *New Youth*" ("Shinseinen no tanjō"), pp. 221–230. For further information about the magazine in English, particularly concerning its female readership and the

careers of female detective writers who published there, see Kawana, "The Price of Pulp."

79. Quoted in Nakajima, *Nihon suiri shōsetsu shi*, vol. 1, p. 221.

80. Kozakai Fuboku, "Kagakuteki kenkyū to tantei shōsetsu," in *Hanzai bungaku kenkyū* (Tokyo: Kokushokan-Gyōkai, 1991), pp. 234–241. Reprinted from *Shinseinen*, February 10, 1922 (supplement).

81. Hirabayashi Hatsunosuke, "Watakushi no yōkyū suru tantei shōsetsu," *Shinseinen*, 1924, no. 10 (summer special), pp. 271–273.

82. Katō Takeo, "Edogawa Ranpo kun no sakuhin," *Shinseinen*, vol. 6, no. 5 (April 1925), p. 162.

83. Hirabayashi, "Nihon no kindaiteki tantei shōsetu," pp. 157–158. Dated February 25.

84. Kume Masao, "Tantei shōsetsu to ningen-mi," *Shinseinen*, 1924, no. 10 (summer special), p. 266.

85. Nagata Mikihiko, "Tantei shōsetsu jidai," *Shinseinen*, 1924, no. 10 (summer special), pp. 271–273.

86. Satō Haruo, "Tantei shōsetsu shōron," *Shinseinen*, 1924, no. 10 (summer special), p. 262.

87. Hirabayashi Hatsunosuke, "Injū sono ta," in Ōwada Shigeru, ed., *Hirabayashi Hatsunosuke tantei shōsetsu sen* (Ronzō misuteri sōsho 2) (Tokyo: Ronzōsha, 2003), vol. 2, pp. 269–276; reprinted from *Shinseinen*, vol. 9, no. 13 (October 1928).

88. Kozakai Fuboku, "Tantei shōsetsu no shōrai," in *Hanzai bungaku kenkyū*, p. 256. Reprinted from *Bungei kurabu*, March 1929. The highbrow writers Kozakai has in mind are probably Satō Haruo (*Shimon*, 1918) and Tanizaki Jun'ichirō ("Tojō," 1920; "Tomoda to Matsunaga no hanashi," 1926).

89. "'Race,' Time, and Modernity" (1991), quoted in Bart Moore-Gilbert, *Postcolonial Theory: Contexts, Practices, Politics* (London: Verso, 1997), p. 122.

Coda: Cultural Borrowing Reconsidered

1. "Fukumen no buyōsha," in Edogawa, *Edogawa Ranpo zenshū*, vol. 2, p. 139; *The Suicide Club* is a collection of tales by Robert Louis Stevenson (1850–1894). At the club's nightly meetings, the members randomly select a murderer and his victim from among themselves by dealing out a deck of playing cards, with the killing to be accomplished before dawn.

2. Edogawa, *Edogawa Ranpo zenshū*, vol. 2, p. 152.

3. Ibid., p. 143.

Bibliography

Adorno, Theodor. "On Popular Music." In *A Critical and Cultural Theory Reader,* ed. Antony Easthope and Kate McGowan. Toronto: University of Toronto Press, 1992.

Anderson, Marston. *The Limits of Realism: Chinese Fiction in the Revolutionary Period.* Berkeley: University of California Press, 1990.

Barthes, Roland. *Pleasure of the Text.* Trans. Richard Miller. New York: Hill and Wang, 1975.

———. *The Rustle of Language.* Trans. Richard Howard. New York: Hill and Wang, 1986.

Bloom, Harold. *The Anxiety of Influence.* New York: Oxford University Press, 1973.

———. *A Map of Misreading.* New York: Oxford University Press, 1975.

Botsman, Daniel. *Punishment and Power in the Making of Modern Japan.* Princeton: Princeton University Press, 2005.

Brooks, Peter. *Body Work: Objects of Desire in Modern Narrative.* Cambridge, Mass.: Harvard University Press, 1993.

Ch'en, Paul Heng-Chao. *The Formation of the Early Meiji Legal Order.* Oxford: Oxford University Press, 1981.

Du Boisgobey, F[ortuné]. *The Consequences of a Duel.* Trans. A. D. Hall. Seaside Library. New York: George Munro, 1885.

Eco, Umberto. *The Role of the Reader: Explorations in the Semiotics of Texts.* Bloomington: Indiana University Press, 1979.

Edamatsu Shigeyuki et al., eds. *Meiji nyūsu jiten.* 6 vols. Tokyo: Mainichi komyunikēshonzu, 1983–1986.

Edo machi-bugyō. Rekishi gunzō raiburarii 3. Tokyo: Gakken, 1995.

Edogawa Ranpo. Shinbungei-tokuhon. Tokyo: Kawade shobō shinsha, 1992.

Edogawa Ranpo. *Edogawa Ranpo zenshū.* 25 vols. Tokyo: Kōdansha, 1978–1979.

———. *Tantei shōsetsu yonjūnen.* Tokyo: Chūsekisha, 1994.

Fujii, James A. *Complicit Fictions: The Subject in the Modern Japanese Prose Narrative.* Berkeley: University of California Press, 1993.

Gaboriau, Émile. *The Widow Lerouge.* No trans. Seaside Library. New York: George Munro, 1874.

Gonda Manji. *Gendai suiri shōsetsu ron.* Tokyo: Daisan bunmeisha, 1985.

———. *Nihon tantei sakka ron.* Tokyo: Gen'eijō, 1975.

Green, Richard Lancelyn, ed. *The Adventures of Sherlock Holmes.* Oxford: Oxford University Press, 1994.

Haley, John Owen. *Authority without Power: Law and the Japanese Paradox.* New York: Oxford University Press, 1991.

Harris, James B., trans. *Japanese Tales of Mystery and Imagination.* By Edogawa Rampo [Ranpo]. Tokyo: Charles E. Tuttle, 1956.

Hatsuda Tōru. *Hyakkaten no tanjō.* Tokyo: Sanseidō, 1993.

Haycraft, Howard. *Murder for Pleasure: The Life and Times of the Detective Story.* New York: D. Appleton-Century, 1941.

Henderson, Dan Fenno. *Conciliation and Japanese Law, Tokugawa and Modern.* Vol. 1. Seattle: University of Washington Press, 1965.

Hirabayashi Hatsunosuke. "Nihon no kindaiteki tantei shōsetsu." *Shinseinen,* vol. 6, no. 5 (April 1925): 156–161.

———. "Watakushi no yōkyū suru tantei shōsetsu." *Shinseinen,* 1924, no. 10 (summer special): 271–273.

Hirakawa, Sukehiro. "Japan's turn to the West." In *The Cambridge History of Japan,* vol. 5: *The Nineteenth Century,* ed. Marius P. Jansen. Cambridge: Cambridge University Press, 1989.

Hirata Yumi. "The Story of the Woman, the Woman in the Story: Takahashi Oden and the Discourse of the Poison Woman." In *Gender and Japanese History: The Self and Expression / Work and Life,* vol. 2., ed. Wakita Haruko et al. Osaka: Osaka University Press, 1999.

Hodgson, John A., ed. *Sherlock Holmes: The Major Stories with Contemporary Critical Essays.* Boston: Bedford, 1994.

Ihara Saikaku. *The Life of an Amorous Woman and Other Writings.* Ed. and trans. Ivan Morris. New York: New Directions, 1963.

———. *Tales of Japanese Justice.* Trans. Thomas M. Kondo and Alfred Marks. Honolulu: University of Hawai'i Press, 1980.

Iida Momo. *Kuroiwa Ruikō.* Tokyo: Riburopōto, 1992.

Imai Kingo, ed. *Hanshichi Torimono-chō.* 6 vols. Tokyo: Chikuma shobō, 1998.

"International Copyright Relations of the United States." Circular 38a. Washington, D.C.: U.S. Copyright Office, 2003.

Ishida Bunshirō, ed. *Shinbun kiroku shūsei: Meiji Taishō Shōwa dai jiken shi.* Tokyo: Kinseisha, 1966.

Ishimaru Hisa. "Bungei kurabu." In *Shinchō nihon bungaku jiten.* Tokyo: Shinchōsha, 1988.

Itō Hideo. *Kindai no tantei shōsetsu.* Tokyo: San'ichi shobō, 1994.

———. *Kuroiwa Ruikō: sono shōsetsu no subete.* Tokyo: Tōgensha, 1979.

————. *Kuroiwa Ruikō: tantei shōsetsu no ganso.* Tokyo: San'ichi shobō, 1988.
————. *Kuroiwa Ruikō kenkyū.* Tokyo: Gen'eijō, 1978.
————. *Shōwa no tantei shōsetsu.* Tokyo: San'ichi shobō, 1993.
————. *Taishō no tantei shōsetsu.* Tokyo: San'ichi shobō, 1990.
Jiji shinpō. Tokyo. August 2, 1893.
Jinnai Hidenobu, ed. *Process: Architecture,* no. 72 (April 1, 1987).
Kanagaki Robun. *Takahashi Oden yasha monogatari.* In Okitsu Kaname, ed., *Meiji kaika-ki bungakushū 2,* pp. 3–61. Meiji bungaku zenshū 2. Tokyo: Chikuma shobō, 1966.
Kasai Kiyoshi. *Tantei shōsetsu ron.* 2 vols. Tokyo: Tōkyō sōgensha, 1998.
Katō Shūichi et al., eds. *Buntai.* Nihon kindai shisō taikei 16. Tokyo: Iwanami, 1989.
Katō Takeo. "Edogawa Ranpo kun no sakuhin." *Shinseinen,* vol. 6, no. 5 (April 1925): 161–163.
Katsura Chiho. "Ranpo shōsetsu no eigaka ni tsuite." *Kokubungaku kaishaku to kanshō,* vol. 59, no. 12 (December 1994): 70–75.
Kawana, Sari. "The Price of Pulp: Women, Detective Fiction, and the Profession of Writing in Inter-War Japan." *Japan Forum,* vol. 16, no. 2 (2004): 207–229.
————. *Sleuthing Japan: Detective Fiction and Modern Culture.* Minneapolis: University of Minnesota Press, forthcoming.
Keene, Donald. *Dawn to the West: Japanese Literature of the Modern Era: Fiction.* New York: Henry Holt, 1984.
Kimura Ki, ed. *Kuroiwa Ruikō shū.* Meiji bungaku zenshū 47. Tokyo: Chikuma shobō, 1971.
Kinkley, Jeffrey. *Chinese Justice, the Fiction: Law and Literature in Modern China.* Stanford: Stanford University Press, 2000.
Kinmonth, Earl. *The Self-Made Man in Meiji Japanese Thought.* Berkeley: University of California Press, 1981.
Kodama Kōta et al., eds. *Meiji jidai.* Zusetsu nihon bunka shi taikei, vol. 11. Tokyo: Shōgakukan, 1967.
Koike Shōtarō. "Takahashi Oden." *Nihonshi daijiten,* vol. 4, p. 645. Tokyo: Heibonsha, 1993.
Kokubungaku kaishaku to kanshō, vol. 59, no. 12 (December 1994).
Kozakai Fuboku. *Hanzai bungaku kenkyū.* Tokyo: Kokushokan-Gyōkai, 1991.
Kristeva, Julia. *Desire in Language.* New York: Columbia University Press, 1980.
————. *The Revolution in Poetic Language.* New York: Columbia University Press, 1984.
Kume Masao. "Tantei shōsetsu to ningen-mi." *Shinseinen,* 1924, no. 10 (summer special): 265–267.
Kuroiwa Ruikō, trans. *Kettō no hate.* Tokyo: Sanyūsha, 1891.
————, trans. *Makkura.* Tokyo: Kin'ōdō, 1889.
————. *Ruikō zenshū.* 7 vols. Numbered irregularly. Tokyo: Takara shuppan, 1979.
Kuroiwa Ruikō kai, ed. *Kuroiwa Ruikō.* Tokyo: Nihon tosho sentā, 1992.

Lewis, H. D. "The Legal Status of Women in Nineteenth-Century France." *Journal of European Studies*, vol. 10, part 3, no. 39 (September 1980): 178–188.

Lippit, Seiji M. *Topographies of Japanese Modernism*. New York: Columbia University Press, 2002.

Liu, Lydia. *Translingual Practice: Literature, National Culture, and Translated Modernity—China 1900–1937*. Stanford: Stanford University Press, 1995.

Lockwood, William W. *The Economic Development of Japan*. Princeton: Princeton University Press, 1968.

MacDonald, Ian, trans. *The Curious Casebook of Inspector Hanshichi: Detective Stories of Old Edo*. Honolulu: University of Hawai'i Press, 2007.

Marran, Christine. *Poison Woman: Figuring Female Transgression in Modern Japanese Culture*. Minneapolis: University of Minnesota Press, forthcoming.

———. "'Poison Woman' Takahashi Oden and the Spectacle of Female Deviance in Early Meiji." *U.S.-Japan Women's Journal*, English supplement no. 9 (1995): 93–110.

Matsumura Yoshio. *Ranpo ojisan*. Tokyo: Shōbunsha, 1992.

Matsuyama Iwao. *Ranpo to Tōkyō*. Tokyo: PARCO, 1984. Rpt. Chikuma shobō, 1994.

Mehren, Arthur Taylor von, ed. *Law in Japan: The Legal Order of a Changing Society*. Cambridge, Mass.: Harvard University Press, 1963.

Mertz, John Pierre. *Novel Japan: Spaces of Nationhood in Early Meiji Narrative, 1870–88*. Ann Arbor: University of Michigan Center for Japanese Studies, 2003.

Mihara Kenzō. *Shikei haishi no kenkyū*. Tokyo: Seibundō, 1990.

Miller, J. Scott. *Adaptations of Western Literature in Meiji Japan*. New York: Palgrave, 2001.

Miyamoto Tadao. "Sōma jiken." *Heibonsha daihyakka jiten*, vol. 8, p. 974. Tokyo: Heibonsha, 1984.

Moore, Cornelia, and Raymond Moody, eds. *Comparative Literature East and West: Traditions and Trends*. Honolulu: University of Hawai'i, East-West Center, 1989.

Moore-Gilbert, Bart. *Postcolonial Theory: Contexts, Practices, Politics*. London: Verso, 1997.

Muramatsu Takeshi, ed. *Shōwa hihyō taikei 2*. Tokyo: Banchō shobō, 1968.

Musashino Jirō. "Kaisetsu." In Okamoto Kidō, *Hanshichi torimono-chō*, vol. 5. Tokyo: Kōbunsha, 1986.

Nagata Mikihiko. "Tantei shōsetsu jidai." *Shinseinen*, 1924, no. 10 (summer special): 271–273.

Nakajima Kawatarō. *Nihon suiri shōsetsu shi*. 3 vols. Tokyo: Tōkyō sōgensha, 1993–1996.

———, ed. *Edogawa Ranpo: hyōron to kenkyū*. Tokyo: Kōdansha, 1980.

———, ed. *Edogawa Ranpo wandārando*. Tokyo: Chūsekisha, 1989.

Nawata Kazuo. *Torimono-chō no keifu*. Tokyo: Shinchōsha, 1995.

Nishikawa, Toshiyuki. "Capital Punishment in Japan." *Asian Thought and Society: An International Review,* vol. 10, no. 29 (July 1985): 81–93.

Nishino Tatsukichi, ed. *Ōoka Seidan.* Genbon-gendai yaku 67. Tokyo: Kyōikusha, 1989.

Okamoto Kyōichi. "Kaisetsu." In Okamoto Kidō, *Hanshichi torimono-chō,* vol. 6. Tokyo: Kōbunsha, 1986.

Okamoto Kidō. *Hanshichi torimono-chō.* 6 vols. Tokyo: Kōbunsha, 1986.

Okitsu Kaname. "Bakumatsu kaika-ki bungaku kenkyū." *Meiji kaika-ki bungaku shū 1,* pp. 415–422. Meiji bungaku zenshū 1. Tokyo: Chikuma shobō, 1966.

———. "Kaidai." *Meiji kaika-ki bungakushū 2,* pp. 425–434. Meiji bungaku zenshū 2. Tokyo: Chikuma shobō, 1967.

———, ed. *Meiji kaika-ki bungaku shū 1.* Meiji bungaku zenshū 1. Tokyo: Chikuma shobō, 1966.

———, ed. *Meiji kaika-ki bungaku shū 2.* Meiji bungaku zenshū 2. Tokyo: Chikuma shobō, 1967.

———. *Meiji shinbun koto hajime: bunmei kaika no jānarizumu.* Tokyo: Taishūkan shoten, 1997.

———. "Tsuzukimono no kenkyū." *Meiji kaika-ki bungakushū 2,* pp. 413–424. Meiji bungaku zenshū 2. Tokyo: Chikuma shobō, 1967.

Ōkubo Toshinori et al., eds. *Meiji jidai.* Zusetsu nihon bunka shi taikei 11. Tokyo: Shōgakukan, 1967.

Ōwada Shigeru, ed. *Hirabayashi Hatsunosuke tantei shōsetsu sen.* 2 vols. Ronzō misuteri sōsho. Tokyo: Ronzōsha, 2003.

Poe, Edgar Allan. *Poetry and Tales.* New York: Library of America, 1984.

Reichert, Jim. "Deviance and Social Darwinism in Edogawa Ranpo's Erotic-Grotesque Thriller *Kotō no Oni.*" *Journal of Japanese Studies,* vol. 27, no. 1 (Winter 2001): 113–141.

———. "Tsubouchi Shōyō's *Tōsei shosei katagi* and the Institutionalization of Exclusive Heterosexuality." *Harvard Journal of Asiatic Studies,* vol. 63, no. 1 (June 2003): 69–114.

Ruikō Shōshi [Kuroiwa Ruikō], trans. *Hōtei no bijin.* Tokyo: Kunshidō, 1887.

———, trans. *Yūzai muzai.* Tokyo: Inoguchi Matsunosuke, 1889.

Sakai, Cécile. *Histoire de la littérature populaire japonaise: Faits et perspectives (1900–1980).* Paris: l' Harmattan, 1987.

Sand, Jordan. *House and Home in Modern Japan: Architecture, Domestic Space, and Bourgeois Culture, 1880–1930.* Cambridge, Mass.: Harvard University Asia Center, 2003.

Sas, Miryam. *Fault Lines: Cultural Memory and Japanese Surrealism.* Stanford: Stanford University Press, 1999.

Satō Haruo. "Tantei shōsetsu shōron." *Shinseinen,* 1924, no. 10 (summer special): 262–265.

Seaman, Amanda C. *Bodies of Evidence: Women, Society, and Detective Fiction in 1990s Japan.* Honolulu: University of Hawai'i Press, 2003.

Seidensticker, Edward. *Low City, High City.* New York: Knopf, 1983.
———. *Tokyo Rising: The City since the Great Earthquake.* New York: Knopf, 1990.
Shih, Shu-Mei. *The Lure of the Modern: Writing Modernism in Semi-Colonial China, 1917–1937.* Berkeley: University of California Press, 2001.
Shinmura Izuru, ed. *Kōjien.* 5th ed. Tokyo: Iwanami, 1998.
Silver, Mark. "The Lies and Connivances of an Evil Woman: Early Meiji Realism and *The Tale of Takahashi Oden the She-Devil.*" *Harvard Journal of Asiatic Studies,* vol. 63, no. 1 (June 2003): 5–67.
Sone Hiroshi. "Toshi no meian." In *Nihon bungaku o yomu,* vol. 6. Tokyo: Yūseidō, 1993.
Steenstrup, Carl. *A History of Law in Japan until 1868.* Leiden: E. J. Brill, 1991.
Suzuki Sadami. "Modan toshi no gensō." *Taiyō,* supplement 88 (Winter 1994): 16–17.
Takahashi Yasuo. *Monogatari yorozu chōhō.* Tokyo: Nihon keizai shinbunsha, 1989.
Takayanagi, Kenzo. "A Century of Innovation: The Development of Japanese Law, 1868–1961." In *Law in Japan: The Legal Order of a Changing Society,* ed. Arthur Taylor von Mehren. Cambridge, Mass.: Harvard University Press, 1963.
Tanizaki Jun'ichirō. *Naomi.* Trans. Anthony Hood Chambers. New York: Vintage, 2001.
Todorov, Tzvetan. *The Poetics of Prose.* Trans. Richard Howard. Ithaca, N.Y.: Cornell University Press, 1977.
Torrance, Richard. *The Fiction of Tokuda Shūsei and the Emergence of Japan's New Middle Class.* Seattle: University of Washington Press, 1994.
Totman, Conrad. *A History of Japan.* Malden, Mass.: Blackwell, 2000.
Toyoda Takeshi. *Myōji no rekishi.* Tokyo: Chūōkōronsha, 1971.
Tsuda Mamichi. "Shikei wa kei ni arazu." *Meirokusha zasshi,* no. 8 (1875).
Tsukamoto Tetsumi, ed. *Ōoka seidan.* Yūhōdō, 1928.
Tsunoda, Ryusaku, et al., comps. *Sources of Japanese Tradition.* New York: Columbia University Press, 1958.
Tsurumi Shunsuke. "Kuroiwa Ruikō." In *Taishū geijutsuka no shōzō,* ed. Katō Hidetoshi, pp. 200–274. Nijisseiki o ugokashita hitobito 8. Tokyo: Kōdansha, 1963.
Vlastos, Stephen, ed. *Mirror of Modernity: Invented Traditions of Modern Japan.* Berkeley: University of California Press, 1998.
Wada Shigejirō. *Kindai bungaku sōseiki no kenkyū: riarizumu no seisei.* Tokyo: Ōfūsha, 1973.
Wakita Haruko et al., eds. *Gender and Japanese History: The Self and Expression / Work and Life.* Vol. 2. Osaka: Osaka University Press, 1999.
Washburn, Dennis C. *The Dilemma of the Modern in Japanese Fiction.* New Haven: Yale University Press, 1995.
Watt, Ian. *The Rise of the Novel: Studies in Richardson, Fielding, and Defoe.* Berkeley: University of California Press, 1957.

Wigmore, John Henry, ed. *Law and Justice in Tokugawa Japan: Materials for the History of Japanese Law and Justice under the Tokugawa Shogunate 1603–1867.* Part 1. Tokyo: Kokusai Bunka Shinkokai, 1969.

Yamamoto Taketoshi. *Kindai nihon no shinbun dokusha-sō.* Tokyo: Hōsei daigaku shuppan, 1981.

Yamashita Takeshi. *Shinseinen o meguru sakka-tachi.* Tokyo: Chikuma shobō, 1996.

Yanagida Izumi. *Meiji shoki honyaku bungaku no kenkyū.* Meiji bungaku kenkyū, vol. 5. Tokyo: Shunjūsha, 1961.

Yanagita Kunio. *Meiji taishō shi: sesō-hen.* Tōyō bunko 105. Tokyo: Heibonsha, 1967.

Yorozu chōhō. Tokyo. No. 1 (November 1, 1892) and nos. 199 (July 18, 1893) to 568 (October 24, 1894).

Yoshida, Kazuo. "Japanese Mystery Literature." In *Handbook of Japanese Popular Culture,* ed. Richard Gid Powers and Hidetoshi Kato, pp. 275–299. New York: Greenwood Press, 1989.

Index

Adaptation, 17–18, 66. *See also* Kuroiwa
 Ruikō
Adorno, Theodor, 194n33
adultery, 90–91, 92
Aeba Kōson (Takenoya Shujin), 58
aka-shinbun (sensationalized
 newspapers), 79
Akechi Kogorō (character), 136, 146,
 148, 158–159
Akutagawa Ryūnosuke, 2, 135
architecture: and inadequacy in the
 Japanese detective novel, 171–172;
 and the locked-room mystery,
 20, 157–158, 160, 162–163, 164;
 Western influence, 102, 144,
 180n13
Ariwara Narihira, 116–117
"asymmetrical cosmopolitism" (Shih), 6
ateji (Chinese characters that
 approximate sound), 72

Barthes, Roland, 38–39, 154
Beeston, L. J., 167, 172
"belatedness" (Bloom), 134
Benjamin, Walter, 189n27
Bentley, Eric C., *Trent's Last Case*, 9–10,
 11, 12–13, 14–15, 152, 176, 180n18
Bhabha, Homi, 173
Bloom, Harold, 134
Boissonade, Gustave, 68, 72, 73
Botsman, Daniel, 25
Bungei kurabu (Literary Club), 101–102
bunka-mura (culture villages), 144, 145

Capital punishment, 17, 25, 75–76, 96,
 183n9
Chesterton, G. K., 135, 167
Chikamatsu Monzaemon, 75
Chūgai shinbun (Domestic and Foreign
 News), 187n43
Collins, Wilkie, 167
colonialism, 4, 97, 173
Conan Doyle, Arthur: "The Final
 Problem," 180n18; influence on
 Edogawa Ranpo, 135; influence on
 Okamoto Kidō, 18, 99, 100, 123, 131;
 published in *Shinseinen*, 167; "The
 Red-Headed League," 5; "A Scandal
 in Bohemia," 113; "Silver Blaze,"
 159; "The Speckled Band," 5–6,
 113–114, 160; use of stock motifs,
 124–125; use of Watson character,
 113–114. *See also* Holmes, Sherlock
confession, 25, 26, 28, 29
Conway, Hugh, *Dark Days*, 65. *See also*
 Kuroiwa Ruikō, *Hōtei no bijin*
copyright, 65
courtroom narrative, 16, 22, 56. *See also*
 Ihara Saikaku; *Ōoka seidan*
criminal biography: as antecedent to
 detective novel, 17, 22; character
 identity in, 42; *dokufu-mono*, 30–31,
 41, 69; narrative strategy, 58;
 portrayal of justice system, 23, 31;
 referentiality in, 23; and the status
 system, 23, 40. *See also* Kanagaki
 Robun

About the Author

Mark Silver received his B.A. from Haverford College and holds master's degrees and a Ph.D. in East Asian Languages and Literatures from Yale University. He has been a visiting researcher at Keiō University and has taught Japanese language and literature at Colgate University. He is currently assistant professor of Japanese at Connecticut College.